The Art of Shrinking Heads

For Michel

The Art of Shrinking Heads

On the New Servitude of the Liberated in the Age of Total Capitalism

DANY-ROBERT DUFOUR

Translated by David Macey

polity

First published in French in 2003 as *L'Art de réduire les têtes* © Éditions Denoël, 2003

This English translation © Polity Press, 2008

Polity Press
65 Bridge Street
Cambridge CB2 1UR, UK

Polity Press
350 Main Street
Malden, MA 02148, USA

Ouvrage publié avec le concours du Ministère français chargé de la culture – Centre National du Livre.

Published with the assistance of the French Ministry of Culture – National Centre for the Book.

This book is supported by the French Ministry of Foreign Affairs, as part of the Burgess programme run by the Cultural Department of the French Embassy in London. www.frenchbooknews.com

Liberté • Égalité • Fraternité
RÉPUBLIQUE FRANÇAISE

ISBN-13: 978-07456-3689-4
ISBN-13: 978-07456-3690-0 (pb)

The publisher has used its best endeavours to ensure that the URLs for external websites referred to in this book are correct and active at the time of going to press. However, the publisher has no responsibility for the websites and can make no guarantee that a site will remain live or that the content is or will remain appropriate.

Typeset in 11 on 13 pt Scala
by Servis Filmsetting Ltd, Manchester
Printed and bound in India by
Replika Press PVT Ltd, Kundli

For further information on Polity, visit our website: www.polity.co.uk

Man is, inside himself, the site of a history.

Jean-Pierre Vernant, Article on Ignace Meyerson,
Encyclopaedia universalis

Henceforth, we are doomed to live naked and in anxiety, which is something we have more or less, by the grace of the Gods, been spared since the beginning of the human adventure.

Marcel Gauchet, *Le Désenchantement du monde*

The final realization of the individual coincides with his desubstantialisation.

Gilles Lipovetsky, *L'Ère du vide*

Where now? When now? Who now?

Samuel Beckett, *The Unnamable*

Smooth, shiny, white, like the Helly Hansen waterproof I've succeeded in nicking at last. *Great plasticity of the ego*. There's also a note on it in my file. Plastic. That's all.

Paul Smaïl, *Ali le magnifique*

Contents

Preliminary Remarks

There is a widespread belief that capitalism is basically 'stupid', and that it is a pure system that is primarily intent upon trying to maximize its profits. And yet, just as capitalism was about to make its neoliberal turn in the early 1970s, Dr Jacques Lacan, a psychoanalyst renowned for his ability to detect the meaning that lies beneath the meaning, warned his audience – which was highly politicized in those days – and put forward a very different interpretation in his seminar: 'Capitalist discourse is something that is madly astute [. . .] it works like clockwork, couldn't work better. The trouble is it works too fast, it gets consumed. It's so good at getting consumed [*ça se consomme si bien*] that it is wasting away [*ça se consume*]' (Lacan 1972a).

So it would seem that capitalism works very well. So well that, one day, it should end up . . . wasting away. The only problem is that it will not waste away until it has consumed everything: resources, nature, everything – up to and including the individuals who are its servants. In keeping with the logic of capitalism, Lacan pointed out, 'the slaves of the ancient world' have been replaced by men who have been reduced to the status of 'products': 'products [. . .] that can be consumed like other products' (Lacan 1991: 35). The eminent psychoanalyst also suggested that slightly euphemistic expressions such as 'human material' and 'consumer society' should be understood in this rather macabre sense.

These malicious remarks have lost none of their relevance in the hour of capitalism's total victory. It now sings the praises of 'human capital', of the enlightened management of 'human resources' and of 'good governance linked to human development'. Lacan's remarks quite simply suggest that capitalism also consumes . . . human beings. It looks so remarkably clever because it has succeeded in transforming into an efficient social system that now operates on an almost global scale what the ironic surrealist slogan used to express with remarkable frankness: 'Eat some human flesh; it's good for you' (cited in Pierre 1980).

Is progress a mask that allows a discreet cannibalism to survive? Quite possibly. But what could capitalism possibly consume today? Bodies? It has been using them for a long time now, and the old notion of 'productive bodies' is there to prove it.[1] The real novelty appears to be the head-shrinking. It is as though the full development of instrumental reason (technology), which was made possible by capitalism, had resulted in a deficit of pure reason (the ability to judge a priori what is true and what is false, or even what is good and what is evil). It is precisely this feature that seems to me to be the truly characteristic feature of the so-called 'postmodern' turn: this was the moment when capitalism began to devote some of its intelligence to 'head-shrinking'.

In order to show how capitalism is now consuming minds, we will, throughout this book, relate their consumption to the rapid extinction of those modern philosophical forms of the subject which until recently served as points of reference and allowed us to think our being-in-the-world. The hypothesis I will be putting forward is basically simple but radical: we are currently witnessing the destruction of the double subject of modernity. I refer to the critical (Kantian) subject and the neurotic (Freudian) subject – and I do not see why I should have any hesitation about adding the Marxian subject to the list. And we are seeing the emergence of a new 'postmodern' subject.

I am of course aware that there is something abrupt and hasty about this judgement, which has to be further specified before it can be developed and compared with the reality that surrounds us.

(1)   The process of the simultaneous scrapping of the modern subject and the manufacture of a new subject (which we can call 'postmodern') is happening extremely rapidly. The critical Kantian subject, who was born in or about 1800, is of course two hundred years old. Similarly, Freud's neurotic subject, who was born in or about 1900, has lasted until our day; indeed, a good proportion of twentieth-century thought was devoted to this subject. But although both

---

[1] The notion that the body is productive to the extent that it is a biological body that has been integrated into the production process is already there in Marx (1976). See book I of *Capital*, entitled 'The process of production of capital'; part IV, entitled 'The production of relative surplus-value'; chapter 13, entitled 'Cooperation'. See also Deleule and Guery (1972).

subjects should, because of their respectable old age, be spared from summary execution, they are disappearing before our very eyes and with astonishing rapidity. We have here a phenomenon amazing to analyse. We thought that these philosophical subjects were safe from the vicissitudes of history, that they were safely installed in a transcendental position, and that they were shatter-proof points of reference when it came to thinking our being-in-the-world – and many thinkers do still spontaneously use them in their reflections, rather as though they were eternal. But, even though they do correspond to distinguished historical constructions, these subjects are no longer as self-evident as they once were. They are becoming fuzzy. Their contours are becoming blurred and we are moving on to a different subject-form.

There is something surprising about their long reign and sudden demise. We find it difficult to believe that figures that were so well indexed, so sophisticated and so tried and tested could disappear in such a short time. But we should never forget that civilizations that have existed for thousand of years can vanish within a few years. To restrict the discussion to recent events, it should be remembered that we have seen Indian tribes in the Amazonian forests, which had survived for centuries in the most hostile environments because they lived under the auspices of deeply rooted symbolic practices, die out within a matter of weeks because they could not resist the inroads of a different form of exchange.[2] It is not by chance that I mention this textbook example: I am prepared to bet that the modern subject, who is defined by a twofold reference to Kant and Freud, is dying in the West because a different form of exchange is spreading.

---

[2] See, for example, Yves Billon's feature-length documentary *La Guerre de pacification en Amazonie* (Les Films du Village, 1973).

When the Trans-Amazonia highway was being built in Brazil, the Brazilian state developed a policy of so-called 'enforced contact' in order to defuse the Indians' self-defence reactions. The documentary, which was made in the early 1970s, evokes the fate of the Parakanas Indians. The technique used to get close to them was simple but remarkably effective. Rudimentary shelters made from leaves and known as *tapini* were built and 'gifts' were hung up in them. Once contact had been established in this way, a 'native entertainment park' was established, and this plunged the Indians into the fatal spiral of commodity exchanges. The process of acculturation was brutal, destructive and extremely rapid. All that remained to be done was to dump the Indians in native reservations, where the suicide rate – both individual and collective – was very high . . .

(2)   The programmed death of the subject of modernity is not, it seems to me, unrelated to the mutation in capitalism we have been observing for a good twenty years now. This new state of capitalism, which can summarily be described as 'neoliberalism', is undoing all those forms of exchange that have survived by reference to some absolute or metasocial guarantor. To get straight to the point, we can say that a standard – gold, for example – was needed to guarantee monetary exchanges in the same way that a symbolic guarantor (such as Reason) was needed to allow philosophical discourses to exist. We have now ceased to refer to any transcendental values when we become involved in exchanges. As Marcel Gauchet puts it (2002: xxv), we are now dealing with 'actors who wish to be free from all ties and with nothing above them to hinder the maximization of everything they do'. Exchanges are no longer valid insofar as they are guaranteed by some higher power (either transcendental or ethical); they are valid by virtue of the direct relationship they establish as commodities. Commodity exchanges are, in a word, beginning to desymbolize the world.

To illustrate how commodities are bringing about a spontaneous desymbolization, I will cite only one example. It appears anodyne but is highly significant. I refer to the recent 'sex-change' undergone by Her Majesty's Ships. The front page of the 25 March 2002 issue of *Le Monde* reported that British ships were no longer female. We were informed that both feminist organizations and the Minister for Transport supported the move to refer to ships as 'it' and not 'she'. The editor of *Lloyd's List* – the oldest British daily, founded in 1735 and widely regarded as the bible of the shipping industry – justified the change on the grounds that ships were products like any other products: 'We see it as a reflection of the modern business of shipping. Ultimately they are commodities, they are commercial assets. They are not things that have character – either male or female.' Ships are a kind of floating real estate. The shipping business has to change in the era of globalization or it will fall behind the rest of the business world. So to hell with using feminine pronouns when referring to ships. The origins of the custom are obscure and it is out of date. The important thing is that ships must be described as mere commodities. Who cares about the ancient custom of decorating the prows of ships with statues of goddesses, or about the sailors' sentimental attachment to ships they so often compared to their wives, mothers and mistresses? Once a ship becomes a 'product like any other', or in other words a commodity that can be exchanged at its market value for other commodities, it loses much of its symbolic value. It is, *ipso facto,* relieved of the excess meaning that prevented it from looking like nothing more than just another product in a neutral and extended cycle of trade.

More generally, all the transcendental figures that once guaranteed values are now being challenged. Commodities that can be exchanged for their strict market value are the only things that are left. Human beings are now being asked to get rid of all the symbolic weight that once guaranteed their exchanges. Symbolic value is being dismantled, and all that matters is the neutral monetary value of commodities. As a result, there is nothing and no other consideration (ethical, traditional, transcendent or transcendental) to stand in the way of the free circulation of commodities. The outcome is the desymbolization of the world. Human beings no longer have to agree about transcendent symbolic values; they simply have to have to go along with the never-ending and expanded circulation of commodities.

The above example demonstrates that language and figures of speech are being affected by this desymbolization. And, as it happens, the polemic usually concentrates on language and the use of language. Whilst the example I have just given is amusing, we will soon be looking at others, which can go as far as to have a profound effect on our aptitude for discourse. It is in fact the whole weight of the symbolic in human exchanges, which was so important to the great anthropologists of the twentieth century (from Mauss to Lévi-Strauss and then Lacan), that is being called into question. It has to be spelled out in no uncertain terms: the triumph of neoliberalism will lead to the debasement of the symbolic. If, as Marcel Gauchet puts it (2002: xxv), ' [the market model's] sphere of application is destined to expand far beyond the realm of commodity exchanges', the weakening, and even the debasement, of the symbolic function is the price we will have to pay.[3] We therefore have to make a new analysis of the symbolic in the era of postmodernity.

(3)   This radical change in the way exchanges take place is leading to a real anthropological mutation. Once all the symbolic guarantors of exchanges between human beings begin to disappear, the human condition itself begins to change. Indeed, our being-in-the-world can no longer be the same when what is at stake in a human life is not an

---

[3] The current decline of universal anthropology and the profusion of local and relativist ethnologies and of other forms of ethnography are witnesses to its debasement.

attempt to come to terms with the transcendental symbolic values that act as guarantors, but something which is bound up with our ability to fit in with never-ending flows of circulating commodities. In short, the old subject is no longer needed. We are beginning to discover that, like all the previous ideologies that were unleashed in the twentieth century (communism, Nazism . . .), neoliberalism wants nothing less than to create a new individual.[4] But the great strength of this ideology, as opposed to its predecessors, is that it has not started by addressing the individual itself, through re-education or coercive programmes. It simply gives objects a new status, defines them as mere commodities and then waits for the inevitable to happen: for human beings to transform themselves while they adapt to the commodities, which are henceforth promoted as the only reality.[5] Individuals are now being knocked into shape in the name of a real, and it is advisable to give in rather than resist.[6] The process always has to look soft, like something we want or desire. It is as though we were talking about a series of *entertainments* (television or adverts, for example). We shall soon see that these 'soft' facades conceal a terrible violence.

And if, by chance, some region in the world insists on adopting the masochistic position of trying to escape this 'soft' breaking in, we now know that this ideology will stop at nothing to introduce these recalcitrant areas to the 'benefits' of the new capitalism, whether they like it or not.[7] In a sense, the United States's overwhelming military

[4] This is beginning to be explored. See for example Le Goff (2002), Michéa (2002) and Flahault (2003).

[5] The work of the psychoanalysts Charles Melman and Jean-Pierre Lebrun (2002) demonstrates that considerable changes are already observable at the clinical level. The authors claim that a 'liberal man' is coming into existence and turning the old psychic economy upside down. We may be making the transition from a culture based upon repression, and therefore neurosis, to a culture that promotes perversion, which is the final defence against psychosis. Now the difference between the old psychic economy and the new appears to relate mainly to the new status given to objects by ultraliberalism.

I had already completed this book when I read Melman and Lebrun. I therefore do not mention the possible connection that may exist between our work, but I note with some (purely theoretical) satisfaction that my philosophical thesis about the destruction of the old subject and the concomitant appearance of a new subject is already supported by precise clinical observations.

[6] Indeed, what is the point of resistance if it is a case of 'TINA', as Margaret Thatcher hammered it home to tell us that 'There is no alternative' to the market?

[7] Here I am picking up a point made by Lacan during the 10 May 1967 session of the (unpublished) seminar on the logic of fantasy. Lacan speaks of the masochistic

intervention in Iraq in the spring of 2003 helps to prove the point. Especially if the regions in question possess strategic resources. When it comes to getting its own way, the invisible hand of the market has no qualms about using the iron fist of the generals.

(4)   It should be noted that when I speak of 'making a new subject', I am using 'subject' in the philosophical sense of the term: I am not talking about the individual in the sociological, empirical or worldly sense. I am talking about the new philosophical form of a previously unknown subject that is now being constructed – and I will come back to this point. Similarly, I use 'subject' in the philosophical sense when I speak of the scrapping of the 'Kantian subject' or of the 'Freudian subject'. These were forms constructed by the understanding as it attempted to stabilize itself on a lasting basis and to take a transcendental stance that would rise above the multiplicity of possible sensations, feelings and experiences. I am basically saying that the things now coming under attack are the two subject-forms that were constructed during modernity, and which defined modernity itself.

I refer, first, to the form constructed in or around 1800, with the appearance of the Kantian critical subject. Hume's empiricism and his scepticism about rationality and classical metaphysics had, as we know, shaken Kant so much that he suddenly awoke from his (famous) 'dogmatic slumber' and felt compelled to found a new critical metaphysics, established within the limits of mere reason, freed from the dogmatism of transcendence yet making no concessions to empiricist scepticism.[8] This is how Kant's philosophy came into being: it drew on the progress that had been made in physics since Galileo and Newton, and was based upon a magisterial synthesis of experience and understanding. It took the Kantian turn to demonstrate that intuition without concepts is blind, but that concepts without intuition are empty.

---

position which consists in putting oneself in such a position as to be rejected by the Other. And he takes as a clinical example . . . Vietnam. He argues that war was being waged on the Vietnamese to 'convince these people that they are very wrong not to want to be admitted to the benefits of capitalism, even though they would rather be refused them'. At this point, Lacan puts forward a very interesting proposition: 'I am not saying that politics is the unconscious, but just that the unconscious is politics.'

[8] 'The Remembrance of David Hume was the very thing that many years ago first interrupted my dogmatic slumber and gave a completely different direction to my researches in the field of speculative philosophy' (Kant 2004: 11).

This new foundation signalled the beginning of Kant's famous Copernican revolution, orchestrated throughout his three *Critiques* (Kant 1999, 1993, 1991a). The route was punctuated by three major questions: 'What can I know? What must I do? What can I hope for?'

In an attempt to answer the first question, Kant refutes the empiricism of the Enlightenment by contending that it is not experience but the power of the mind that organizes knowledge. Of course all knowledge begins with experience, but it is irreducible to experience. My knowledge is indeed dependent upon my sense-perception of objects. But Kant identifies two a priori forms of sensibility – space and time – which exist prior to any experience and which are, in his view, part of the very structure of the mind. Experience is then organized by the understanding. Thus I constantly intervene in the field of knowledge by establishing relations between objects through categories that refer to the rational principle of causality. Kant identifies the twelve categories, universal and necessary, which allow us to unify the field of experience.[9] What I can know (the *phenomena*) is therefore given to me both by pure forms of sensibility (these are the object of transcendental aesthetics) and by categories (which are the object of the transcendental analytics). This is contrasted with what I cannot know, namely things as such, or as they exist in themselves independently of all points of view. Similarly, the phenomena given by sensible intuition are contrasted with the pure beings of thought or *noumena* (God, the soul, and so on), which classical metaphysics claimed to be able to know. That ambition was in fact a pure illusion on the part of

---

[9] 'The function of thinking in a judgement can be brought under four titles, each of which contains under itself three moments' (Kant 1999: A 70/B 95). They may be suitably represented in the following table:

1 *Quantity of judgements*
   Universal
   Particular
   Singular

2 *Quality of judgements*
   Affirmative
   Negative
   Infinite

3 *Relation of judgements*
   Categorical
   Hypothetical
   Disjunctive

4 *Modality of judgements*
   Problematic
   Assertoric
   Apodeictic

classical metaphysics, which produced nothing but antinomies. To take a well-known example: 'Is the universe finite or infinite?' As I can prove both the thesis and the antithesis, the proofs cancel each other out. It is precisely because these antinomies are insoluble that Kant inaugurates the Copernican revolution of critical philosophy which, he hopes, will 'resolve the scandal of the ostensible contradiction of reason with itself', as he put it in his letter of 21 September 1798 to Christian Grave (Kant 1967: 252).

The answer to the second question ('What must I do?') is an imperative (Kant 1964: 55): 'For enlightenment of this kind, all that is needed is *freedom*. And the freedom in question is the most innocuous of all – freedom to make *public use* of one's reason in all matters.' I must therefore make use of my freedom to think. Such is the moral imperative incumbent upon thinking human beings, and it obliges them to use their critical faculties. As Descartes had already stated, they have a duty to think for themselves.[10] Kant does not shy away from the implications of this principle, insofar as 'criticism is the preparatory activity necessary for the advancement of metaphysics as a well-grounded science' (Kant 1999: B cccvi).

The question 'What can I hope for?' is bound up with the need – which is much more practical than theoretical – for a principle of justice in the world. Kant therefore does not posit it as an a priori given but as an effect of the work of criticism. We see here an essential feature of the great inversion effected by Kant: it is the ethics of the work of criticism that founds metaphysics.[11]

It is no exaggeration to claim that, for the last two hundred years, all critical thought has stemmed from Kant's critical subject. Hegel and Marx had to be Kantians in order to elaborate their philosophies of history, and Hegel did remark that Kant inaugurated modern philosophy. Even Nietzsche's radical critique of morality relied heavily upon the critical intellectual power advocated by the man he called, with some affection, 'the great Chinaman of Königsberg' (Nietzsche 1990: §210). Nietzsche is of course very critical of what he calls the dual role Kant ascribes to reason when he sets it up as both judge and accused (Nietzsche 1982: Preface §3), but his own criticisms still derive from the 'unshakeable moral law' revealed by Kant, and which is synonymous with 'its inner Idea of freedom' (Kant 2006: 443).

[10] For this ethics of thought, see the *Critique of Judgement* (Kant 1991a: §40).

[11] If we cease to do the work of criticism, 'we no longer know what is good'. Cf. Rogozinski (1999).

Had he not been a Kantian, Freud himself could not have constructed the Freudian subject. He had, that is, to rely upon the synthetic power of the mind in order to elaborate a theory capable of
explaining what had hitherto been regarded as disparate and accidental phenomena (dreams, slips of the tongue, bungled actions). We
know that Kant wanted metaphysics to be thought of in the same way
as physics, and Freud adopts exactly the same position with respect to
the psyche – this is precisely what is meant by his 'physicalism'.[12] It is
not, however, just his formal stance on science that makes Freud a
Kantian; it is also the content of his science. According to Paul-Laurent
Assoun, who is one of Freudianism's best epistemologists, Freud
basically wanted to reveal the 'radical "psychological truth"' of Kant's
theory of the subject (Assoun 1995: 'Freud, lecteur de Kant'). He does
so by introducing a 'double equation' modelled on Kant: 'conscious =
phenomena' and 'unconscious = thing in itself' (1995: 'Kant et
Freud'). It is therefore no exaggeration to say that Freud comments on
Kant by 'taking his text and metaphors literally' (1995: 348).

This Kantian subject, which is an ideal form and could therefore
preside over the formation of all modern individuals, now comes in
for sharp criticism. What is this critical subject worth, now that buying
and selling commodities are the only things that matter? According to
Kant (2002: §36), not everything has a monetary value: 'Everything has
either a *price* or a *dignity*. Whatever has a price can be replaced by
something else as *equivalent*. Whatever by contrast is exalted above all
price and so admits of no equivalent has a dignity.' We could not put
it more clearly: dignity is irreplaceable, 'priceless' and 'has no equivalent'. It refers only to the autonomy of the will and can be contrasted
with anything that does have a price. This is why the critical subject is
ill-suited to commodity exchanges. The critical subject is the very
opposite of what is required in the door-to-door selling, marketing and
advertising (much of it mendacious) of commodities. They try to reas-
sure us by saying that this challenge to the critical subject marks the
triumphant return of utilitarianism and Hume's posthumous revenge
on Kant. But how can we fail to see that this utilitarianism has been
twice watered down? On the one hand, it does more to promote the

---

[12] When I refer to 'Freud's physicalism', I refer to the fact that Freud always stated
his wish to make psychoanalysis one of the Sciences of Nature (*Naturwissenschaften*)
rather than one of the sciences of the mind (*Geisteswissenschaften*). This decision is
the combined outcome of his background in medicine, physics and chemistry, of the
scientific context of the day and of his positivist position. See Micheli-Rechtman
(2002).

pursuit of individual happiness than the search for the happiness of the greatest possible number; on the other, it reduces and circumscribes individual happiness by restricting it to the dimension of appropriating commodified objects.

The Kantian subject is in a poor state in what we can describe, in shorthand, as the era of neoliberalism. But this is not all: the other subject of modernity, namely the Freudian subject, who was discovered around 1900, is no better off. Neurosis, with its compulsive fixations and repetitive tendencies, is not the best source for the flexibility that is needed for multiple 'inputs' into the flow of commodities. The figure of the schizophrenic unveiled by Deleuze in the 1970s (Deleuze and Guattari 2004; 1992), with the multiple and irreversible polarization of his desiring machines, is much more efficient in that respect.[13] So much so that, when the fashion for neoliberalism began, Deleuze thought he could outflank capitalism, which he suspected of not deterritorializing fast enough. He thought that a so-called 'paranoiac' reterritorialization would be able to block the machinic flows (of Capital or identity) by invoking the figure of the schizophrenic, who could disrupt normed flows and throw them into confusion by plugging everything into everything else. What Deleuze failed to see was that, far from making it possible to get beyond capitalism, his programme merely predicted its future. It now looks as though the new capitalism has learned its Deleuzean lesson well. Commodity flows must indeed circulate, and they circulate all the better now that the old Freudian subject, with his neuroses and the failed identifications that always crystallize into rigidly anti-productive forms, is being replaced by a being who can be plugged into anything and everything. I am basically putting forward the hypothesis that the new state of capitalism could not be better at producing the schizoid subject of postmodernity.

[13] It will be recalled that the 'schizophrenic' described by Deleuze and Guattari has little to do with the schizophrenic described by classical psychiatry. Or, if he does exhibit some of the same features, Deleuze and Guattari make a positive virtue of them. The Deleuzean schizophrenic might therefore be defined as a modality of subjectivation which escapes the great dichotomies that usually supply the basis for identity. Neither man nor woman, neither son nor father, neither dead nor alive, neither man nor animal, the Deleuzean schizophrenic is, rather, the locus of an anonymous, never-ending and multiple becoming. The schizophrenic individual resembles a crowd, a people or a mob traversed by various cathexes that are both external to him and potentially heteroclites. In *Anti-Oedipus*, Deleuze and Guattari (2004: 401f) make a distinction between two social poles of libidinal cathexis: a 'paranoiac' pole that is reactionary and has fascist tendencies, and a revolutionary 'schizoid' pole.

Given the desymbolizing tendency we are now experiencing, a critical subject who puts forward arguments constructed in the name of the moral imperative of freedom is surplus to requirements. So, too, is the neurotic subject trapped into compulsive guilt. We now require a precarious, acritical subject who displays psychotic tendencies. When I say 'displays psychotic tendencies', I refer to a subject who is open to all kinds of fluctuating identities and who is therefore ready to be plugged into every commodity. The heart of the matter [le vif du sujet] is gradually being replaced by a subjective void [le vide du sujet] that is open to the four winds.

It is obvious that not all individuals have become psychotic as a result. The fact that an acritical subject with psychotic tendencies is now the dominant subject-form does not mean that the whole of postmodern humanity is becoming psychotic. Not everything in the world has become postmodern. There are still vast zones that are modern, or even premodern. And besides, even when the postmodern offensive is at its height, there is still some resistance, for the time being at least. Critical thought and neurosis are still in good shape and still have a good future ahead of them. Basically, wherever there are living institutions, or wherever not everything has been deregulated or emptied of all substance, something will resist this dominant form. To argue that a new subject-form is beginning to dominate the human adventure is not to say that all individuals will surrender without striking a blow. I am not saying that all individuals will go mad, but simply that, because the advent and success of that ideal subject-form are guaranteed, those who are promoting the new capitalism are making a great effort to drive them mad. Mainly by plunging them into a 'world without limits' (Lebrun 1997) that encourages acting out and puts individuals in a borderline state.

I will attempt in chapter 1 to identify the key stages in the transition from the modern subject to the postmodern subject. Chapter 2 will look at how that subject is being manufactured, whilst chapter 3 will try to demonstrate that the construction of that subject implies the denial of important realities. Chapter 4, finally, attempts to sum up what accompanies the production of this subject: the destruction of culture and the promotion of a new nihilism.

1 From Modernity to Postmodernity: Mapping the Transition

It should already be obvious that my hypothesis is that, in our societies, the human condition is undergoing a historic mutation before our very eyes. This mutation is no theoretical hypothesis; it appears to me that, on the contrary, we can verify it if we look at a whole series of events that are affecting the populations of the developed countries, even though they are not always very clearly defined. We have all heard of these events: the ascendancy of commodities, difficulties with subjectivation and socialization, drug addiction, the growing incidence of acting out, the appearance of what we call – rightly or wrongly – 'new symptoms',[1] the explosion of delinquency amongst sizeable fractions of the young population, new outbreaks of violence, new sacrificial forms . . .

When confronted with these events, many people who specialize in psychosocial questions (youth workers, psychologists, sociologists, even psychoanalysts . . .) simply remind us that there is nothing new about these problems. The main reason why we notice them now is that we have a surfeit of information, and the main reason why we take an interest in them is simply that the workings of the mass media need their daily diet of news. So move along, there's nothing to see. That is more or less what the specialists tell us to do. At best, they try to deconstruct the discourses that stage these events. They can deconstruct to their hearts' content, but all too often they forget that, when they have finished deconstructing, the real work has still to be done: they now have to produce a new construction and a new intelligibility

---

[1] For example anorexia, bulimia, drug addiction, depression, panic attacks . . . in other words disruptive practices that reject the bond with the Other. These symptoms are often encountered and evoked in diagnoses of so-called 'prepsychosis'.

of the facts. And, as Bachelard remarks in his study of air and dreams (Bachelard 1943), facts are stubborn things.

I basically think that, far from being accidents, artefacts or epiphenomena constructed, to a greater or lesser extent, by the media, these elements and events must be seen as signs of the very serious crisis which is affecting the populations of the developed countries and especially their young people, who are their most vulnerable members.

I will be putting forward the hypothesis that these difficulties are closely bound up with the transformation that the human condition is undergoing in our democracies. We cannot, in other words, go on ignoring the fact that, given the crisis currently facing our societies, being a subject now means something very different from what it meant in previous generations. In short, I have no hesitations about conjecturing that the subject who is now emerging is far from being the subject who emerged a generation ago. The subjective condition is also subject to historicity, and in that sense we have probably turned a corner. This is having a particular impact on the great institutions responsible for our political life, education, physical and mental health, justice and so on.

A crack in modernity

I am certainly not the first to have noticed the signs of the transformation affecting forms of self-being and being-together in modernity. As several philosophers have noted, each in their own way, the emergence of this new subject actually corresponds to a crack in modernity. Some time ago, we entered an era that we readily describe as 'postmodern'. Jean-François Lyotard, who was one of the first to identify this phenomenon (Lyotard 1986), used the term 'postmodern' to describe an era characterized by the exhaustion and disappearance of the grand narratives of legitimation, and especially of the religious and political narratives. I do not intend here to discuss the expression's legitimacy, and other expressions have in fact been suggested ('supermodern', 'hypercontemporary' . . .). I would, however, simply like to note that we have reached an era which has seen the dissolution, or even the disappearance, of the forces on which 'classical modernity' was based. Whilst the collapse of the great dominant ideologies and of the grand soteriological narratives is the primary feature of postmodernity, we might add, to complete the picture, that we are also witnessing the disappearance of the avant-gardes, and then other significant elements such as the spread of democracy and the concomitant rise of individualism, the reduced role of the state, the gradual ascendancy of commodities – to the detriment of all other considerations – the rule of money, the transformation of culture into a series of fashions, the massification of lifestyles, which goes hand in hand with a growing individualism and exhibitionism, the reduction of history to immediate events and instant news, the important role played by very powerful technologies, many of them uncontrolled, increased life expectancy, the insatiable demand for perpetual good health, the deinstitutionalization of the family, growing doubts about sexual identity and even human identity (there is now, for instance, talk of an 'animal personality'), the avoidance of conflict and the gradual loss of interest in the political, the transformation of the law into a procedural legalism, the making public of private space (one thinks of the vogue for webcams), the privatization of the public domain, and so on. All these features should be seen as symptoms of the mutation modernity is undergoing. They tend to indicate that the advent of postmodernity is not unrelated to the advent of what we now call neoliberalism.

It is precisely this mutation that I will try to reflect upon insofar as it corresponds to what we might call an acceleration of the process of individuation, which began so long ago in our societies. This process does have its positive aspects as the growing autonomy of the individual affords new pleasures, but it also causes new forms of suffering. Whilst the autonomy of the subject indeed has an authentically emancipatory goal, there is nothing to indicate that this autonomy is a demand to which all subjects can respond from the outset. The whole of philosophy appears to suggest that autonomy is the most difficult thing in the world to achieve, and that achieving it is a lifetime's work. It is not surprising that young people, who are by definition dependent on others, should be so vulnerable to this demand, and in such a problematic way. This creates a new and difficult context for all educational projects. There is much talk of 'young people's loss of direction', but, in these conditions, it would be surprising to find that they had any sense of direction at all. Of course they are lost: they are experiencing a new subjective condition, and no one – and least of all those responsible for their education – can understand it. It is therefore pointless to talk about a loss of direction, if all we mean by that is that a few old-fashioned lessons about morality can repair the damage. It is morality itself that is not working, because it can only work 'in the name of . . .'. In a context in which individuals are constantly becoming more autonomous, no one knows in whose name (or in the name of what) we should be acting. And when we no longer know in whose name, or in the name of what, we should be talking to young people, things become as difficult for those who have to talk to them every day as they are for those they are talking to. This new situation, in which there is no longer any credible collective enunciator, is making it more difficult than ever to gain access to the subjective condition. It affects everyone, and especially young people. What are the subjective effects of the demise of the agency that interpellates and addresses all subjects, and to which all subjects must respond? That agency has always been present throughout history and always mobilized by it, notably in the educational system. One of our most urgent needs is for studies in contemporary psychology which can identify this new disposition, of a subject basically called upon to create oneself – a subject whom no historical or generational antecedent is addressing, or whom none can continue with any legitimacy to address.

But what precisely is this autonomous subject? Does the notion mean anything, given that, as we tend all too often not to want to know, the Latin for 'subject' is *subiectus*, which describes the status of someone who has been *subjected*? The subject, then, is first and foremost the one who has been subjected or submitted. But submitted to what?

A short treatise on submission to being, to the One, and to the Subject

By a 'short treatise' I mean a succinct account that deals with the essential points. Let us begin by saying that the question of submission has always been of great interest to philosophy: man is a substance whose existence is not self-sufficient; it depends upon another being. The many ontologies that have developed around this question have suggested various possible names for that being: Nature, Ideas, God, Reason or . . . Being. It might even be said that the whole of philosophy is nothing more than a sequence of propositions about the first principle of being – beginning with the proposition put forward by the sophists, which appears paradoxical at first sight: in order to nip philosophy in the bud, they assert that being does not exist and that everything is a becoming.[2] Naturally enough, the sophists soon fell

[2] See Barbara Cassin's fine study of the sophists. Cassin demonstrates (1995: 13) that, for the sophists, 'being [. . .] is not that which is revealed by speech, but that which discourse creates'. Hence her coinage 'logology', as opposed to 'ontology'. We must therefore always listen to the enunciation that underpins statements and force ourselves to relate the objectivity of things to the performativity of discourse.

into the trap they had set for the emergent philosophers. They very quickly found that their proposition had been ontologized in the form of a thesis about becoming: 'becoming exists'.[3] We are also familiar with the Presocratic proposition which posits that Nature, in its very multiplicity, is the first and last being. We then have Plato's proposition, which posits an ontology of intelligible entities (mathematical beings and ethical beings). Aristotle's proposition asserts an ontology of the concrete (thing, living being, person) which has always been a great inspiration to empiricists. Onto-theological propositions posit the existence of one divine creator, whilst science posits an ontology of true propositions (that which is true, or that which has been proved to be true, exists). Kant's proposition posits Reason 'in itself' as a supranatural principle and an a priori given. Hegel's proposition posits that history is the site of the self-realization of the absolute spirit. Husserl's describes consciousness as that which constantly transcends itself because it encounters that which is not consciousness. According to Heidegger's proposition, Being is an absolute principle and man is its exclusive guardian. Sartre's proposition is that being is part of existence. Philosophy is, in a word, the sum of propositions put forward by transcendentalism, immanentism and empiricism.

As we can see, these are highly speculative forms – and yet I am not afraid of asserting that all these propositions are eminently political.

One might think that ontology takes us far away from the field of the political and still further away from politics, which always has to deal with the very practical business of organizing day-to-day life and which presupposes a sense of acting on the real and the maintenance of maintaining the vital contact with the environment. This is far from being the case, and ontology is very close to the political and to politics. When we are discussing the form and organization of the community, the *polis* and the state, we are discussing nothing less than giving human beings access to the truth of being and freeing them from the simple domination of their immediate passions. Plato's *Republic* and Aristotle's *Politics*, which are models of the genre, demonstrate that the political is the ultimate goal of philosophy. But the same is true of all ontologies: they all involve a politics that

[3] In my view, Deleuze's philosophy of becoming should be related to this current. I therefore do not share the view of Alain Badiou, who describes Deleuze as an unwitting Platonist attempting to find a univocity of being beneath the pragmatic assertion of multiplicities (Badiou 1999).

celebrates, organizes or prepares for the human realm of being. In that sense, all ontologies are political. Agamben (1998: 8) even goes so far as to say that 'politics . . . appears as the truly fundamental structure of Western metaphysics insofar as it occupies the threshold on which the relation between the living being and the logos is realized.'

Being is therefore never pure. It always has a political translation or, one might even say, stand-in. And we can call that stand-in the 'third' or the 'One'.

In his *Esquisse d'une philosophie du droit*, Kojève (1981) remarks that 'the law exists when a *third party* view intervenes in human affairs', but he traces the existence of the third party to a pre-legal stage, or back to the very moment of the constitution of political space, when a third party – chosen from a number of possible candidates – is constructed and put on stage by a group of speaking subjects. It is in this respect probable that the political disposition of human beings is very long-standing and begins with the very process of humanization itself.[4] Societies have always been political in the sense that they have always adopted a third party, to whom sacrifices can be made. They have not, however, always been aware of this fact. They became aware of it thanks to the 'Greek miracle' of the fifth and fourth centuries BC. Until then, human beings had invented the third parties from which their being derived without realizing what they were doing. Greek philosophy changed everything: deliberations about the organization of the *polis* now influenced the choice, form and organization of the third party. There is therefore a close link between pure ontology and political ontology: Plato has as much to say about the *eidos* as about the Republic.[5]

That is what the term 'political' means: the *polis* or Greek city was the third party that Greek society invented for itself in the fifth and fourth centuries BC; and *politikos* is the science that takes the *polis* as its object. The term remains the same, no matter which third parties societies adopt, and obviously applies in all circumstances.

When I speak of 'political philosophy', I am therefore referring to a body of thought that tries, on the one hand, to identify the various third parties that humanity has adopted and, on the other, to analyse

---

[4] The theory of human neoteny (which holds that human beings are, as is generally recognized, incomplete when they are born) allows us to take a new approach to the question of the primitive third party – the totem – which Freud resolves by resorting to a scientific myth in *Totem and Taboo* (Freud [1912]). See Dufour (1999).

[5] *Eidos* is usually translated as 'form' or 'idea' and relates to Plato's 'theory of Forms'.

the modes in which individuals have constructed and reconstructed those third parties throughout history. Basically, speaking subjects, which can be symbolized as *I* and *you*, have never ceased to construct third parties or eminent *theys* such as the Gods, who can authorize their existence. At the beginning of the *Politics*, Aristotle rightly notes that our status as 'political animals' is bound up with our status as 'speaking animals'.

We might therefore say that, because they speak, subjects never cease to construct the entities which they elect as the unifying principle – as the One or the *Subject* around which other subjects are organized. The notion of a discursive construct is important. Constructing Subjects that look like perfectly natural entities is probably the political's greatest ambition, and striving to achieve their naturalization is the very meaning of political power [*puissance*]. But the notion is specious in all the cases, because all such agencies are produced by little subjects in their need to create a Subject who, in return, allows them to exist. The third party at the centre of symbolico-political systems is therefore a fictional structure, but the fiction is supported by all speaking beings. That is why the political can never be divorced from a certain number of myths, stories and artistic creations, which are designed to prop up that fiction. These various narratives in fact prescribe what the Subject must look like if two interlocutors are to be able to devote themselves, more or less peacefully, to the inexhaustible vocation – speaking – which supplies the model for all their other activities.

In the field of political ontology, this political stand-in of Being is referred to as the *One*. In the section of his *Principe de souveraineté* devoted to 'Foundations' (those of modern political power), the political scientist Gérard Mairet (1997: 185ff) remarks that 'politics is concerned with what is common to human beings who are living together in a given time and space'. Politics therefore relates to the *common being* of humans. Human collectivities cannot exist without a principle of unity: the community, the *polis*, the state . . . This is why Mairet tells us that the political cannot exist without 'an ontology of the *one*'. Many different forces were obviously at work in the Greek *polis*, but it looked like a unitary body. In the Christian city, the state is a microcosm modelled on a macrocosm which is organized and caused by one God. In the modern state, the political order is no longer based upon God. 'The order of the state and the state as order' no longer stem from a divine cause but from a human cause, as revealed by Machiavelli in *Il Principe* (1513) and then by Jean Bodin in the *Six Livres de la République* (1576). This, however, does nothing to alter its ontological structure, which is still organized around the *one*.

Of course the One does not exist and has never existed. It is a purely fictional construct. What we actually find in its place is discord – no matter whether we call it *stasis* (quarrel, differend), as Nicole Loraux indicates in the case of the Greek *polis* (1997), where the One is no more than a counterweight to permanent divisions and dissidence, or, following Jacques Rancière (1995), 'dissension' [*mésentente*]. For Rancière, politics always has to do with a 'false count, double count or miscount' of the parts of the whole. The role of the fiction is to unify what is heterogeneous.

The Other

Throughout human history, being – however defined – has always been made incarnate and it is that aspect, or 'ontology as politics', that really interests me here. Informed readers will probably have realized that the question of the *Other*, as formulated by Lacan, is not very far removed from what I am saying here about being and the One. We also know to what extent, in the 1950s, Lacan has used Heidegger's ontology, which is very radical, as the basis for his own theory of the symbolic, in which the Other figures as third locus, of speech. The Other is a third locus as well as the locus of the third party or of what Lacan, who openly evokes religion here, calls the 'Name-of-the-Father'.* The Name-of-the-Father is, barring accidents, that which appears in the place of the Other because it is, as Lacan puts it ([1958b]: 485) 'the signifier of the Other qua locus of the law'. I could therefore use the Lacanian term Other and correlate it to Name-of-the-Father, which is also a Lacanian term. I am trying to bring together three registers that are normally kept separate – the purely speculative register associated with Being, the purely political register associated with the One, and the symbolic register associated with the Other – in order to show that, even though it is not often clearly perceived, there is a real continuity between the ontological, political, symbolic and clinical aspects of the problematic of the subject.

What I am putting forward here does not seem to me to contradict Lacan's theory of the Other. On the contrary. But as I take the view that books can also allow us to enter into a dialogue with the dead, I will

---

* In French, *nom-du-père* is phonetically indistinguishable from *non du père* (' "no" of the father').

put it this way: I have several serious remarks to make to Lacan about his theory of the Other. In fact I think that some very specific aspects of the Lacanian theory of the Other must be further developed before we can deal with the question that concerns me here: the postmodern mutation undergone by modalities of subjectivation.

The incompleteness of the Other

My first remark picks up and develops Lacan's point about the incompleteness of the Other. The indispensable property that allows the Other to be constituted as such is, paradoxically, its incompleteness. There is in fact always some viewpoint that allows us to perceive that the Other is incomplete. The Other, which appears to be complete, is found to be lacking. Let me take the example of Kafka's incomparably logical parable 'Before the law' [1916], which was later incorporated into chapter 9 of *The Trial*. Kafka gives us to understand that what constitutes the law is the fact that someone asks: 'What is the law?' It is not in fact the answer which defines it that constitutes the law, but the question which is asked of it. It is in fact the (partial) defect in the Other that allows me, small subject, to pin a demand onto it and to demand an explanation: Why . . .? By what right . . .? If the Other was a plenum, everything would be smooth and I would be unable to ask for anything. I am therefore the Other's subject only if I can ask the Other to explain itself. Basically, I am the Other's subject to the extent that I can resist the Other. In that sense, *the subject is both one who is subjected and one who resists subjection*. In other words, *the subject is the Other's subject and one who resists the Other*.

If the subject is, in the last analysis, the one who resists, it is immediately apparent that there is one mistake we must not make when we attempt to make the subject autonomous: no one who has not previously submitted to the Other can escape the Other. How can we possibly resist the Other unless we have first been alienated in the Other? If we infringe that law, and escape it before we come under it, we may well find that we are free, but we will also find that we are nowhere. We will find ourselves in a chaotic space in which there are no signposts and which exists in a non-place and a non-time. As we shall see later, it is probably this kind of mistake that is being made today.

It can basically be said of the Other – understood as existing within the limits of mere reason – that it allows the symbolic to function insofar as it gives the subject something to lean on. This gives the subject's discourses some foundation, even if it is a fictional one.

On the structuralization of the Other

My second remark concerns the element of structuralism in Lacan's theory of the Other. For the contingent reasons that I am about to examine, and which have major theoretical implications, Lacan structuralizes the big Other and therefore turns it into a big Other transfigured throughout all eternity, self-identical at all times and in all places.

It will be recalled that Lacan was due to give a seminar on 'The names of the father' in 1963. The plural (names) is important by way of indicating a certain phenomenological approach to the Other – which is not surprising, if we think of Lacan's links with Merleau-Ponty. The attempt to find a principle behind the multiple was in keeping with the spirit of the times. We can, for example, find something similar in Claude Lefort's work on social and political phenomenology; he too was close to Merleau-Ponty. In his early work, Lefort was attempting to explain historical change in terms of what gives every society its specificity, whereas during the same period Lacan was exploring the many names of the father in order to find possible forms of unconscious social meaning. In the first – and only – session of that seminar (20 November 1963) Lacan speaks of, I quote, the 'various incarnations' of the Other and goes on to evoke Freud's mythical father of the horde, Lévi-Strauss's totemism (where 'the father can only be, in mythical terms, an animal'), the question of the father in St Augustine, the name of Elohim in the burning bush of the Jews, El Chaddaï, the Phoenician pottery of Upper Egypt, 'where the name is situated . . .'.

The seminar on the 'names of the father' was interrupted after this first session.[6] We never had 'The names of the father' that Lacan might otherwise have listed in the seminar, but we did later get a concept of the 'Name-of-the-Father' that was set in structuralist stone. It was, namely, a unified concept that was structuralized for all time, and with hyphens to hold it together. Its plurality was now restricted to a 'three-in-one' form (imaginary, real and symbolic; see Porge 1997). But it was no longer subject to any historical or geographical variation (or any other form of variation). All that remained of the 'names of the father' was a phantom appellation which returned in the form of 'les non-dupes

[6] The interruption was the result of Lacan's 'excommunication' from the International Psychoanalytic Association. Lacan's name was removed from the IPA's list of recognized training analysts on 13 Ocober 1963; the pretext used was his practice of 'short sessions'. On this period see the work of Elisabeth Roudinesco (1997: 301–8; 1990: 359–72).

errent', the title of the 1973–4 seminar.* This had different heuristic effects and displaced the original problem without solving it.[7]

I am not challenging this structuralization at all. Being able to think with a fixed category is probably a big step forward, but only on condition that it does not take away the variations and the diachrony, or the specificity of every figure of the Other. It must not, in other words, abolish the differences between the historical scenes in which the life of the subject unfolds. We can always try to repeat Freud's adage to the effect that the unconscious has no sense of time. True, but that does not give us adequate grounds for thinking that time has no sense of the unconscious! It is quite possible, in other words, to argue both that the unconscious has no sense of time and that the subject's condition undergoes historical variations.

If we try to understand why Lacan had to abandon the original pluralist project – which seemed fine – we will find only one explanation. Having been excommunicated from the IPA and obliged to interrupt his seminar, he was probably 'forced' to give guarantees to the few university institutions that were open to new ideas: the École Pratique des Hautes Études and the École Normale Supérieure in Rue d'Ulm. They allowed him to go on teaching in a context worthy of him and with an audience worthy of him. We know that the transfer was engineered by Althusser, who was also at odds with his own institution, namely the French Communist Party. Elisabeth Roudinesco describes the two conspirators wandering the streets of Paris one cold night in December 1963. I should imagine that Lacan, who was asking for a favour, had to conclude a sort of pact with Althusser: winning over the young intellectuals of France was the only way to put a stop to the exclusions and excommunications that were going on in their respective churches.[8] The project would not go through without massive

---

* A Lacanian pun on *les-noms-du-père*, 'the names-of-the-father', read as *les non-dupes errent* 'those who are not duped are in error'.

[7] It is significant that, ten years after he abandoned the seminar on 'Les Noms du père', Lacan seemed to challenge his listeners and future readers to find what was concealed in his teachings: 'What I was planning to say about the names of the father . . . might have been of use to them [the psychoanalytic societies]. That is precisely what I did not want. In any case, I know they won't find them by themselves.' (*Les Non-dupes errent*, 13 November 1973).

[8] 'We have to tell them something,' we read in the letter Lacan wrote to Althusser before they met. The 'them' refers to 'all those who are gravitating in your vicinity and who respect, or so you tell me, what I was doing'. Letter of 21 December 1963, *Magazin Littéraire*, no. 304, November 1992, p. 49.

input from what was then the most radical current within contemporary thought, namely structuralism. This does not mean that I doubt Lacan's commitment to structuralism. I simply want to show that, being extremely shrewd, Lacan was always able to exploit circumstances and opportunities in order to advance his theories. He succeeded in turning every obstacle to his own advantage. Structuralism certainly served his purposes for the moment, and Lacan exploited it to great advantage. But he never had any scruples about changing his theoretical mounts whenever they began to lose their wind – and this is precisely what he did with structuralism. Within five years, he was denouncing the 'so-called structuralist tub' everyone was dipping into (Lacan 1968), after having talked about the 'cultural sewer' no one could escape 'even by joining the Party'. The allusion to Althusser and his membership of the (Communist) Party, which he never left, seems quite clear.

I cannot stop myself from seeing the interrupted seminar as a sort of suppressed or censored chapter that stuck in Lacan's throat. The strange thing is that, having been excluded from the IPA and having been forced to stop his seminar, Lacan decided not to go on with it less than two months later, in January 1964, even though he had every opportunity to do so when he was back in the saddle at ENS.

I think that we are now, at long last, paying some of the costs of Lacan's excommunication. When he went to ENS, he had to refound his teachings on a new basis and to teach in ways that would ensure that he found an audience. This was a time when a powerful structuralism was making its presence felt. Now the defining feature of structuralism is its deliberate disregard for history. This is not to say that the structuralization was a mistake. On the contrary: Lacan had to preserve the Other in its entirety, together with its structure and its lack. But he also had to learn to list its different figures. And does not Saussure, who was the precursor of structuralism, tell us that there is no contradiction whatsoever between synchrony and studies in diachronic linguistics (which he called 'historical or dynamic')? So that, whilst we do in fact have a structural theory of the Other, we have no history of the Other: and that is becoming a tragedy now that we have reached a stage where the question of the Other, or of the absence of the Other, arises in a new modality, which forces us to rethink the models of subjectivation.

What the structuralized 'Name-of-the-Father' gives us to understand is that the Father has always already been deposed, and that this has certain implications for the subject. There is, however, no word about his permanent removal throughout history or about his new and unexpected stumbles. But this is precisely what we need if we are to be able to understand the contemporary exhaustion of the figures of the Other, which is specific to postmodernity, and its effects on psychical structures.

The Other as fiction

My third remark has to do with the nature of the Other: even the Other that sits at the centre of symbolic systems is in fact *imaginary*. I mean that the only things that can guarantee the symbolic function are figures with a fictional structure. A shared fiction is all we need in order to posit an Other that can provide us with an answer to the question of origins (which are lacking as such). In short, we have to believe in, and construct, the Other; if we do not, that question really will come back to torment us. That is the meaning of what Freud, at the end of the thirty-first 'New introductory lecture on psychoanalysis' (Freud [1933]: 80), calls *Kulturarbeit* ['the work of culture']: every culture tries in its own way to shape subjects by leaving on them a specific imprint that allows them to confront the question of origins, which can never be resolved. That is why we paint the Other, sing the praises of the Other and lend the Other a face and a voice. That is why we put the Other on stage, represent it or even over-represent it, sometimes in the form of something that cannot be represented. We kill for the Other. We become the Other's administrator. The Other's interpreter. The Other's prophet. The Other's stand-in. The Other's lieutenant. The Other's scribe. The Other's object. The Other wants. The Other dictates. But behind all these social masquerades, the only thing that matters about the Other is that, when it is transformed in this way, it tolerates on our behalf the things that we ourselves cannot tolerate. That is why the Other takes up so much room and demands so much from its subjects. It occupies the position of the *third party* which provides us with a foundation.

At the centre of the subject's discourses, we find, therefore, a figure, in other words one or several discursive beings in which the subject believes as though they were real. These are gods, devils, demons – beings who, in the face of chaos, guarantee the subject a permanence, an origin, an end and an order. Without that Other, that metasocial guarantor, it is difficult for the subject to be a self. She does not know which way to turn, and all being-together is itself in peril because a common reference to the same Other is the only thing that allows different individuals to belong to the same community. The Other is the agency through which a foundational authority is established for the subject, and it is that authority that makes a temporal order possible. The Other is also a 'there', an external point that allows the foundation of a 'here', or an interiority. If I am to be here, the Other basically has to be there. Unless I make that detour through the Other, I cannot know where I am, cannot accede to the symbolic function and cannot construct any spatiality or temporality. Lacanian psychoanalysis has made a great contribution to discussions of the key question of access to symbolization. On the other hand, it has nothing to say about the question of the variance of the Other. It is as though, goaded on by the dominant structuralism of the day and its desire to grasp the subject, it had hypostasized the Other in a form that was valid once and for all. Whereas in fact the Other has constantly changed throughout history. Indeed, history is the history of the Other or, to be more precise, the history of the figures of the Other. We therefore really do have to construct a historical psychology because, without it, we will have great difficulty in understanding the origins of what is happening to us now. A whole intellectual field has to be re-explored. In France, the task was begun by Ignace Meyerson, followed by Jean-Pierre Vernant for the ancient world, and Marcel Gauchet is attempting to explore the modern period in similar ways.

Figures of the Other

Having reached this point, a question arises: what Others, or what figures of the Other, have human beings constructed in order to submit to them, so as to present themselves as subjects of those Others?

Given that the 'subject' is *subiectus*, or one who has been *subjected*, we can say that history is a series of subjections to great figures placed at the centre of symbolic configurations. Drawing up a list of those figures is easy: the subject was subjected to the forces of *physis* in the Greek world, to the Cosmos or to Spirits in other worlds, to God in monotheisms, to the king in monarchies, to the people under the republic, to the race in Nazism and other racial ideologies, to the nation in nationalism, to the proletariat in communism. In other words, the subject has been subjected to a variety of fictions and a great deal of effort was required to construct each of them. Each of these fictions was a major production or a very demanding scenography.

I am certainly not saying that all these figures are the same; on the contrary, the whole of economic, political, intellectual, artistic and technological life changes, depending on which figure of the Other is chosen and placed at the centre of the politico-symbolic system. All constraints and all social relations change, as does our being-together; the one thing that remains constant is our common relationship with submission.

In that respect, the important thing is that texts, dogmas, grammars and a whole field of knowledge have always had to be developed to subordinate the subject, that is, to produce the subject as such, and to regulate an enormous variety of ways of working, talking, believing, thinking, living, eating, singing, loving, dying, and so on.[9] Thus it seems that what we call 'education' has never been anything more than the instutionalization of the type of submission that has to be induced in order to produce subjects.

The subject, qua speaking subject, is basically the subject of the Other. A subject is a subject only because he or she is the subject of a Subject or an Other: we have only to list all the figures that have succeeded one another in the place of the Subject or the Other: *physis*, God, king, people . . .

If we hypothetically assume that this is the right way to state the identity of the Other and to establish the premises for a history of the Other, it is immediately apparent that the distance between me and what founds me as a subject constantly decreases as the figure of the Other changes. If we follow the transition that takes us from *physis* to the people, we can see certain key stages in the Other's return to the human world. In polytheism, we have the impassable distance between us and the multiple gods of *physis* (humans can never reach the world of the immortals, but the gods – identified as 'Gods of the moment' by the great German Hellenist Walter Friedrich Otto (1954) – can at any moment appear instantly in the human world and even 'ride' whoever they like, to use the language of trance cults). Then we have the infinite distance of the transcendental monotheisms, and the median distance that separates the throne from both heaven and earth in the divine-right monarchies. Finally, we have the intermundane distance between individual and collectivity in the republic . . . As we move from one figure to the next, the distance between subject

[9] Mention should be made here of the work of Claude Lefort (1978), which looks both at what individualizes societies and at what allows one social meaning to be transformed into another.

and Other or Subject decreases. It obviously does not do so at a constant rate; there are advances and retreats and even some aberrant deviations (such as race), but it does decrease. As we shall soon see, this distance is reduced to zero during the transition to postmodernity. But, before we get to that point, we have to deal with a crucial issue: that of how the forms of the unconscious vary depending on the distance between us and the Other.

Are there ages of the unconscious?

This finally brings us to one of those major questions which are very rarely discussed but which nonetheless represent a decisive issue for contemporary thought. I have been wondering about the possibility that the Other might undergo historical variations. As soon as we advance that hypothesis, we can legitimately ask if its variance does not, *ipso facto*, mean that manifestations of the unconscious also vary, simply because the unconscious is a relationship with the Other. If the Other actually does appear in different forms, then the unconscious must also take different forms. Assuming that I know what the unconscious looks like today, I am basically entitled to ask what it looked like prior to modernity, or in what is conventionally termed traditional societies.

Marcel Gauchet has a powerful suggestion to make (2002: 251): 'the world of the traditional personality is a world without an unconscious to the extent that it is a society in which the symbolic reigns in an explicitly organizational manner.' These societies are indeed constituted by the exclusive hegemony of a Subject which is the sole determinant of their prevailing ways of life (ways of speaking, telling stories, working, eating, loving, dying . . .). The characteristic feature of these traditional worlds is submission to the Other on a mass scale. But does this necessarily mean that they are societies without an unconscious?

If we are to answer this question, we must, I think, make a distinction between two very different types of traditional society: societies in which there is a monolithic Other, as in monotheistic societies, and societies in which there is a multiple Other, as in polytheistic societies. I will not discuss the former, except to say that they are societies in which an individual's every action is constantly monitored to ensure that it conforms to dogma. Polytheistic societies introduce an important nuance: individuals living in archaic societies are also dominated by higher forces that transcend them in the absolute sense, but their dependency upon that power is transformed by the fact that it is

multiple. One of the characteristics of individuals living in polytheistic societies is that their narratives show that they are constantly at
odds with an elusive multiple Other. Ultimately, as we can see from
the great Greek narratives of the *Iliad* and the *Odyssey*, these individuals are turning to seers and prophetesses for oracles that can inter-
pret the signs sent them by the gods. This is the only way they can find
their direction in a world which is governed by multiple and potentially contradictory forces.

These forces, which can, as Vernant puts it (1974), be 'grouped
together, associated, contrasted or differentiated', intervene directly in
human affairs, either through external manifestations (the unleashing
of natural elements such as storms, winds and earthquakes, the appearance of animals, illnesses . . .) or through internal manifestations
(ideas that come to mind, premonitory dreams, amorous impulses,
warlike ardour, panic, shame . . .). The *tragic* is a product of this religious conception of a world which is being torn apart by conflicting
forces. As Vernant remarks of the Greeks, 'destiny is ambiguous and
opaque'. The two levels never overlap, and the subject is therefore
always torn between, and baffled by, contradictory forces to such an
extent that he is both unable to act and unable not to act. Whatever the
individual does, he cannot escape the destiny that awaits him. He constantly reads and interprets his destiny, but it is always written in code
and ciphers. Like Oedipus, who fled Corinth when the Delphic oracle
revealed to him that he would kill his father and marry his mother, he
will meet his destiny even as he attempts to avoid that terrible fate.

In terms of their relationship with the unconscious, these traditional societies can, I believe, be characterized thus: the reason why
this world appears to have no unconscious is, as Marcel Gauchet
argues, that the unconscious is not constituted by acts of repression
that have been internalized by a subject. On the contrary, it is made
fully visible by the oracles and narratives of the prophetesses, rhap-
sodes, aedes and inspired poets, who reveal the Other's plans. Once
we have established this major difference, the formal similarity
between the two states is revealed by two characteristic features of the
formations of the unconscious: on the one hand, and as in the
Freudian conscious, the distinction between true and false does not
exist in these mythical narratives;[10] on the other, these narratives

---

[10] In a crucial passage, Vernant makes the point that 'myths mobilized a form of
logic [. . .] of the ambiguous [. . .] which is not that of the yes/no binary' (Vernant
1974: 'Conclusions').

constantly reveal scenes of sacrifice, scenes in which the boundary between divinity, humanity and animality is crossed, scenes in which the boundaries that separate the living from the dead are crossed, and incestuous scenes that transgress the generation gap. The great book of prohibitions which, in the modern unconscious, are usually thoroughly repressed appears to be strangely open and immediately readable in these traditional societies. It is as though this direct and exclusive relationship with a multiple and contradictory Other in some way displayed the existence of the unconscious rather than concealing it.

It is as though, as Nietzsche put it so long ago (Nietzsche 1971: Preface §4), the Greeks put everything on display: 'Oh, those Greeks! They knew how to live. What is required for that is to stop courageously at the surface, the fold, the skin, to adore appearance, to believe in forms, tones, words, in the whole Olympus of appearance. Those Greeks were superficial – *out of profundity*.'

It is because the unconscious was put on display 'on the surface' in this way that Freud went in search of the organizing concept of psychoanalysis – the Oedipal knot – in the Greek myths of the House of Thebes. This strange and disconcertingly direct access to the archaic form of the unconscious is still of contemporary relevance. Any informed reader senses this on reading Vernant's or Détienne's studies of Greek myths and archaic powers. To confirm that this is the case, one has only to look at the long list of the psychoanalysts who have turned to Vernant to find there such and such feature more vividily expressed than in their clinical material. Some of them actually suspect that Vernant is doing psychoanalysis but is either unwilling to admit it or is doing so without realizing it. And his studies do indeed appear to be informed by psychoanalytic categories. The similarity must, however, be problematized; if it is not, it will be called into question – and Vernant himself has questioned it.[11] If Vernant's analyses are not inspired by psychoanalysis, we have to assume that his inspiration comes not from this immediately visible (non-Freudian) 'archaic unconscious', but from some other feature of the polytheistic societies he studies.

[11] Vernant (1972: 77) wonders 'in what sense can a literary work belonging to the culture of fifth-century Athens and which is itself a very free transposition of a much older Theban legend, which predates the *polis*, confirm an early twentieth-century doctor's observations about the patients who haunted his consulting room?'

These brief remarks about archaic societies do at least allow us to put forward a major hypothesis: just as there is a history of the Other, there would appear to be a history of the unconscious, and it could appear to have left its mark on us. The unconscious is indeed bound up with a historical sequence of figures of the Other. And that is why Lacan said in such provocative terms that 'the unconscious is politics'.[12] Given that it is a relationship with the Other, the unconscious is of necessity political, to the extent that the Other organizes the social realm in which the subject appears. And this Other changes throughout history. This is in fact clearly what Lacan is suggesting when, in the next sentence of his aphorism, he defines 'the Other [as] the locus for the deployment of a word [*parole*] that is, in the circumstances, contractual'. It is significant that Lacan uses the Lockean (and then Rousseauist) term 'contract' to define the Other after he has opened the unconscious to politics in this way. Indeed, if the Other is a product of the (social) contract, it is obviously an agency that is always being remodelled and subject to never-ending social negotiations (which, in Locke, can also take the form of the People's right to rebel). And it therefore inevitably determines distinct forms of the unconscious, corresponding to the type of contract that is in force.

There would, then, appear to be different ages of the unconscious. We have suspected that this is the case for the last fifty years: it is no accident that the same Lacan should, in the 1950s, have described neurosis, which is modernity's prerogative, as an 'individual myth' (Lacan 1979).[13] This appears to be a clear indication that, before it manifests itself at the level of the individual, the unconscious finds expression in archaic societies and in the collective narratives of oral societies. The unconscious manifested itself openly in the collective myths of periods which had a multiple and contradictory Other. The hypothesis

---

[12] Lacan, *La Logique du fantasme* (10 May 1967, unpublished). Lacan refrains from commenting on his aphorism. Whilst it may have amused the highly politicized members of the École Normale of the day, I suspect that it left the analysts in the audience very perplexed.

A commentary on this proposition can be found in M. Plon's 'L'In-conscient de la politique' (2001).

[13] He did so in a lecture given to Jean Wahl's Collège de Philosophie on 4 March 1953: 'If we proceed from the definition of myth as a certain objectified representation of an epos or as a chronicle expressing in an imaginary way the fundamental relationships characteristic of a certain mode of being human at a specific period, if we understand it as the social manifestation – latent or patent, virtual or actual, full or void of meaning – of this mode of being, then it is certain that we can trace its function in the actual experience of a neurotic' (Lacan 1979: 408).

that there are ages of the unconscious will lead me to deal with the question of the form the unconscious takes in our postmodern contemporaneity. But we must look first at the form it took in modernity.

Modernity: elements for a history of the Other, continued

Now that we have defined traditional societies, which are characterized by the exclusive hegemony of a Subject – simple or multiple – it is much easier to define modern societies: modernity is a collective space in which the subject is defined by several of these instances of the Other. At this point, my typology will then be as follows: there are societies with a multiple Other (as in monotheisms), and societies with several Others. The latter correspond to the coming of the modern period. Since then we have been governed by several Subjects rather than by one. Modernity therefore appears to correspond to the end of the unity of the spirits that once assembled around a single Subject.

This is what 'modernity' would mean: that several Subjects coexist, but their coexistence is not necessarily peaceful.

Just when did our world enter modernity? Braudel's answer, which displays a certain wit, is 'somewhere between 1400 and 1800'. If we really have to set a date, I would trace modernity back to the moment when exchanges of all kinds (cultural, commercial, but also warlike and colonizing) began to take place, between Europe and America on the one hand, say in 1492, the year of Columbus's conquest of America, and between Europe and the Orient on the other, say in 1517, when the Portuguese reached Canton in China. We could then say that the turn of the sixteenth and seventeenth centuries in Europe corresponds to the beginning of modernity. It also corresponds to the beginning of the globalization of trade and to the first contacts, many of them violent, between the world's various populations. Very different Subjects* met and had to learn to live together by learning the lessons of their earlier encounters (one thinks, in this respect, of the cities of Cordoba, Toledo, Granada and Seville which, between the twelfth century and the fifteenth, saw the encounter between Judaism, Islam and Christianity. These centres were the real precursors of modernity). This period also corresponds to an unprecedented phenomenon: the establishment of a link between technology and

---

* Henceforth Subject (*le grand Sujet*) is capitalized in order to distinguish between it and the subjects that organize themselves around it.

scientific grammars (it has a name: Leonardo da Vinci). This articulation lead to a general redeployment of representation and narrative: the Renaissance was explicitly conceptualized by the Florentine Vasari, who was the first art historian: a *moderno* age was about to be ushered in by the *rinascita* of the 'good art' of the *antico* golden age, which would transcend the 'bad art' of the dark, *vecchio* age of the Middle Ages.

The generalization of these contacts and this new cultural landscape had major implications, because it was at this historical moment that the West began to fling itself into a frantic attempt to transcend itself. The modern era therefore began with a moment of civilizational upheaval. It was an upheaval both inside and outside Europe, in that it led to a search for a way of life that could articulate permanent change in every domain: technological, scientific, political, aesthetic, philosophical . . .

Since then, nothing has been able to resist this aggressive way of life, which is intent upon destroying all the old fixed values, the old rites and the old habitus of societies which had a single centre, even if this means instilling a feeling of instability, permanent crisis and tension in the subjectivity and a recurrent 'discontent of civilization'. Definitions of our subjective condition of 'being ourselves' and 'being-together' are not the same when our relationship with the Subject is simple, and when it is complex. And, in modernity, that relationship is complex.

We became modern when the world ceased to be closed, shut in and shut up by, and for, a single Subject, and when it was transformed and became, as Koyré puts it, a world that was open, multiple or even 'infinite'.[14] It therefore seems to me that we can think of modernity as a collective space in which the subject is subjected to several figures of the Subject. This diversification of the Subject and this openness were not, however, sudden events. First, there had to be an encounter between different economies which came into contact suddenly and violently as a result of the discovery of several worlds. And there then had to be an encounter with other cultures. This involved the execution of plans both for their conquest and for their mutual understanding.

---

[14] I refer to Alexandre Koyré's theses on the history of philosophical and scientific thought in the sixteenth and seventeenth centuries (Koyré 1957), and especially on the role played by Neoplatonism in the invention of the new Galilean order, which evicted man from his place at the centre of the universe and led to the rejection of fixed views on the universe.

This diversification of the figures of the Subject was concomitant with the decline and then the collapse of the church's control over scientific discoveries: 1663 was the year when the Vatican condemned Galileo for his discoveries about the movement of the earth, but it also marked the end of the control of religious dogma over scientific discoveries.

The same openness then appeared at the philosophical level with the rise of philosophies that preserved the principle of submission to the Subject but which also tried to define specific zones of freedom and action. The Cartesian subject, defined by her own capacity for thought (the famous 'I think, therefore I am' is still, however, a correlate of the God who guarantees that knowledge), is obviously the most important example. (It is no accident that Descartes, whose definition of the subject goes far beyond that of a subject who is merely the subject of a king, should have chosen exile in the United Provinces, which was a truly advanced laboratory for modernity in the domains of economics, politics, aesthetics and philosophy.)[15]

At the level of political philosophy, the real beginning of this openness came at the end of the seventeenth century in England (Locke defined the theory of contract, popular sovereignty and the natural rights of man in 1690) and at the end of the eighteenth century in France.

The openness became more pronounced in the eighteenth century with the *Aufklärung* and the Enlightenment, which marked the definitive philosophical emancipation of the subject. Europe then developed the more radical project of extracting a subject from nature. Rousseau began to define it all by himself, as he believed he had discovered it in various accounts of voyages to the West Indies.

The culmination of this process was the birth of the critical Kantian subject. This is obviously a subject who is never at peace, who is

[15] Witness Descartes's letter of 5 May 1631 to Guez de Balzac (Descartes 1953: 941–2): 'I urge you to choose Amsterdam for your retreat and to prefer it, I would say not only to all the Convents of the Capuchins and the Chartreux, but to all the finest houses of France and Italy . . . In this great city, where I am living, there is no man apart from myself who is not being involved in trade [*marchandise*], everyone is so intent on his profits that I could spend my whole life without being seen by anyone . . . In what other country could one enjoy such complete freedom, and in what other country could one sleep with fewer worries, as there are always armed men afoot to guard us? I do not understand how you can love the air of Italy so much. When one breathes it, one often breathes in the plague . . . and there the darkness of night covers larcenies and murders.'

always decentred in such a way that his very decentering can give rise to the work of reason. All that remained to be done was to promote that permanent decentring as a 'supreme practical principle' in order to demonstrate that 'rational nature exists as an end in itself' (Kant 2002: §32) and is accountable only to itself.

Reason, or modernity as multireferential space

Modernity is now five hundred years old, but it was not until the nineteenth century, when it was fully established in political terms, that it became possible to take stock of the civilizational upheaval it had provoked. It took a poet to describe the new course that the boat on which humanity had embarked was following, to see that civilization was drifting and, more importantly still, to realize that civilization marked the end of the absolute monopoly of a Subject: civilization was adrift. It was in fact Baudelaire, one of the greatest romantic poets of the nineteenth century, who coined the term 'modernity' around 1850. He describes its new subject in 'The painter of modern life':

> And so, walking or quickening his pace, he goes his way, for ever in search. In search of what? We may accord that this man, such as I have described him, this solitary mortal endowed with an active imagination, always roaming the great desert of man, has a nobler aim than that of the pure idler, a more general aim than the fleeting pleasure of circumstance. He is looking for that indefinable something we may be allowed to call 'modernity'. (Baudelaire 1972: 402)

One suspects, on reading this definition, that this very Kantian-looking 'solitary mortal' may well be chasing after modernity, but that he will never catch up with it because its defining feature is that it transcends itself, so to speak, because it is constantly questioning its own foundations. Modernity is in fact that which attacks everything. We have only to look at the last hundred years to see that nothing in Europe has escaped it: the traditional forms of man's submission to gods, kings and powers, values in philosophy, genres in literature, fixed metres in poetry, harmony in music, ornamentation in architecture, perspective and figuration in painting, the foundations of language, logic and mathematics, the stable structure of the space-time continuum in the universe, not forgetting the stable position of the subject at the centre of the universe and of itself within a general physics, metaphysics, ontology and psychology . . .

Modernity is therefore a space in which we find subjects who are, as such, subjected to several Subjects: to spirits and gods, to one God in a variety of monotheistic guises (Judaism, Catholicism, the various Protestantisms, Islam . . .), to the King, the Republic, the People, the Proletariat, the Race . . . All these elements can be found in modernity, which likes nothing better than changing from one definition to the next – which explains the mobile, crisis-prone and eminently critical side of modernity. *Reason is therefore not so much a new Subject that has outlived all the others as a space that has opened up within thought. It is a space where all possible disagreements as to Subjects past, present and future are endlessly discussed.*[16] Modernity is a space in which, because the basic referent is continually changing, the whole of symbolic space has become complex. There is, then, a Subject in modernity, an Other – if not many Others, or at least many figures of the Other.

With modernity, the space and time of thought escape their local determinations: we no longer live in the immemorial time of myth, in the referential time that revealed God to men, in the chronicled rural time of the works and the days, the historical times of a succession of reigns, or any other possible time: *we live in all times at once*. It is, of course, thanks to Kant that thought ceases to be conditioned by local temporalities. For Kant, it is a generalized cosmopolitanism that gives us access to the universal.[17] On this point, I am at least in partial agreement with Deleuze when he, following Kant, remarks that the time is 'out of joint' (Deleuze uses Shakespeare's expression in *Hamlet* I v): 'Kant's historical situation allowed him to grasp the implications of this reversal. Time is no longer the cosmic time of an original celestial movement, nor is it the rural time that was derived from meteorological movements. It has become the time of the city and nothing other, the pure order of time' (Deleuze 1998: 28; translation modified).[18] I agree with Deleuze when he attempts to demonstrate that

---

[16] There were, however, attempts to turn Reason into a new Subject. A political attempt to do so was made during the French Revolution, when temples dedicated to the cult of Reason were built (on 5 frimaire of the year IV, or 25 November 1795, the Convention officially dedicated all the churches in Paris to Reason.) Positivism represents a philosophical attempt to do the same thing – that of Comte in the *Positivist Catechism* (Comte 1966).

[17] So much so that, according to Kant ([1784b]: §8), this form of philosophy will lead to 'a perfect political constitution as the only possible state within which all natural capacities of mankind can be developed completely'. Kant even regarded the realization of this 'universal cosmopolitan state' as a 'hidden plan of nature'.

[18] See also 'Quatre leçons sur Kant', at www.webdeleuze.com.

Kantian time is a new and multiple time, which is in keeping with the cosmopolitan time of the city, but not when he concludes from this multireferential time to a time subject to continuous variations. I do not in fact think that Kant was a Deleuzean: he did not take the step leading from the multiple to the vertigo of the continuous variations which Deleuze celebrates so much under the description of 'tensor'. For Kant, Reason is still a battlefield forever articulated around successive times.

The three features of the modern subjective condition: differend, neurosis and criticism

Because it is characterized by a plurality of Subjects, modernity has generated new discursive forms expressed in new ways of speaking and new forms of linguistic self-realization. The first of these forms is bound up with this: modernity sanctioned the development of the new and extremely violent modalities of domination (such as colonization and slavery) that Europe implemented in its struggle against other civilizations. These modalities were characterized by what Lyotard calls 'the *differend*' (Lyotard 1983; cf the excellent commentary in Amorim 1996: 51–7). A differend is not the outcome of a form of subjugation imposed by some Subject or other; it derives from a special terror, which is without dispute because it comes from elsewhere – from a different world, determined by a Subject who is different and hands down judgements and sanctions which have been decided in advance and are not open to discussion. These are always carried out summarily and transgress the principles of a discursive sequence.

As the differend spread beyond Europe, modernity saw the creation of a new discursive space, characterized by an internal *critique*. The paradox of modernity is that it generated such radically different discursive forms. This antinomy caught the attention of J. M. G. Le Clézio, who has devoted a fine book to the conquest of the New World: 'at the very moment when it [. . .] was inventing the foundations of a new republic, the West inaugurated the era of a new barbarism' (Le Clézio 1988: 228). The unprecedented deployment of a critical discursive space in the West was correlated with a deafening silence: 'the silence of the Indian world is probably one of humanity's greatest tragedies.'

The critical discursive form arises because all definitions of the Other can be found in modernity, which, from this point onwards, can no longer function except as a space which is open to multiple, or even contradictory, references and in which the signposts are constantly being moved.

This multiplicity of the forms taken by the Subject and of the figures of the Other in modernity has further major implications: the subjective condition is not defined solely by *criticism* (in the realm of secondary processes, be they conscious or unconscious), but also, as Freud has taught us to say, by *neurosis* in the realm of primary processes, that is, in the unconscious.

The modern subject is *critical* to the extent that she can no longer be anything but a subject who plays on references that constantly compete, or even come into conflict, with one another. This latter aspect is obviously decisive for thought when it is in a situation of modernity: it can only exist as a space defined by criticism, as no dogmatic reference can, in principle, last long before fire is returned. Modernity is, in effect, a site where distinct, or even contradictory, *ideologies* supported by different Subjects clash. It is also significant that the concept of 'ideology' emerged in Kantian circles in the early 1800s.[19] It is basically this clash of distinct ideologies, which is characteristic of modernity, that gives reason no rest and institutes it, as Kant has done, into a 'universal practical law'.

But this critical subject is *ipso facto* subject to *neurosis*. It is the fact that no normally constituted individual can obey all the action-oriented moral maxims the transcendental subject is required to obey (as expounded in the *Critique of Practical Reason* (Kant 1993)) that gives birth to the Freudian subject. That is why the Freudian subject (who is subject to guilt) and the Kantian subject (who submits to ethics) are a pair. The former is, in some way, born of the impossibility of satisfying the critical freedom that is demanded of the latter. The individual never quite matches up to the critical freedom required of him, that is, to what desire requires of him. For, as Lacan puts it when he talks about what he is trying to exhume in his text on Kant and Sade (Lacan [1963a]), 'the moral law [. . .] is simply desire in its pure state [. . .] That is why I wrote "Kant with Sade" ' (Lacan 1994: 276).

The subject can accede to desire or to the transcendental only when she identifies with a Law that is a pure empty form devoid of all content and of all feeling. Now there is a mismatch between this Law,

[19] According to Destutt de Tracy, who knew his Kant, 'ideology' refers to a system of intermediaries between matter and spirit, in other words to the representations that dominate the human mind or the spirit of a social group (Destutt de Tracy 1970). The term is later used in the same sense by Marx, especially in his *German Ideology*.

which Lacan identifies with desire insofar as its wants and desires are imperative,[20] and the satisfaction afforded to the individual by empirical objects, not to say – as psychoanalysts do say – part-objects.

We now have to qualify Lacan's surprising discovery that desire in its pure state is equivalent to the ethical Law – and we also know that it caused a stir, since it was thought until then, thanks largely to the influence of Sartre, that desire was inevitably the opposite of the Law. Lacan's identification of the two was a gradual process. In 'Kant with Sade', he merely posited that 'the law and *repressed* desire are one and the same thing'. A year later, he asserts, as I have just recalled, that the ethical law is perfectly identical with desire *in its pure state* (my emphasis).

I agree with Lacan about this equivalence, but I disagree with him when he asserts that it is Kant's contemporary Sade who has revealed what remained repressed in Kant's moral law: 'Sade represents [. . .] the first step of a subversion of which Kant [. . .] represents the turning point [. . .]. I shall be able to claim that it [*Philosophy in the Bedroom*] yields the truth of the *Critique*' (Lacan [1963a]: 645–6). According to Lacan, Sade demonstrates that the law includes the desire to transgress the law.[21] Lacan basically believes that sadism, like any essentially perverse impulse, can catch Kantianism in the trap of the ethical Law because it takes this Law to the point of transgression.[22] I fear that Lacan goes astray over this point: sadism in fact interrupts the movement of Kantian reason rather than transgressing it. It becomes fixated on an Other who is assumed to be stronger than all Others, by making that Other its ultimate reference. This Other is Nature. Sade's 'philosophy in the bedroom' is a philosophy of Nature. It is in fact Nature that experiences *jouissance* [*qui jouit*] thanks to the actions of Sade's libertines (male and female). Appearances to the

---

[20] Desire, like the law, wants. This is the major theme of Lacan's 1959–60 seminar on 'The ethics of psychoanalysis': 'The breakthrough is achieved by Kant [. . .] To the extent that it imposes the necessity of a practical reason. Obligation affirms an unconditional "Thou shalt" [. . .] Now we analysts are able to recognize that place as the place occupied by desire' (Lacan 1992: 315–16).

[21] In the 1950s, Bataille and Blanchot did a lot of work on the theme of obeying the law by transgressing it.

[22] In 'Kant with Sade', Lacan remarks that, to the best his knowledge, the link between *Philosophy in the Bedroom* and the *Critique of Practical Reason* had 'never been pointed out before' (Lacan [1963a]: 645). Yet almost twenty years earlier, Horkheimer and Adorno demonstrated in their excursus on 'Juliette or Enlightenment and morality' that Sade's characters obey a Kantian categorical imperative (Horkheimer and Adorno 1973: 81–119).

contrary notwithstanding, Kant, in his wisdom, seems to me to go much further than Sade because, for him, all Others are equally valid and their only role is to perpetuate the endless, restless motion of reason in action. Nature does not have any special pre-eminence in Kant. That is why I do not think that sadism reveals what is repressed in Kant's ethics or that, if it does, it does so in order to interrupt its course. We might therefore say that, paradoxically, it is Sade and not Kant who interrupts reason (and desire) by introducing a permanent transgression. And this is also why I do not think (like Adorno) that the dialectics of reason, and especially the development of instrumental reason and technological progress, is 'ultimately self-destructive' (Horkheimer and Adorno 1973: 4) and leads to the catastrophe of Nazism. The Nazis did indeed invoke Nature to block the progress of Reason – but their Nature obviously had nothing in common with Sade's, as it was supposedly embodied in a superior race. Their imprecations against cosmopolitanism, which constantly revives Reason in all its forms, demonstrate that they were anything but Kantians. It was therefore the fact that the progress of reason came to a halt that led to Nazism, and not its continuation.

The only thing about which we can really agree is, in short, that desire and the moral Law are equivalent to one another. And that the individual, who is forced to seek satisfaction in objects that always remain part-objects, cannot accede to desire. The individual is prevented from doing so, but does not really know why, and that ignorance obviously instils a feeling of guilt. Lacan makes this point when he demonstrates that 'the only thing one can be guilty of is giving ground relative to one's desire' (1992: 321). The moral obligation to obey reason, generated by a multiple time, cannot therefore be followed in all its practical implications (except by the one whom Lacan will call 'the hero'). The outcome is a moral debt, and it has fallen to Freud to demonstrate that it was also a symbolic debt.

We know that guilt is absolutely central to Freud's theory. Neurosis is the currency in which each and every subject pays its symbolic debt to the Other (the father, according to Freud), who takes care of the question of origins. Neurosis flourished in the period of modernity simply because the debt is owed to an Other who appears in different guises, and hence takes many different forms.

In that respect, it is no accident that psychoanalysis should have come into being in Austria at a time when history had so many figures of the Other: it should not be forgotten that Austro-Hungary was a 'KK' (*Kaiserlich und Koeniglich*) kingdom, under the tutelage of a twofold Subject: the King–Emperor Franz-Josef. The Kaiser and the Koenig derived their authority from gods who were not always dead (that of the Old Testament, worshipped by Ashkenazy Judaism, and that of Christianity) and who represented several nations and homelands (the Austro-Hungarian compromise of 1867 recognized the existence of a Hungarian state, the Austria of the Habsburg-Lorraines, and an assortment of countries with the hereditary Emperor of Austria as their sovereign). To complicate things still further, in the effervescent Vienna, the implications of new ontologies deriving from logic, philosophy, aesthetics and physics were adding even more names to what was already a long list of fathers. This was probably the first time in history that there had been so many concomitant figures of the Other in one place. Basically, there were a lot of fathers in Vienna. Probably too many. This plethora of fathers can be seen as an indication that the paternal figure was beginning to break down. It will be recalled that, for Musil, the KK kingdom had become one big 'Kakania'. Psychoanalysis was born of an excess which signalled a lack and a decay of the paternal figure.[23] When there are lots of fathers, there are lots of scores to be settled with them, and that means a lot of hysterics, because hysteria is characterized by rivalry, guilt, seduction, and debts to the Other. I speak, therefore I owe. And my *guilt* – the word is, as I have said, the key to Freud's discovery – is the debt that I cannot pay back to the Other, who allows me to speak. The debt therefore revolves around the question of the father: the father as name, as he who names and he through whom we gain access to the symbolic. The father [*père*] functions as a marker [*re-père*] and starting point for spatial and temporal sequences, narrative lines, histories, space and time.

Freud's stroke of genius was to build a specific stage or a discursive theatre where this relationship with the Other could be acted out or re-enacted. The stage built by Freud was specifically modern and was in keeping with a time when, as I have already shown, the unconscious was being put on show in individual narratives, as well as in the collective oral stories that were constantly being passed on and reworked, as they are in traditional societies.

The twin determinants of the modern subject appear to be contradictory. How can someone who is neurotic be truly critical?

---

[23] See Gay (1991). The author relates the invention of psychoanalysis to the crisis in paternity described in the work of Hermann Broch, Robert Musil, Karl Kraus, Joseph Roth and Elias Canetti.

Neurosis, with its propensity for repetition, does seem to be incompatible with the free deployment of criticism. But, precisely because they are trapped in repetition, neurotics are in fact the best at encouraging criticism. We also know how the hysteric can keep the master on his toes [*faire courir*] by signalling to them 'that's still not it'. 'The hysteric is the unconscious in action, and puts the master up against the wall and tells him to produce' (Lacan 1970b: 89). To put it in more general terms, if we assume that criticism and neurosis are incompatible, we forget the neurotic's ability (no matter what kind of neurotic he is) to want the world interpreted in terms of his symptoms, in terms of what is insistent in his discourse without his realizing it. The Freudian subject and the Kantian subject form a pair. They are sibling rivals who eventually find that they can get along fairly well together: neurosis can, in certain conditions, become the best spur to criticism. At all events, modernity owes everything to these two subjects, who are so closely related thanks to its characteristic relationship with the multiple figures of the Other. Where the modern subject is concerned, we might say that he is characterized by a 'Kant with Freud'.

Postmodernity as the decline of the Subject

This twofold definition of a modern subject who is both neurotic and critical collapses, in my view, during the transition to postmodernity. Because of the critical and crisis-prone space in which it moves, the defining feature of modernity is its tendency to attack everything – including itself. It ends up by being caught in its own snares. Marcel Gauchet, who describes the moment when modernity's pre-eminent political creation – democracy – turns on itself, argues, however, that 'there is no such thing as postmodernity because there is nothing in the "post" that wasn't there in the "pre" ' (Gauchet 2002: xv). That does not, on the other hand, prevent him from immediately adding, 'this does not alter the fact that there is a break'. Marcel Gauchet appears to have chosen to work on continuities; I propose to work on breaks. What discontinuity and what basic change do we observe as we move from modern space to so-called postmodern space?

Why has this twofold description of the modern subject – neurotic and critical – broken down? Quite simply because no figure of the Other and no Subject has any real validity in our postmodernity. What Subject could impress today's younger generation? What Others? What figures of the Other do we now have in our postmodernity?

It seems that, whilst all the ancient Subjects and all those of modernity are obviously still available, none of them has enough prestige to impress. They all seem to be affected by the same symptom of decadence. The decline of the figure of the Father in Western modernity has often been noted: in his first published work on family complexes, Lacan himself was already talking about the decline of the paternal imago (Lacan 1938). The paternal imago is of course the Father in his symbolic dimension, but all figures of the Father are in decline too: our heavenly Father, the Fatherland and all the other ways of celebrating the Father.

I think we can trace the irreversible decline of all possible figures of the Subject back to Auschwitz. After Auschwitz – a catastrophe that occurred in the heart of the most cultivated region in the world – there is nothing to suggest that we can still invoke a Subject capable of guaranteeing the possible existence of speaking subjects. Auschwitz has made the *differend*, which destroys the principle of discursive logic and which was once characteristic of the situation of colonization, central to European culture. No form of Subject is possible now. The civilization which has produced the successive Subjects supposed to save us has devoured itself. Auschwitz has destroyed all possible laws. The poet Ghérassim Luca (2001) puts it in terms that could not be more scathing or more concise: 'How can we condemn in the name of the law/A crime committed in the name of the law?' So long as the crime committed in the name of the law (the genocide of the Indians or the slave trade, for example) remained outside European territory, it did not detract from the authority of the West's Subjects. On the contrary. But when the crime was committed in Europe and led to the self-destruction of the European civilization, all those Subjects lost their legitimacy. All at once, they looked like cleverly constructed but terrible illusions, which would ultimately lead us to nothing but the most disconcerting antinomy of all: the antinomy that transforms – or inverts – law into crime, and crime into law. Since then, we have been left completely to our own devices, and we cannot really come to terms with it.

In postmodernity, there is basically no Other in the sense of a symbolic Other, or an incomplete set onto which the subject really can pin a demand, of which he can make a demand or ask a question and to which he can raise an objection. In that sense, we could say either that postmodernity is a regime without Others or that postmodernity is full of semblances of Others that immediately reveal themselves for what they are: humbug.

Nothing will come to our rescue. In postmodernity there are no more soteriological narratives, whereas modernity was full of them.

At first sight, the collapse of the central fiction that once organized our lives seems to be a twilight of the idols – which sounds rather like good news, especially to anyone who has read Nietzsche. Some are even prepared to believe that we are once more reliving the unique moment of grace that occurred between Stoicism and Scepticism. Flaubert was talking about it when he wrote: 'After the gods had gone and before the coming of Christ, there was, between Cicero and Marcus Aurelius . . . a unique moment when man was alone.'[24] Has that blessed moment returned?

I think not. I am very much afraid that those who try to convince themselves of it confuse escaping our symbolic subjection by rising above it with escaping it by debasing ourselves. We obviously escape it in both cases, but the end result is far from being the same. We can strive to achieve autonomy thanks to an extremely demanding asceticism: let us not forget that the Stoics frequented the master assiduously, and therefore attached great importance to spiritual guidance and to examining their conscience. The alternative is to lapse into a completely illusory autonomy: we are free only to want what commodities constantly offer us. If we escape the fiction by debasing ourselves, in other words before we enter into it, reject all masters from the outset, and grant ourselves autonomy before we have acquired the means to construct it, we find ourselves going in the opposite direction to the Stoics. We find ourselves within a space that is neither 'autonomic' nor critical, not even neurotic; we are in an anomic space where there are no signposts and no limits, and where everything is inverted.[25] Not all individuals in this space will necessarily become psychotic, but almost everything encourages them to do so.

What remains of the grand narratives?

A few surviving forms are all that now remain of the grand narratives. These survivals delineate relative localized areas of extension and of narrative pertinence. But, although they are still told in the name of a Subject, these narratives no longer supply foundational references. At best, these Subjects still have what Benjamin called an *aura*. The idea

[24] Marguerite Yourcenar comments on this phrase at length in her *Mémoires d'Hadrien* (Yourcenar 1951).

[25] I describe this as a *unary* space ['*unaire*'] (Dufour 1996a).

of an *aura*, which derives from the aesthetics of the sublime, bears witness to an 'Other presence' and to 'the unique apparition of a distance' (Benjamin 2002: 104–5). But, as Hegel remarked of the statues of a different period, namely ancient Greece, we may well admire it but it 'leaves us somewhat cold' (Hegel 1975: vol. 2, p. 392). At best, aesthetic emotion is perhaps tinged with nostalgia (and it is a fact that postmoderns like visiting museums), but we no longer believe in it.

So what narratives do we have left?

The monotheist religious narrative

The strength of the religious narrative is that it posits the existence of a God who can supposedly take responsibility for answering the question of origins on everyone's behalf. The religious narrative therefore claims to be able to resolve the huge problem of the subject, or the problem of how the subject is founded by becoming subject to an Other – subject to God. To that extent, it can always be called to the aid of the subject should the individual prove to be too fragile a support, as is often the case in democratic societies. God is the last recourse. It is therefore not surprising to find that symbolic acts performed in what is supposedly the greatest democracy in the world – the United States – are constantly and universally grafted onto religious discourse. Oaths in court are, for example, sworn on the Bible, as are all major public acts. Basically, it is very useful to have a pocket Other in the form of a little Bible to prevent the subject from *running [fuir]* (in the double sense of 'leaking' and 'running away from danger').

We must not, however, restrict the discussion to the religious narrative's role as an adjuvant to democracy. For a long time, that narrative claimed to be in absolute control over spiritual and intellectual questions (and, in consequence, over bodies). Everything to do with the Spirit had to be subjected to the Church's *imprimatur*. If it was not, the pyres could easily be lit. Thus many scientists had to keep quiet about their discoveries if they did not want to be reduced to ashes. To take only one example, mention should obviously be made of Galileo, who was the hero of the great Copernican–Galilean revolution. He owed his life to the fact that he officially recanted his discoveries *in extremis*. Condemned by the Vatican in full classical seventeenth century and in the very age of Descartes because he had argued that the earth indeed revolved around the sun, Galileo ended his days as a recluse and in great moral and physical pain, whilst his writings and his example became, to the consternation of his judges, the ferment of intellectual Europe. Yet despite its attempts to adapt to modern times, it was not before 31 October 1992 that the Catholic Church rehabilitated Galileo!

Although it has made some attempt to remain compatible with the modern and postmodern worlds, religious discourse still wants to have as much influence as possible over both minds and bodies. It still wants to be in complete control. One might think that this will to power had been blunted by the passage of time, but that is far from being the case. Critical thought has only to relax its vigilance for a moment for religious discourse to return, in forms we thought it could never take again. Darwin, for example, recently became *persona non grata* in Kansas. In this state deep in America, the ten members of the Kansas State Board of Education decided, on 11 August 1999 and by six votes to four, to remove all references to the Darwinian theory of the evolution of species from the public school syllabus because the conservative churches, which are powerful and well organized in the Kansas region, had successfully defended the creationist thesis against the evolutionist thesis.

The narrative of the nation-state

Both major referents of the nation-state narrative are now in a state of complete confusion.[26]

The first one is that of *land* (*ius soli*).[27] Anyone born on French soil is deemed to be French, this being the reference that functions in France. The origins of the narrative which is told about French soil must go back in time as far as possible (for example, to 42 BC, when Vercingetorix defeated Caesar outside Gergovia). A few inaccuracies need not stand in the way of the attempt to prove how old the land is: Charlemagne, for example, was supposedly king of the Franks, even though he actually ruled over the Germanic regions of Austrasia, Western Friesland, Hesse, Franconia and Thuringia, and even though he established his main residence in Aix-la-Chapelle in what is now Rhineland–Westphalia [Aachen in German]. In the mid-nineteenth century, or at the very moment when Victor Hugo was singing the praises of the emperor, German nationalists were adopting the latter's

---

[26] On the nation-state, see Delannoi and Taguieff (1991); Dumont (1991); and the remarkable study of Beckouche (2001).

[27] On *ius soli* and *ius sanguinis*, see Schnapper (1992) and Weil (2002). What follows is a greatly simplified version of their theses.

name as their totem. That, however, is of little importance. The signifier is more important than the reality, and it is the land that matters. Basically, we are French from the ground upwards: I set foot on this land, this land is French, therefore I am French. Everything else – language, spirit, tradions – is, so to speak, an optional extra. The earth shapes its subjects from head to foot. But we increasingly find that it leaves the brain untouched. We paw at the ground and stamp our feet, but nothing happens: Frenchness and its supposedly universal values refuse to appear . . .

The second referent is *blood* (*ius sanguinis*). For example: anyone who can prove that they have German ancestors is German. It follows that, if blood is the sole guarantor of nationality, the shape and size of the land can vary. If blood does more than soil to certify citizenship, it is possible to deduce a corollary: those who have German blood can live only on German soil. From time to time we hear the demand – its strength can vary – that the two should match and that German soil should correspond to German blood. The demand is for a 'Greater Germany'. The problem is that there is no reliable way of identifying German blood – which is only natural, given that ultimately German blood, like any narrative, escapes all verification (no blood sample will ever prove that a given individual is German). Real criteria therefore have to be replaced by symbolic criteria. Blood is linked to language (as it is today): anyone with German blood, in other words anyone who speaks German (or even 'spoke' it in previous generations) is German. Basically, if Herr Schmidt, who is currently living in Poland, has parents or grandparents who spoke German, he must be German, even if he has forgotten how to speak the language. Giving him back the German language he has lost will be enough to make him German once more. It should be noted that the rise of Nazism is not at all inconsistent with the centrality of the German reference to blood: blood was not only linked to language, but also to the other criterion of *race*. It was linked to the so-called 'Aryan race', which thus became the centre of, and a reference for, a new grand narrative, which was grafted on to the blood narrative in order to glorify it. References to, and stories about, blood are therefore bloody, and perhaps more than bloody, because they are more abstract than references to, and narratives about, soil.

It is quite obvious that nation-states always need a truly political agency to make the reference to *soil* or *blood* incarnate for all to see. So there is a king (who tends to signify blood) or an emperor (tending to signify land) (Demorgon 1996) who has the responsibility to personify the permanence of these great references. Just to make sure, this agency is usually linked to another (religious) narrative. Kings and emperors ruled by divine right (at least until Napoleon decided to crown himself, in a fine display of self-foundation). Being guaranteed by two grand narratives, dynasties can be long-lived and could last for several generations. But when the king or emperor turns out to have no clothes, it is the *People* who takes over. Subjects now need a new agency to govern them: the Republic.

Because they are based on similar references, there is a great rivalry between the grand narratives of nation-states. They have always used war to settle problems over partition walls, because their complex systems of alliances are subject to all sorts of reversals. Frontiers, which place territorial limits on the expansion of grand narratives, also constitute sacred boundaries. Once they are crossed, or merely threatened, they trigger the *casus belli*.

For a long time, the narrative of the nation-state claimed to be the most important narrative of all. Its dominance was also signalled by a metaphor which very clearly indicated the pre-eminent role this narrative should play for every subject: the nation-state claimed to be the father and mother of the individual (compare the 'mother-country' [*la mère-patrie*]). A very compelling intimate imaginary was mobilized, and it should be analysed in terms of social psychology and social psychiatry. It mobilized, in other words, the drives. The narrative can be summarized as follows: every sacrifice can be demanded of an individual in the name of the debt she had contracted with the parents to whom she *owed* her life. In other words, all individuals owed their existence to the nation-state in the same way they owed their lives to their parents. Foucault (2003) could thus define the traditional sovereignty the state exercises over its subjects as the power to 'take life or let live'. Nation-states have obviously not denied themselves the power to 'take life', not least because they were constantly turning on one another.

Be that as it may, in the grand narrative of the nation-state, peoples were constantly called upon – by the narrative – to recall something that never existed (the immense Battle of Bouvines,[28] Charlemagne, Emperor of the French, France united in the Resistance, German

[28] I am course referring to the famous 'Battle of Bouvines'. On 27 July 1214 a very minor clash took place between King Philippe-Auguste, flanked by a few knights from the royal provinces, and Otto of Brunswick, Emperor and King of Germany, flanked by the Count of Flanders and the Count of Boulogne, and supported by John Lackland, King of England. Contrary to all expectations and almost without a fight, Otto fled and the King of France won. Although it was very minor, the event

blood . . .). So the narrative worked by forcing subjects to go on indefinitely settling a debt that could never be repaid.

But today what unites nation-states is the very thing that once separated them. Although they were founded on the basis of their differences, all nation-states took on, with greater or lesser rapidity, the same political form: democracy. This form now provides Europe with its point of reference and reduces antagonisms between the continent's nation-states to second-order matters. They now see themselves as homogeneous rather than mutually hostile. Their homogeneity derives from a few founding principles: the separation of powers, free elections, equality of citizens before the law, equality between men and women, freedom of enterprise, the right to own property . . . These principles are the key features of the democratic systems of all European states.

The frontier has therefore been displaced: it once divided nation-states, but they are now united behind the frontier of the democracy, that keeps democratic states in and non-democratic states out. The proof is that democracy is the number one criterion for entry into the European club. Although confined to Europe and, more generally to the West or to what is known as the North, the democratic form lays claim to a new universalism, which sails under the flag of human rights. We are all familiar with the debates pursued in order to introduce a right of intervention which could allow democratic states to cross their borders and intervene in states which flouted democratic principles a little too openly.

For good measure, we are now witnessing the revival of the *regional narrative* that accompanies the withering away of the narrative of nation-states, whose national frontiers are rapidly disintegrating in Europe. The regional narrative celebrates Corsica, Brittany, the Basque Country, Catalonia, Lombardy . . . This narrative presents itself as a miniature reproduction of the narrative of the nation-state (it is fuelled by a reference to *land, blood, language* or *race,* and sometimes a combination of three. There are right-wing versions of this narrative (promising a return to the primal local purity – it was not for nothing that Yann Goulet's Parti National Breton allied itself with the Nazis). There are also left-wing versions (with a promise of the final coming of direct local democracy).

---

became the kernel of a great monarchical legend in the thirteenth century and was then forgotten about until it reappeared in nationalist colours in the nineteenth century. In 1914, it became one of the strongest expressions of the anti-German revanchist spirit. See Duby (1985).

The narrative of the emancipation of the working people

This grand narrative (which was liberating) was meant to abolish all other grand narratives (which were alienating), together with the frontiers created by nation-states ('Workers of the world . . .'). It promised us that we would find ourselves in a homogeneous, classless world. As we know, we soon became disenchanted with the future when the societies that were supposedly building communist happiness were rapidly transformed into vast prisons. Both versions of this narrative – the Russian and the Chinese – look very depressed now that the wall has come down and that China has made the transition to a very unbridled market economy. This brutal collapse came about after a period of one hundred years of violent outbursts (the Paris Commune, the Russian Revolution, the Chinese Revolution, the worldwide youth movements of the 1960s, guerrilla campaigns, Third World struggles). Minor pockets of resistance, some of them quite bizarre, continue to hold out in some countries and go on perpetuating this narrative.

What these groups have come up against is not, however, the political death of the proletariat. The proletariat might reappear, as history has never spared us sudden appearances and reappearances (it should be remembered that China, which represents one quarter of humanity, was governed in the name of a proletariat that had scarcely ever existed in that country). The real problem with the proletariat is the possibility of its theoretical death. In the so-called neoliberal economy, the production of value is no longer essentially based upon labour. Capital is no longer made up of the surplus-value (Marx's *Mehrwert*) generated from the surplus appropriated in the process of the exploitation of the proletariat. Increasingly, capital gambles on high value-added activities (research, genetic engineering, the internet, information, the media . . .) in which unskilled or semi-skilled wage labour often plays only a very small role. But what is much more important is that capital now relies heavily on the financial management of large-scale speculative movements. The share of the 'real' economy is falling because the economy has become more and more 'financialized' over the last twenty-five years thanks to the introduction of new financial mechanisms and new tools for managing capitalism: the junk bonds that allowed the raiders of the 1980s to finance takeovers, operations based on leverage buy-out techniques, dot-coms established thanks to acrobatic financial manoeuvres, managers who are paid in stock options instead of cash. It is as though some all-conquering epiphenomenon has been grafted on to a real economy; we now have a virtual economy which essentially consists in creating large amounts of money out of almost nothing by charging very high prices for things that do not exist, no longer exist or never existed in the first place. The danger is that these paper empires might be suddenly torn up (as in the Enron, WorldCom and Tyco scandals).[29] The stock exchanges have effectively become huge casinos, where managers with vested interests and powerful computers constantly calculate just when they should place their bets. They can make such huge profits (Microsoft's Bill Gates, for example, has a personal holding of some 80 billion dollars in shares – and still owns a flourishing business, unlike George Soros, a pure speculator who has more or less repented of his sins)[30] that there is obviously no place left for Marx's producer of surplus-value. In this financial climate, the proletariat no longer supplies the greater part of capital.

Marxists are certainly not mistaken when they point out that workers (and especially those in the Third World) are still exploited in the sense that Capital still profits from a part of their unpaid 'surplus-labour'. But when they are offered a choice between slave labour and waged labour, as they were in all Western countries and as they are in more and more countries, populations are not slow to choose. They opt for the collective wealth (which is real, even if unequally distributed) and the enjoyment of the extra commodities that capitalism usually brings.

The death of the proletariat does, however, raise one real question: in the shattered world of postmodernity, someone or something still has to take responsibility for collective issues, for sharing things out and for the common good. Very disparate political, social and philosophical forces are now trying to give a possible form to a collective reason that no longer has a rightful owner.

A candidate Subject: Nature

As Subjects go into decline, various candidate Subjects put themselves forward. One of the most serious is Nature, and it is now very

---

[29] 'If normal accounting techniques had been used, Enron, with a turnover of something like $6 billion, would have looked like a relatively small company in the energy sector. With the help of its auditors, it declared a turnover of $100 billion and had a market value of $90 billion' (Rohatyn 2003). The author of these comments is a businessman and the former American ambassador to France.

[30] George Soros was the founder of the Quantum Fund, which was one of the most daring investment funds in the history of finance. His *Crisis of Global Capitalism* (Soros 1998) gives a very instructive account of these techniques.

popular: now that modernity has removed all limitations on practice, and especially on prosthetic practices, we are experiencing what
Denis Duclos calls 'catastrophic short circuits'.[31] If we want to
secure reterritorialization at last, what could be better than our great
mother-earth? This would mean that the myth would no longer be
celebrating a cultural referent; it would be celebrating the real referent, now that we have at last found it once more. It would be
celebrating our origins: Nature. Now that the great totems of history
have pretty well collapsed, geography is making a comeback. And
indeed, the narrative of Nature no longer celebrates the father: it
celebrates the mother. We must stop making the mother who gave
birth to us all suffer. Let's stop scarifying her with useless human
signs, draping her in roads and railways, festooning her with cities,
soiling her with rubbish and exploiting her so shamelessly . . . This
candidate great narrative can adapt to all the forms taken by the
decline of the father in our societies, or coexist alongside them. It is
the apocalyptic forecasts it carries with it that give the ecological narrative its great strength. They have become much more credible
than the old apocryphal forecasts religion was rehashing for thousands of years. This narrative therefore has a great appeal for crowds
who are prepared to be really frightened – and we can quite understand why.

Whilst some of the troops who sustain this narrative are prepared
to take part in any political operation that pays heed to their options so
as to avoid the worst – which is quite likely to happen[32] – others, who
rely on the same apocalyptic forecasts, are tempted by the fundamen-
talist fantasy of retreating into specially prepared havens so as to preserve a few patches of real Nature – while there is still time.

For the ecological narrative, Nature is a referent that invalidates all
other referents because it can annexe them. If we take Nature away
from the nation-state, the proletariat or the churches, there will be no
land left for them to construct their territories. That is why, now that
the grand narratives are in decline, a number of the ideologues of the

---

[31] See on this point, among other works by Duclos (especially his regular contributions to *Le Monde Diplomatique*), Duclos (1996).

[32] On the principle: Prepare for the worst . . . to prevent it happening. See Dupuy
(2002). Jean-Pierre Dupuy adopts the opposite approach to Hans Jonas's 'precautionary principle' (Jonas 1984). According to Jonas, we have to act immediately because
we do not know what the future impact of a technology will be, whereas 'enlightened
catastrophism' insists that, because it is certain that catastrophic events will happen,
we have to act now to stop them happening.

old Subjects, and especially of the proletariat, are joining Nature's ranks.

The only problem of this candidate Subject is the reality of human nature – it does not exist.[33] That is why human beings had to create a second nature: culture. It follows that the neotenin cannot devote himself to preserving natural equilibria, which his second nature really does threaten, without also attempting to make his second nature viable. Basically, the discourse of Nature is not self-sufficient: that is why there will be no ecologists of our first nature without what I would call an *ecology of our second nature* – and that is precisely the main threat of dissolution to the ecological narrative. There is a danger that it will be absorbed into other narratives.

Postmodern democracy as the end of grand narratives

Having *declined* the figures of the Subject that were celebrated in the grand narratives, today we have to accept that the Other is in *decline*. Being could once be declined [*se déclinait*]; now it *admits defeat* [*il s'incline*]. Postmodernity no longer has any presentable figures of the Subject to offer. Whilst earlier periods defined spaces marked by the distance between the speaking subject and that which founded him, postmodernity is a space defined by the abolition of the distance between the subject and the Subject. Postmodernity, which is democratic, corresponds in fact to the age in which we began to define the subject not in terms of its dependency on, and submission to, the Subject, but in terms of its juridical autonomy and total economic freedom. We have begun to define the speaking subject in *self-referential* terms: the new subject is no longer the subject of God, King or Republic. She is her own subject.

As I have already said, I, like Lyotard, trace the irreversible decline of grand narratives back to Auschwitz, to the catastrophic moment when it became apparent that the West's successive Subjects had led only to the absolute dominance of the terrifying narrative of Race. After that paroxysmal point, where civilization in a sense devoured itself, there can be no more grand narratives, which is why we postmoderns find ourselves without a grand narrative.

At this moment of civilizational collapse, it has become apparent that nation-states, which were in permanent conflict, had finally constructed, precisely because of their antagonism, a completely

[33] See my work on neoteny (Dufour 1999).

homogeneous whole. What the most powerful states have in common after two world wars, so many shameful wars of decolonization and the ontological debacle of Auschwitz? Democracy.

Democracy's referent is no longer *soil* or *blood*, but the free individual. This paradigm shift had existed *in nuce* ever since the Enlightenment, and especially since Rousseau, who, throughout his work, used deep introspection as a way of rediscovering his universal 'nature' and of learning to speak 'in the name of the entire human race' (in the famous epigraph to the *Confessions*; see Dufour 1996a).

The subject was once a subject insofar as he was referred to this *God*, this *land* or this *blood*. An external Being conferred being onto the subject. With democracy, that hetero-reference was transformed into an auto-reference. The subject became, in a sense, his own origin. This auto-reference raises a lot of problems. Perhaps more than it solves! It hurt when human beings discovered that they could be subjects only by being the subjects of a fiction, but it hurts even more when they discover that they have no fiction, as there is now a danger that there will be no more subjects. This mutation does not, however, raise only ontological problems. It also – and more importantly – raises some formidable political questions – in the broad sense of government in general and self-government in particular.

Neopagan narratives, or the generalized floating of values

Modernity resembled a complex space in which we constantly had to move from one regime of values to another. Postmodernity establishes a new type of space: moving space. Everything within it, including values, becomes flexible. If, as has already been pointed out (Goux 2000), there is one event that signals our entry into postmodernity, that is the transition from the absolute reference of the gold standard to a regime in which all currencies are flexible. Fiduciary (*fiducia*, from the Latin *fidus*, 'trust', *fidere*, 'to trust') was based on something different. The trust that once bound together the contracting parties was based upon a grand referent that founded a system and a regime for the exchange of all values (semiotic, symbolic, financial . . .). It now 'floats' in the same way the relative values of currencies have floated since 1972.

We can now see, taking shape in all the domains, little narratives designed to be used in specific places and circumstances (Lyotard describes them as 'pagan'). They allow for the establishment of little ternary networks, each one with a narrated, a narrator and a narratee.

As a result, we witness the appearance of a lot of tribes (Maffesoli 1996):[34] computer scientists, Buddhists, bikers, net surfers, opera buffs, people into body-piercing, people with tattoos, rock, punk and rap musicians, lone yachtsmen and yachtswomen, lovers of extreme sports, bungee jumpers . . . The social bond is breaking down into a multitude of sociabilities, each with its own referential fixations. Every brotherhood has its code of honour, its knowledge, its contractual obligations, its local liturgies, its passwords, its initiation rites, its rituals, its totems, its membership badges (clothes, hairstyles, tattoos, costumes . . .). But they are all based upon the sacrificial reference around which the group rallies.

I do not know whether grand narratives (for instance, the monotheist narrative) inspired more enthusiasm, but they did have at least one advantage over today's little narratives: the sacrifice was focused on one central figure, and that prevented it from spreading throughout the social body. The sacrifice of Isaac in Judaism (where after the staying of Abraham's hand, his seed was multiplied as the stars of the heaven) and, in Christianity, the sacrifice of Jesus (who died for the salvation of humanity) were sacrifices made once and for all and then inscribed in Scripture. They accepted human abjection – living in order to die – and turned it into its opposite: being shared in this manner, the horror became sacred. When this great sacrifice no longer works, all we can do is resort to local forms of sacrifice. When something goes wrong in social relations, we gather together locally and throw down a challenge which will lead to the death of the individual who is made to feel all our anxieties. That reassures our minds until the next time. Bikers, for instance, will go on with their runs until someone dies. And then they will sing the praises of the dead man who dared to defy the danger. Even the good viewers who spend hours in front of the box, watching formula-one cars doing lap after lap on Sundays, are waiting for one thing only: to see someone like Ayrton Senna crash! Communities gather around their glorious dead, who left common mortals in order to choose the hour or manner of their death. Death itself is not always the goal. Sometimes the goal is to reach the breaking-point beyond which death is certain. Once a diver goes beyond a certain depth, there is a possibility that he will never return to the surface (as in Luc Besson's *The Big Blue*, the adolescent cult film of the 1990s). The net surfer who spends too long in front of the screen is in danger of entering another

[34] Maffesoli's interpretation of the 'time of the tribes' as signalling 'the decline of individualism in mass societies' (the book's subtitle) was very ill-considered.

world or of becoming seriously cut off from this one (see Kiyoshi Kurosawa's fine film *Kairo*, which came out in 2001: the frozen surfers turn into ghosts). When body art (scarification, piercings) goes beyond a certain point, there is a danger that the individual will disappear behind the tattoos.[35]

There are as many forms of sacrifice as there are floating narratives.

These little narratives, which have a local value, obviously give us a strange feeling of déjà vu: they are grand narratives that have been shattered in marginal situations. To adopt a clever formula from Gianni Vattimo (1988), they bring into play 'an immense construction site of traces and residues' that testifies to the survival of 'the primitive in our world'.

Communitarian narratives

As the grand narratives, and especially the narrative of the nation-state, break up, we see the rise of narratives calling for communitarianization, or in other words for the atomization of all the universal principles endorsed by modernity. We should have judges who are black or *beur* [of North African origin, born in France] to hear cases involving black or *beur* delinquents. The community should be accountable only to the community, because the world consists of an infinite number of juxtaposed communities, each with its own laws. There is a constant tendency to divide every community into still smaller communities. There is a price to be paid for this, as the outcome is an absolute relativism in which nothing is commensurable with anything else. This is a way of re-establishing tribes, and it is by no means incompatible with the existence of an empire (the American empire, for example) which has no difficulty in dividing and ruling.

The market as new Subject?

The postmodern would therefore appear to correspond to the absence of Subjects, and this is something without a historical precedent. One might, however, wonder if, in these neoliberal times, 'the Market' isn't in the process of becoming a new Subject.

The dominant narrative at the moment is probably the narrative that glorifies commodities. For various reasons, its irresistible rise has been facilitated by an ideal economic situation:

[35] For a clinical study, see Chassaing (1999).

• The relativization of the absolute sovereignty promoted by the narratives of the nation-state. Commodities, like capital, must be able to circulate unhindered at the frontiers, and without any frontiers, if possible – one thinks of the norms that have been proposed by the agencies which manage foreign investment and international trade (see, for example, the recent controversies over the Multilateral Agreement on Investment).[36] The commodity narrative wants there to be no borders; it does not want to have any territory of its own, it simply follows distribution flows that penetrate spaces in arborescent fashion.

• The simultaneous rise of democratic discourse and utilitarianism. There has to be a product to satisfy every desire of every democratic subject. Commodities must, in other words, be able to function within the framework of the libidinal economy. Ultimately, it is the connection between the two economies (the commodity economy and the libidinal) that explains the power and contemporary ascendancy of the commodity narrative. The goal is to bring every desire face to face with a manufactured object that can be found on the market for consumer goods. This applies to the cultural, practical and aesthetic domains, to the desire for social distinction, to real or imaginary medical needs, to the desire to have a great presence and good clothes, to sexual desires . . . Desire has, by definition, 'no object',[37] but in the commodity narrative every desire must find its object. Commodities must provide a solution to every problem. The commodity narrative describes objects as the guarantors of our happiness. What is more, they can make us happy in the here and now.

We therefore find that manufactured objects are becoming increasingly personalized: their infinite diversity is constantly increasing because they must correspond as closely as possible to the needs of individuals who are 'constrained' by democratic discourse to regard themselves as unique and to display insignia that allow them to believe they are unique. The illusion of individuality instilled by this ever-expanding production of objects is in fact intended to be an effective way of managing large masses of people.

---

[36] See, for example, 'L'AMI nouveau va arriver', Le Monde Diplomatique, May 1999 (p. 13) for a discussion of agreements which aim at 'subordinating States', with a view to doing away with the last obstacles to 'free market forces'. After the failure of the Multilateral Agreement on Investment (MAI), new projects were circulated under the names of Transatlantic Economic Partnership (TEP) and the World Trade Organization's 'Millennium Round'.

[37] Freud said that the drives have no object.

Because they are targeted as goals, objects reduce desire to need. Now we know what this functionalization of desire usually leads to: it inevitably quickly revives the desire which sought satisfaction in its object. The subject, having sought to satisfy her desire through the object, inevitably discovers, given the nature of the drives, that 'that still isn't it', and that the lack which stimulated her desire is still there. The disappointment that follows the reception of each object is the best ally to the expanded extension of the commodity because it inevitably restarts the cycle of desire for an object. If 'that wasn't it', we have to go on demanding. The disappointment we experience when we get the object is the ultimate source of the commodity narrative's power.

• The rise of the narrative of neopagan tribes. Because humanity is being diversified into an infinite number of tribes whose predictable needs can be identified and even predicted, there will always be an outlet for the commodity cycle. Vast numbers of market researchers are therefore always taking the pulse of consumers and surveying their sexual and emotional lives, so as to anticipate their needs and to give their desires possible names and credible destinations. Every micro-group which has been identified must be able to find the products which supposedly correspond to it on the market. No group can be ignored. There is no such thing as a small profit. A profit can be made from babies who 'want' their favourite shampoo, senior citizens who 'want' to occupy their spare time and invest their savings, poor adolescents who 'want' cheap brand names and rich adolescents who 'want' their own cars. They must all be satisfied. 'I' is now central to every advert: there is not one of them which doesn't emphasize 'I want . . .', 'I do . . .', 'I decide . . .'

• The collapse of the narrative of the emancipation of the working people. Now that the commodity narrative no longer finds its way blocked by the antithetical narrative of the emancipation of the working people, its development is unfettered. The present absolute dominance of the market was greatly facilitated by the implosion of the only other reference that insisted on its universality, namely the proletariat (after years of ultra-leftism, so-called 'red' China, which was in theory communism's last bulwark, finally became the land of 'market-Leninism' long ago). God was already dead when the madman in *The Gay Science* ran into the marketplace with his lantern 'in the bright morning hours' and shouted to the passers-by: 'Whither is God? . . . All of us are his murderers' (Nietzsche 1971: §125). It was the same with the proletariat. Already very ill in economic terms because it was no longer the only source that could produce value, it died its political death in Berlin in 1989, when the East Berliners tore down the wall with their picks . . . and gave market forces an unlimited freedom.

• The decline of the religious narrative. The commodity narrative has infiltrated the places of worship left empty as a result of the decline of the religious narrative. The market's most practical expression – the American-style mall, with its supermarkets and hypermarkets surrounded by boutiques – now claims to have replaced the church in its role of cementing the social bond: families go there to commune on their days of rest in the same way they used to go to mass on Sundays. The churches, both Catholic and Protestant, are empty, and the shopping malls are full. They are our new places of worship. Belief in the omnipotence of the market is sustained by a never-ending sequence of edifying little stories (advertisements) which are as inane as those of an exhausting catechism. They sustain the illusion that, because it has hyperfetichized the commodities and turned them into a spectacle, the market can, like an omnipresent and omnipotent God, meet all our needs. The trick is to fill the consumer's time and space with all the little stories about commodities that are constantly being spun and spread (think of the advertising hoardings, and especially of the TV commercials that saturate our screens). Some sociologists even think (seriously) that the ads should be seen as the myths of our times. Of course Ajax, who was just as brave and strong as Achilles, is now a cleaning powder, but the dubious equating of myth and advertising still seems to me both to undervalue mythology greatly and to overvalue advertising greatly . . . Nevertheless, the 'ad' style is so compellingly pregnant and is invading high culture itself to such a degree that it is becoming a point of reference (both music videos and art-house movies borrow their aesthetics from promos and clips; some books are market leaders, and intellectual creations are treated like commodified products . . .).[38]

---

[38] Article 22 of Italy's *legge finanziaria* for 2002 included a long list of privatization projects: the museums came just below the hospitals. This prompted the director of MOMA and the Guggenheim in New York, the Prado in Madrid, the British Museum and the National Gallery, and the Louvre and the Musée National d'Art Moderne in Paris to launch an appeal to the Berlusconi government pointing out that 'a museum is not a supermarket' (Padovani 2001).

The commodity narrative is so effective because it has a whole priesthood at its disposal. It has market researchers, and we confess our wildest fantasies about bars of soap. It has actors who stage shows in which we see the daily miracles that commodities can perform. It has its preachers who constantly spout their promises of redemption through objects. Its marketing men preach the gospel and spread the good news about good products . . . . The market leads to a real voluntary servitude: it is all the more powerful in that it is recognized by the world's consumers, who have been trained (by the new media) since their early childhood to consume all sorts of commodities.

The commodity narrative is also celebrated by the agents, analysts and commentators of all kinds who work in the economic and financial sectors. It is promoted as a remedy for all our ills, and as a universal panacea. By preaching that there should be no trade restrictions and by promoting investment, the market has, like some all-conquering religion, swamped even the most impregnable parts of the whole world. We no longer so much as notice its most serious and most visible disadvantages (the destruction of nature, growing inequality, the emergence of a fourth world . . .), because the new gospel (the miraculous growth of wealth) is constantly being spread. The market is sweeping everything away to such an extent that Subjects all over the world have made amends and said to themselves that it is better to ally themselves with it than to try to stand in its way – even China's communists. Breviaries have been prepared and they are recited in all the institutions of economic–financial power, in order to disseminate what we know about its versatile laws and to bring it to light, even though it hurts. The need to submit to market necessity is presented as an injunction to which everything else has to be subordinated at once, rather as though we were dealing with some new and inescapable rationality.

And the market is indeed powerful. It is more powerful than all the other Subjects, and they have to bow before it one after the other. Globalization implies the disappearance or relativization of nation-states, republics and kingdoms and of all their so-called universal laws, which suddenly look very specific to them.

Finally and most important of all, even its bitterest enemies see the market as a new demigod, and this symptom is particularly significant. To take only one example: José Bové, who is one of the most widely respected leaders of the struggle against globalization, writes a well-argued article (Bové 2001) in a major evening paper where he more than once describes the market as a new god. Of course José Bové is denouncing this new god, but he still acknowledges its power. This is how he begins his article: 'Humanity is struggling against a formidable *belief*' (my emphasis). He goes on to explain that this new belief has its '*gurus*', who assert that 'there is no *god* but the Market' and describe the market's opponents as '*heretics*'. José Bové then denounces the 'liberal *credo*', which is no more than a '*dogma*', and so on. The vocabulary that is used throughout the article is obviously that of a secular militant attacking the suffocating stranglehold of a new religion that is conquering the world. The same kind of talk could be heard at Davos, the Mecca of the World Economic Forum, in early 2003. Lula, the former metal worker who had become President of Brazil three weeks earlier, began his speech by saying: 'Here in Davos today, there is only one God, and that God is the free market' (*Le Monde*, 26 January 2003).

We therefore have to ask ourselves whether the market is not a new way of producing a Subject. When we are granted an unconditional freedom to indulge in economic and commodified activity, it is indeed possible to create an ever-expanding zone in which values can be produced and exchanged (we can, for example, acquire legal and commercial rights over nature, the human genome and all the living things). Will this not also facilitate the emergence of a Subject whose power will be far greater than that of all the system's actors? Has not the market become power itself, precisely because it is so uncontrollable? When the outcome of a process is so much greater than the sum of its parts, are we not confronted with an irresistible phenomenon?[39]

Now that the market, in its current form, extends to all human activities, we appear to have reached the final stage of a process which Adam Smith had already described as being controlled by an 'invisible hand', with all the religious connotations the expression implies. This theory tells us that everyone must be free to pursue their selfish interests in order to promote the collective interest of society. The 'miracle' that is wrought thanks to this invisible hand regulates everything, and that replaces divine providence and its works.[40] It would be

[39] I discuss this further in Dufour (1996b).

[40] 'Every individual necessarily labours to render the annual revenue of the society as great as he can. He generally neither intends to promote the public interest, nor knows how much he is promoting it, he intends only his own security [. . .] he intends only his own gain, and he is in this, as in many other cases, led by an *invisible hand* to promote an end which was no part of his intention. Nor is it always the worse for society that it was no part of his intention. By pursuing his own interest he frequently promotes that of the society more effectually than when he intends to promote it' (Smith 1996: vol. 2, 477; emphasis added).

futile and presumptuous, if not dangerous, to try to escape this 'hidden spirit' (another of Smith's metaphors, again with religious connotations). This might explain why most of those who were until very recently the market's bitterest enemies surrendered one after another in mid-campaign.

Briefly put, all we have to do to ensure that all goes well is in fact to surrender to a force which, because it cannot be coerced, represents a higher degree of regulation and an ultimate form of rationality that is *true*. In a word, the market would be as powerful as God, but it would have the advantage of being *real* – it would even be the only reality in the fictional world of the neotenin. We should therefore give the market and its laws a free rein, on the understanding that its main law is that it obeys no law.

The market in fact obeys only an internal requirement which tries to avoid the imposition of all external controls: *commodities must be produced in ever greater quantities and at a lower cost*. On the one hand, we have to produce more and more, and the Market owes it to itself to go on creating new uses for commodities and at the same time to expand until it takes control of spheres which were previously regulated by communitarian, interpersonal or personal relations (as we shall see, there is now a market in identities and sexuation). On the other hand, production costs must be lowered, mainly by automating production and cutting, or even marginalizing, labour costs.[41] According to this logic, there must be no restrictions on the circulation of capital. It must be able to invest immediately wherever costs are lowest, and then pull out as soon as conditions improve elsewhere.[42] What is called 'market dynamism' is no more than a nice euphemistic way of describing the market's uncontrollable side. The market is to the economy what a nuclear reaction is to energy: it works very well, and perhaps too well. The longer the reaction goes on, the greater the risk that it will get out of control.

---

[41] In the neoliberal economy, labour is no longer the main producer of value. I am therefore quite happy to add the Marxian subject, who is defined, as I have just noted, by its ability to produce surplus-value, to the list of subjects who are, like the Kantian and Freudian subjects, under attack by neoliberalism.

[42] I am simply repeating what the defenders of the market and globalization are saying. See, for example, the following statement from Percy Barnevik, Vice-President of the Davos Forum (cited in Geuens 2003: 41): 'I would define globalisation as my group's freedom to invest wherever it likes and for as long as it likes, to produce what it likes and to buy and sell what it likes, and with as few constraints as possible when it comes to legislation on labour and social conventions.'

The market may look like a new Subject insofar as it is the ultimate, true rationality, but that can only be because the previous Subjects have thrown in the sponge and bowed down before the new master: the very entity which was instituted as the collective agency's political guardian (the Republic) is now prepared to give up its supervisory and regulatory role. Nothing could be more stupefying than the spectacle of a political agency blandly explaining that it has to sabotage itself at the very moment when the Market has to be kept under constant surveillance precisely because it pursues an absolute empire. The politicians who ask for the state to be dismantled are in much the same position as the manager of a nuclear power station who tries to explain why the reactor should be left unsupervised. Of course it could generate more energy, but it could also cause a few societal Chernobyls. Once the external controls have been loosened, no society and no culture can resist the exclusive ascendancy of the market. Indeed, a society that was completely subordinate to the market could function only if it destroyed much of its own fabric (industrial, social and cultural) in order to redistribute it in accordance with market flows and on an emergency basis. Given that it would have to absorb capitals that may leave as quickly as they were invested, and frequently even more quickly, it would ultimately become necessary, even in peacetime, to organize large sectors of society as though they were refugee camps. In intellectual terms, we have gone so far down the road of establishing the market as the ultimate rationality that we are ready to agree that our era's greatest ethical need is for permanent humanitarian interventions to help the victims of what looks like a new blind 'fate': the uncontrollable socio-economic disasters that all our specialist weather forecasters have given up trying to predict. The growing number of charitable appeals with neither a sender nor an addressee proves that we are afraid of the market in the way that we are afraid that some new 'natural' disaster will strike.[43] As these disasters appear out of nowhere; the only possible response is a vague but intense exhortation in which everyone asks everyone else to be brave, rather as though a cyclone was on its way. Organizations like UNESCO are now asking millions of people to sign petitions (against scourges) and then solemnly return them a few years later . . . to UNESCO

[43] See Amorim, 'O branco da violência' (2000). The author identifies this form of enunciation on the basis of an analysis of the 'marches for peace' discourse. The marches were meant to be demonstrations against the violence in Brazil's big cities, but nothing was said about the causes of the violence.

officials.[44] It is this rejection of politics that allows the market to triumph and to look like an uncontrollable and unpredictable force which can do anything: unprecedented development in some regions (the dazzling new Shanghai) and devastated landscapes in others (as in Argentina).

Perhaps the process is irresistible. But, powerful as it may be, there is at least one sense in which the 'Market' cannot function as a new Subject, and this is an important point. Far from taking responsibility for the question of origins, of foundations, of the first element, that is to say, of the eminently Hegelian question of the human desire for the infinite, all it can do is bring every individual face to face with the torments of self-foundation (and, no doubt, its associated new joys). It is probably at this point that we encounter the limitations of the market economy's claim to be able to take responsibility for all personal and social bonds: it is neither a general economy nor a symbolic economy, but merely an 'economic economy'. It obviously has an effect at the libidinal level, as it still claims to be able to give every subject a manufactured object that will supposedly satisfy his desire, but it fails to function as a general economy in that it leaves the subject to his own devices when it comes to the most important thing of all: founding himself. Now, if this (impossible) question of origins is not dealt with, it will inevitably return in the form of an irrepressible *torment*. This is a question that cannot be abrogated. It can only be dealt with in, and by, the cultural order, what Freud called the 'work of culture – not unlike the draining of the Zuider Zee': 'where id was, there ego shall be' (Freud [1933]: 80).[45] As the specific work that must be done if 'ego' is to 'be' cannot be performed by the market, the most insane demands are therefore voiced, being predicated upon identity (fundamentalism, ethnicisms, regionalisms . . .).

Given that the 'Market' is a network for exchanging commodities and values, being connected to the market is never a matter of plugging only into the *horizontality* of the network. Pierre Levy (1990) seems to me to have provided the best account of the logic of the network. He integrates the technical functionality specific to the

---

[44] In 1997, it launched a '2000 Appeal for a Culture of Peace and Non-Violence'. The closing date for signatures was 2002!

[45] This is where we find the famous formula *Wo Es war, soll Ich werden. Es ist Kulturarbeit etwa wie die Trockenlegung der Zuydersee.*

information network into the philosophical logic of Deleuze's rhizome.[46] In the rhizome network, everything happens in real time with positive feedback. We have everything we need. An individual with a normal supply of productive and/or desiring machines has only to plug some of them into the network for the 'miracle' to happen: it works. The network's principles, which are very simple but profoundly subversive precisely because they are so utilitarian and so immanentist, can be stated in four points:

- the principle of multiplicity states that the network is organized in a fractal way; any given point proves to be made up of a whole network, and so on;
- the principle of exteriority states that the network has no organic unity, its extension, diminution and recomposition always depending on its being plugged into other networks;
- the topological principle states that, in a network, messages, information and commodities do not circulate within a universal or homogeneous space; they create the space within which they circulate – indeed, the network does not exist in space, it is space;
- the principle of the mobility of centres states that the network always has several centres and that they are in constant motion.

As we can see, what has simply disappeared from the rhizome network is the very idea of the Third that once functioned in symbolic sets, in other words the 'one not there', which made it possible to establish a homogeneous ensemble. Everything in the rhizome exists on the same level, there are only interrelations which bring the actors together. There is no exteriority, only interiority. No transcendence, only immanence. The ternary has given way to a dual relationship. No actor has to explain herself to a third party who is at once very distant and infinitely close (present in all of us in the form of the superego, for example), but every actor is caught up in a set of purely dual relations. Which, of course, has the effect of depoliticizing the whole network while multiplying the conflicts inside it. When conflict does break out between two actors, there can be no appeal to a law (a universal law laid down in the name of a Third), but only to a (local) procedure which gets the circuit working again.

[46] 'A rhizome has no beginning or end; it is always in the middle, between things, interbeing . . . the rhizome is alliance, uniquely alliance' (Deleuze and Guattari 1992: 25). The introduction to A Thousand Plateaus is a veritable treatise on the rhizome.

And so it is that, even when it expands to the furthest corners of the globe, as it does in contemporary globalization, the market, being a network, has no room in it for lack or for anything that lies beyond meaning. The actor can plug anything into the network, except, perhaps, the very questions that ought to mean most to him: 'What's it all for?', or 'Why and how should we live?'

As Deleuze and Guattari note (1992: 25), asking a rhizome ' "Where are you going? Where are you coming from? Where are you heading?" . . . are totally useless questions' because, in this world, there is 'no beginning and no end'. They seem to like it that way.

This strange proposition does at least have the virtues of clarity: the rhizome network deprives us of questions about origins and ends.

Of course these questions are totally pointless. But we do not seem to be any better off when we avoid asking them. Isn't it strange, after all, that it should be philosophers agreeing to deprive human beings of their 'pointless' questions? I always thought that, on the contrary, philosophers were the only people who could justify them. Hence I wonder whether the unconditional surrender to the rhizome network of the market does not do great harm to human beings by explicitly depriving them of the useless things that nonetheless interest and even torture them. As, for example, when a man wagers that there is something beyond his own self and rejects the assertion and choices of the ego. Or when he backs the definitely impossible against the indefinitely possible. Or a pure absolute against the rhizome's generalized relativism. Or a poem against the data.[47] Or a phrase that has never been heard before, or a heroic gesture, against all forms of utility. Dispossessing the human being of things that are useless is the surest way to turn him, if not into a schizophrenic, at least into a hebephrenic – that is, into a suffering human.

The new forms taken by mental illness in our societies are testimony to the market's failure to establish itself as a new Subject. Because the market does not acknowledge the Third and can offer only dual relationships, in other words interactions, it does not allow the subject to establish an umbilical link with something which goes beyond her. Now a subject prevented from asking impossible

---

[47] The writer Pierre Michon (2002: 74–5) seems to respond to Deleuze and Guattari's dismissal of questions about beginnings and endings when he states that 'Poems [. . .] can do that. They can see the Big Bang and the Last Judgement in the same blink of the eye [. . .] What good are poets in our times, which are times of distress? . . . Only for that.'

questions about origins and ends is a subject deprived of access to being, that is, a subject prevented from being a subject in the full sense. The network therefore constitutes a sort of zero degree of sociability, because it forecloses any relationship with being. And yet this is the type of relationship that is now being put forward as a model for all possible societies. Everything – commodities, information, artists, the users of various services, the ill (including the schizophrenic and the autistic), emerging associations, pressure groups and so on – has to form a network. The only alternative is not-being. Now the network inevitably confronts everyone with the question of their own foundation, leaving the person absolutely alone in the face of a subjectivation they are forced to come to terms with, without necessarily being able to do so. All the trinitarian workings of the subjective condition are thus under threat, and this has a devastating effect on the speaking subject. The network model takes us from a regime in which the unconscious tended to manifest itself in the form of neurosis (a debt to a third party) to a regime in which it manifests itself in near-psychotic forms as a result of the foreclosure of 'what religion has taught us to invoke as the Name-of-the-Father', to put it in Lacanian terms (Lacan [1958b]: 464). It would, however, be a mistake to believe that what we know about a good old-fashioned psychosis (paranoid or schizophrenic) is enough to explain this phenomenon. On the contrary, we are just beginning to explore postmodernity's new and near-psychotic forms.[48]

The fall of ternary definitions and the rise of self-referential definitions

In postmodernity, the subject is no longer defined in terms of a relationship of dependency on God, king or republic and is forced to define himself. I find the best illustration of this in the new definition of the speaking subject given after the Second World War by the great linguist Émile Benveniste (1971: 224): '"Ego" is he who says "ego"' ['*Est je qui dit je*']. In postmodernity, the speaking subject is no longer defined hetero-referentially but auto-referentially. By giving this definition, Benveniste in a sense ratifies the emergence of a new and

---

[48] I therefore support the hypothesis of the psychoanalyst Jean-Pierre Lebrun (2001: 66), who suggests that we use the expression 'subject in a state of limit-experience' to describe the 'new clinical modalities' we see in 'today's subject': 'a subject left unable to accept subjectivation on his own'.

self-defined speaking subject by granting that subject his semiotic rights.

What Lacan puts forward in his famous text on the mirror stage (Lacan [1949]) is a further index of the emergence of this new definition of the speaking subject. I think that I have been able to demonstrate (Dufour 1998) that Lacan's mirror involves, in addition to its well-known sources (narcissism, neo-Darwinism, Gestalt-psychology and Hegelianism), a specific but unrecognized allusion to theology. The mirror stage in fact contains a reference to Boehme, who argued that God used a mirror in order to know himself in all his infinite diversity. When he elaborates his theory of the mirror stage, Lacan in a sense hands over God's mirror to the subject who says 'I', as we can see from the title of his paper: 'The mirror stage as formative of the I function'. After having dethroned God in this way, Lacan really did have to reintroduce the Other – and he did so in no uncertain terms. The thesis of the mirror stage is, however, still present in the idea that the subject, like God, is shaped by her own image – in self-referential fashion.

These specular and self-referential definitions of the subject are historically congruent. They appeared at the moment when the successive hetero-referential definitions of the subject used in the West had, in the end, led only to the catastrophic Nazi definition in terms of Race. In the last article he published in 1994, Serge Leclaire, commenting on the remarks I made in 1990 about the third party (Dufour 1990), noted that the twentieth century 'saw the collapse of all the figures that gave the third party its prestige. Once God had been pronounced dead, a whole series of disillusionments ensued. They inevitably centred around the Holocaust, and finally destroyed any possibility that there could be a mausoleum for an institutionalized third party, or a symbolic corpus to preserve the spirit of the law' (Leclaire 1998: 194f). After a disaster like that, what else could we do but do away with third-party hetero-referential definitions and adopt a self-referential definition of the subject? For my own part, I see the work of Benveniste and Lacan as establishing the semiotic and psychical rights of a new subject, who is defined self-referentially. I mean by 'semiotic rights' the unconditional right to use the 'I': basically, you can say 'I' without having to explain yourself to anyone, not even to God, the king or the republic.

The new semiotic definition has many implications. Given that postmodernity, which is democratic, corresponds to the period in which we began to define the subject in self-referential rather than hetero-referential terms, that is, in unary rather than trinitarian terms (Dufour 1988; 1996a), it follows that we postulate that the subject has, on the one hand juridical autonomy and, on the other, economic freedom. What I am saying is that both juridical autonomy and commercial freedom, and possibly the total freedom of neoliberalism, are absolutely congruent with the self-referential definition of the subject. That is why I believe that an analysis of the decadence of the Other, which is characteristic of postmodernity, must understand the neoliberal times in which we live. They are defined by the maximal economic freedom given to individuals.

Establishing the semiotic rights of the new, self-referentially defined subject is one thing; looking at their clinical-symbolic consequences is another. Benveniste was not really prepared to do that. He was reluctant to see what Lacan saw so clearly: a subject who is defined self-referentially is also a subject riddled with holes because she has no definition. Lacan was not the only person to understand this: our great literary authors were also keeping watch. Someone else was at the same time contemplating what the advent of a self-defined subject implied for the speaking subject. Although I cannot develop the point here, it was in 1946, that is, at the time of Benveniste's 'discovery', that Beckett, who did not know the linguist, comes up with the same formula, the 'Ego is he who *says* ego'. Except that it was immediately obvious to Beckett that this formula inevitably leads to the worst of disorders. Indeed, Beckett is the author of a memorable anti-Benveniste formula: 'I say I, knowing that it's not I' [*Je dis je en sachant que ce n'est pas moi*] (Beckett 2003: 408). The formula appears in Beckett's greatest novel, which is – appropriately enough – entitled *The Unnamable*. It is pointless to argue that the 'I' ['*je*'] is not the 'ego' ['*moi*'] and that Benveniste and Beckett are talking about different things. What Beckett is calling into question is essentially the first person; hence the imprecation: 'Enough of this cursed first person' (2003: 345). Which removes all ambiguity. If the 'I' produces nothing, it follows that, even though the formula is used and proliferates, something essential which should be working remains in abeyance, if not in check, and is blocking the access to the subjective condition that the formula ought to guarantee.

What strikes me is that this formula gives us a definition of the subject that relies upon self-referentiality. This means that it no longer relies on hetero-referentiality or on anything that defines the subject with reference to some Other. Once we enter a period in which there are no more presentable Others, other problems begin to arise. Why?

Because it is of course at the point when the subject is enjoined to be herself that it is most difficult, if not impossible, to be a self.

From hysteria to hysterology

It is quite possible that the requirement to submit to the self is even more onerous than submission to the Other. How can we count on a self that does not yet exist?

As I have already noted, the price we used to pay for our submission to the Other was a mental disorder known as 'neurosis'. A hundred years ago Freud identified various forms of neurosis, a central one among them being hysteria, which is characterized by a debt. This debt revolves, of course, around the question of the father – that is to say, as Lacan has demonstrated, it revolves around the question of the father as name, as the one who names, the one who grants access to the symbolic, the one to whom we owe a debt.

Well, in moving from modernity to postmodernity, we have moved from hysteria to hysterology.

We will speak of hysterology (or *hysteron-proteron* or *hystero-proton*) to evoke a figure of rhetoric based upon the inversion of anteriority and posteriority. Here is a (literary) example of hysterology borrowed from Jarry: 'I'll light the fire while I wait for him to get the firewood.' The term 'hysterology' comes from the Greek root of [the word] *husteros*,[49] which means 'subsequent', being possibly associated with *proteros*, 'what comes before'. Hysterology therefore means that what is 'after' comes 'before'. In a narrative, hysterology describes a circumstance or incident that should come afterwards, but which in fact comes first. The figure therefore refers to the inversion of the natural order of ideas or facts and describes, as the *Gradus ad Parnassus* so helpfully notes, 'the mental disorder of the speaker'.

To employ hysterology is basically to postulate something that does not yet exist in order to derive authority for engaging in action. This is the situation in which the democratic subject finds herself, placed as she is under the constraint 'Be yourself'. She postulates something that does not yet exist (herself) in order to trigger the action through which she must produce herself as a subject. Now, given that this support is bound to be shaky, not to say non-existent, the act either

---

[49] Its etymology is therefore not the same as that of 'hysteria', which derives from the Greek *hustera*, meaning 'uterus'. As everyone knows, the uterus of hysterical women was thought to contract.

fails by getting always deferred, or is accomplished but puts the subject in the situation of seeing herself perform an act she cannot believe in. The subject then feels herself to be an impostor. That is in the nature of the hysterological subject, as opposed to the hysterical subject. Whereas the hysterical subject is alienated in an Other and constantly reproaches both the Other and herself over her self-imposed dependency, the hysterological subject, who does not have the support of the Other, is inevitably confused inside because she is at once half a subject and a reduplicated subject. She is lost in a distended temporality which lies between a before and an after. She has no presence but still inhabits an extremely dilated present, which is isolated between a here and a there. And it is precisely this world that Beckett explores in *The Unnamable*. This is the world of a subject who finds herself in the position of having to found herself.

In postmodernity, the distance between self and Subject becomes a distance between self and self. The postmodern subject is not just split, but 'schizo'. Any subject in this position has to struggle to found himself. The subject can certainly succeed in doing so, but not without constantly having to be brought face to face with his failures, some serious, some not so serious. This internal distance between the subject and the subject's self proves to be inherent in the postmodern subject, and it alters Freud's diagnosis of the modern subject considerably. The modern subject tended to be neurotic, and psychosis was the exception to the rule. The postmodern subject is evolving towards a subjective condition defined by a borderline neurotic-psychotic state. This subject is increasingly trapped between a latent melancholy (the depression we hear so much about), the impossibility of speaking in the first person, the illusion of omnipotence, and the temptation to adopt a false self, a borrowed personality or even the multiple personalities that are made so widely available by the market. Postmodernity, in other words, may be witnessing the decline of what Freud called the transference neuroses and the rise of narcissistic psycho-neuroses. The ultimate defence against the psycho-neuroses is usually perversion.

Postmodernity and new forms of unconscious manifestation

Alain Ehrenberg has established (1998) that depression is now the most common mental disorder. He shows that the spectacular rise in the incidence of depression corresponded to the moment when disciplinary models for managing behaviour, the rule of authority and conformity with the prohibitions laid down by the Subject, which assigned individuals a ready-made destiny, gave way to injunctions that encouraged everyone to take individual initiatives by enjoining them to become themselves. Depression is, in a sense, the price we pay for our freedom and our emancipation from the authority of the Subject. It finds expression in sadness, asthenia (fatigue, or in other words the 'acedia' of times past), inhibitions or the inability to act that psychiatrists call 'pyschomotor slowing down'. It is a reflection of an inability to live.

The 'sad passion' is now said to affect, either permanently or cyclically, large sections of the population (estimates range from 15 to 20 per cent of all individuals).[50] We can neither act nor take the initiative. This is why we see so many self-help manuals in our postmodern societies. This is what television programmes on ordinary lives are about. So is the widely distributed exhibitionism marketed as literature, and so, obviously enough, is the use of the psychotropic mood-elevators and stimulants designed to boost individual performances. Many individuals in our societies now take anti-depressants on a regular basis. Prozac is the emblematic anti-depressant, and the fact that it has become as common a household name as 'aspirin' illustrates the extent of the phenomenon. It would, however, be a mistake to believe that this situation gets the democratic process into any kind of debt whatsover. Far from it. Taking Prozac or any other drugs belonging in the category of so-called 'comfortable' anti-depressants is one of the new 'democratic' possibilities that allow depressed subjects to work on their inner selves so as to 'feel better', or even 'better than themselves'. One of the side-effects is that the distinction between taking medicines and taking drugs tends to become blurred in our democratic postmodern societies. The other is that, now that moods can be altered artificially and on a permanent basis, it is becoming difficult to tell which is the self and which is the artificially reworked self. Does 'doing philosophy' mean anything today? What has become of the authenticity Heidegger associated with listening to Being? It is even becoming difficult to tell just what the self is – and once again Beckett was prophetic.

I will permit myself two remarks on Ehrenberg's important work on depression. First, now that he must found himself singlehandedly, the speaking subject is in exactly the same depressive position as the Subject of old. Remember Pascal's king. Pascal was a remarkable

[50] Figures from World Health Organization annual report on mental health (OMS 2001).

clinician *avant la lettre*, and he pointed out that a king who is left to his own devices reverts to being what he always was: a subject *like any other*. This is exactly the phrase used by Pascal: 'Put it to the test; leave a king entirely alone [. . .] and you will see that a king without diversion is a very wretched man, and he feels it *like any other*' (Pascal 1966: §137). The king was the foundation of all the rest but, having nowhere to found himself, he inevitably suffered from a persistent melancholy and needed constant diversion. Depression is the modern name for the old illness that Pascal identified perfectly so long ago. The same melancholy that once affected neotenins and forced them to play at being the Subject now affects speaking subjects who are forced to play at being themselves. And, as Pascal notes: 'The man who loves only himself hates nothing so much as being alone with himself. He seeks nothing but himself and flees nothing so much as himself; because, when he sees himself, he does not see himself as he desires himself to be, and finds in himself a heap of inevitable sorrows and a space empty of the real and solid goods, which he is incapable of filling.'*

My second remark has to do with the phenomenon of depression and its very nature. Depression appears to be an obvious clinical given, but it is in fact merely the result of the subject's encounter with the figure of hysterology. The subject becomes melancholy or depressed when she finds that her subjective path is blocked by the figure of hysterology, which makes all action impossible: how can she possibly use something that does not yet exist (herself) so as to trigger the action that will finally make her a self? Depression does not, therefore, relate to some feature that can be identified in psychological or sociological terms, but to the impossible logic of postmodern subjectivation; we cannot use ourselves to become ourselves for the very good reason that the initial support is not there. It therefore seems to me that depression should not be hypostasized into a natural 'mental illness'. It should be seen as a difficulty with subjectivation, bound up with the fact that we are faced with a logical impossibility or, to be more specific, a hysterological impossibility.

What is more, we must not become obsessed with depression. If we do, we will not see the wood for the trees. The hysterological constraints under which we are forced to live in posmodernity can certainly lead to depression, or even to the extreme states we call

---

* This fragment from the posthumous 'Port Royal' edition of the *Pensées* (1670) does not figure in the editions on which the English translation is based.

'panic attacks', but it can also lead to other things. Here are some of them:

(1) *Dishevelled narcissism and subjective infatuation.* In the old psychic economy, the self-referential process was determined by a structural third party. In the Bible, for example, the famous 'I am that I am' (Exodus 3: 14) was assumed by Yaweh, which means precisely 'He is.'[51] The Third basically assumed the unary form. In the new economy, the self-referential movement does away with the *he* to concentrate on the *I*. The unary ambivalence which, in theology, was characteristic of God (who was, when viewed in positive terms, the *totality* itself and, when viewed in negative terms, the *nothingness* of negative mysticism) has been transferred to a speaking subject who is responsible for his own foundation. The outcome has been a notable and highly problematic loss of individual inhibitions about the Subject.

Althusser's autobiography, which was written after he murdered his partner Hélène, is a significant illustration of my point. Althusser (1993: 81) describes his entire life as having been governed by the fantasy of 'giving myself an imaginary father yet behaving as if I were in fact his father'. This is the famous Althusserian fantasy of becoming 'the father's father' or 'the master's master': 'I did not have a father and continued indefinitely to play the role of "father's father" to give myself the illusion that I did have one, or rather to assume the role in relation to myself, since all those I met or who might have acted as fathers were not up to it. I disdainfully placed them beneath me, though my own position was clearly subordinate' (1993: 171). Yet Althusser has only to begin to manipulate things in this way, related to omnipotence, to realize immediately that his life 'consisted of nothing but endless artifice and defeat [. . .] was totally inauthentic' (1993: 277). We have here a perfect hysterological trope. Now Althusser finds in this fantasy, which is obviously designed to be self-foundational, the same theorem that he finds in negative theology, as is proved when he says of himself: 'A total incapacity to be equals total omnipotence' (1993: 278). In his great intelligence (and it is as great as it is insane), Althusser is well aware of the theological origins of this motif: 'We are constantly faced with the same terrible ambivalence, the equivalent of which is found in medieval Christian mysticism: *totum = nihil*' (1993: 278). He does not, however, draw any conclusions about the historical emergence of this subject, probably because,

---

[51] On this ternary structure, see my comments in chapter 8 of Dufour (1996a).

being an individual whose involvement in modernity is exemplary (witness his very Kantian definition of philosophy),[52] he fails to realize that, far from being a matter of individual trajectory and individual accidents, his case had far wider implications and was already a reflection of the era to come. In that sense, Althusser's subjective tragedy was to find himself confronting postmodernity's subject-form with 'only' the philosophical tools of modernity, in other words with considerations about God and then the proletariat, broad and free as they may have been. He was powerless against this 'terrible ambivalence' and he alternated between the omnipotence and impotence that overwhelmed him because it was the ambivalence of a newly emerging historical subject: the postmodern subject.

Leaving aside the case of Althusser, which is in many respects exemplary, we must now look how the social bond and being-together have been affected by the modern diffusion of a subject who is as powerful as it is powerless. The implications are inevitable: if individual actions are no longer referred to something that transcends and guarantees them, then there is no longer any difference between the freedom which is now unconditionally ours and the abuse of the right to freedom. The *Faktum der Freiheit* which was so important for Kant – the meaning which people give to their freedom – has no legitimate heirs and there is no longer anything to prevent public space from being a theatre for individual exploits. We live in *'narcynical'* times, so much so that we should be writing a new treatise, distancing it from Freud's 'On narcissism' (Freud [1914]). We could call it 'On narcynicism: an introduction'. Narcynicism means that everyone today tends to practise what Lacan used to call 'the politics of the stepladder'. This consists basically in the fact that, as soon as you meet someone else, you feel a spontaneous need to move up to the next rung. There are serious cases of narcynicism (they affect those

---

[52] Althusser explicitly defines philosophy, with reference to Kant's *Kampfplatz* ('arena, battlefield'), as putting forward 'theses in opposition to existing theses' (1993: 169). It should, however, be noted that Althusser's treatment of Kant is somewhat cavalier. Although Kant does indeed speak (in the preface to the first edition of the *Critique of Pure Reason*) of a *Kampfplatz*, he does so precisely in order to criticize the state of metaphysics, which is 'a battlefield of endless controversies' (1999: A viii). Whilst logic, mathematics and physical science had reached a state of legitimacy that made objective certainties possible, metaphysics was still, at the moment when he took it up, in a de facto state in which opinions clashed in vain. Far from being content with this *Kampfplatz*, Kant wanted to introduce some order into this 'battlefield' by setting up a tribunal chaired by reason. Hence the need for a critique of pure reason.

who now accord themselves a spectacular right of life and death over others). There are also minor cases. I am thinking, for example, of the pornographic exhibitionism which is now demanded by the mass media.[53] And of mobile phones. I obviously have nothing against mobile phones as such – they are fine sensory prosthetics – but I do dislike the postmodern use which is made of them. They allow everyone to be in permanent contact with everyone else: we are always where we aren't and never where we are. Thanks to these 'communications' devices, public space is now saturated with totally private discourses. We are all so 'free' that not only are we unafraid of putting our private lives on public display; we are forced to do so, thereby indulging in one of the postmodern forms of *jouissance*. In that respect, it is highly significant that putting private lives on display is now being promoted as the great postmodern standard for literature.[54] These 'literary' confessions, which are straight out of the so-called 'popular' press, are far removed from the exemplary stance of Blanchot – one of the authors of recent modernity who spent his life in hiding so as to call attention to his work, in other words to his writing, and not to his private life (by definition of little importance; see Bident 1998). The accursed share in the old libertinage, which was deeply negative and by definition asocial, has been put to death by the false ideal of transparency and sincerity (see Muray's remarkable article (2000)). This is a significant feature of postmodernity: this cult of spontaneity, which is as naïve as it is stultifying and presupposes the existence of an ego whose sole task is to tell other egos its life story in order to exist. It is invading literature and abolishing great fiction.

[53] To take only one out of countless examples. On a famous public service programme broadcast on Saturday evenings, and described as 'cultural', a top presenter was seen asking Michel Rocard: 'Isn't oral sex a form of infidelity?' The point of such programmes is to demonstrate that no function is any longer sacrosanct – not even that of the Prime Minister of the French government. There are only individuals who must at all cost reveal all, even about their private lives. The strange thing is that, when asked, they are perfectly willing to do so, sometimes to the consternation of the presenters. I am, however, prepared to bet that we have seen nothing yet and that this is just the beginning.

[54] On a television programme of literary news (Guillaume Durand's *Campus*, TF1, 5 September 2002), the writer Christine Argot, whose tales of incest and promiscuous love life are adored by the media, explained with a perfectly straight face that 'obscenity' nowadays consists, not in putting one's private life on show, but in keeping it private. Which is why, not wishing to be obscene, she had to tell us all about her sex life in her novels.

(2)   In addition to *narcynicism* and its 'politics of the stepladder' ('which makes everyone think they are handsome', as Lacan puts it), we also encounter an *egalitarian drive* which strives to negate the very hard work that goes into producing ourselves as subjects (Stoicism, for example, gives some idea of what is involved). We are equal from the outset because we are democrats and because we all spontaneously have an ego. All we have to do is to promote our egos in our exchanges (and preferably make a profit). The idea that we might have to make an effort to *become what we are* now meets with great resistance. Pleasure is now the only reason for learning, and anything that hurts is bad. According to this egalitarian drive, we are all spontaneously artists, thinkers and writers, and we are all the more accomplished for having abandoned the reactionary idea of creating. The work no long matters; the intention is the only thing that counts. We promote 'life histories', which is a cheap way of convincing ourselves that our lives are works of art. We readily rail against anyone who still attempts to pass on to others what he has spent a lifetime trying to construct. Who does he think he is? He's no better than we are!

(3)   Whereas depression is characteristic of a subject who is less than himself, the so-called *'multiple personalities' syndrome* (Beckett outlined its general features in *The Unnamable;* David Lynch is now exploring it in films like *Lost Highway* and *Mulholland Drive*) introduces us to the opposite form of a subject who is greater than himself. There has been, we are told, a considerable increase in the number of cases of 'multiple personality' in the United States, even though some orthodox Freudians tend to see them just as cases of hysteria[55] (and thus they fend off what Marcel Gauchet calls the need to 'redefine the unconscious'). The subject is not simply divided, but cut in two and/or

[55] The Freudian schema which is then invoked is the one inherited from Charcot's description of hysterical crises: 'In one case which I observed, for instance, the patient pressed her dress up against her body with one hand (as the woman), while she tried to tear it off with the other (as the man)' (Freud [1908b]: 166). If this case of dual personality is obviously a case of hysteria, does this inevitably mean that the same can be said of all cases of 'multiple personality'? What about those cases which are not related to bisexuality, or those that take the form of successive personalities rather than of personalities who are simultaneously present? Freud himself ([1923]: 30–1) seems to have accepted the possibility of multiple personalities already from 1923 on: 'If [the ego's] object-identifications gain the upper hand and become too numerous, unduly powerful and incompatible with one another, a pathological outcome will not be far off. It may come to a disruption of the ego in consequence of the different identifications becoming cut off from one another

reduplicated. The twenty-first century could well be the era of post-identitarian subjects and bodies: several identities in one body, or a single identity shared by several bodies.[56]

(4) *The denial of the real* should also be mentioned (for example, the essential one of generational difference, as the postmodern subject fails to recognize the principle of anteriority which allows the father [*père*] to function as a marker [*re-père*]; or the denial of sexual difference, which is just as significant). I will come back to this in the next two chapters.

(5) *New sacrificial forms.* I have already explained elsewhere (Dufour 1996a) that one way to overcome the internal confusion of a subject who is forced to supply his own foundations is to provide him with an external support. I examined, amongst other cases, that of a young woman who attempted to found herself as a social subject by suing a whisky distiller when her unborn baby died. She had downed a bottle of whisky in a single evening because she was depressed. She hoped that, if she took the case to court, she would be able to found herself anew by being recognized as the subject of a trauma, in other words a subject supposed not to know how to behave in normal social life or, in this case, not to know that it is inadvisable for pregnant women to drink bottles of spirits. It now seems to me that this was a kind of sacrificial exploit which allowed the subject to found herself thanks to a partial amputation.[57] Founding oneself on the basis of an amputation: the amputation becomes a sort of marker in the real which compensates for a lack of markers in the symbolic. Henri Frignet, a psychoanalyst who has worked on cases of transexualism (Frignet 2000), tells

---

by resistances; perhaps the secret of the cases of what is described as "multiple personality" is that the different identifications seize hold of consciousness in turn. Even when things do not go as far as this, there remains the question of conflicts between the various identifications into which the ego comes apart, conflicts which cannot after all be described as entirely pathological.'

For a critical approach to the issue of multiple personality, see the remarkable collection edited by F. Sauvagnat (2001).

[56] This was foreseen by Artaud; see Grossman (2002).

[57] I therefore disagree with Gilles Lipovetsky (in postface of 1993 to Lipovetsky 1983) when he claims that 'sacrificial culture has died' in postmodernism. Sacrificial forms have not disappeared – far from it. They have simply changed: they no longer relate to the Other, to whom the sacrifice was done, but to the narcissistic dynamic.

me that requests for the ablation of the penis can also be regarded as one of the postmodern forms of sacrifice that allow markers to be laid down so as to 'avoid' internal hysterological confusion. He has also told me about another form of sacrifice that is currently practised in Britain. It involves the amputation of a limb – usually a leg – and sometimes both legs. As in transsexualism, the operation allows the subject's body to be experienced as 'regenerated'; the subject can then claim to have the identity of an amputee. There is even a name for this – *apotemnophila* – and it seems that some British surgeons and psychiatrists do get a lot of patients asking for this type of operation.

Then there are the extreme forms of sacrifice which go far beyond the ablation of a part of the self, as their goal is nothing less than the total ablation of the self. They often occur during violent episodes of acting out. It is increasingly common for individuals who have committed truly murderous acts of violence to ask to be killed on the spot. The postmodern era is witnessing the spread of a new sacrifical form: sacrifice squared. This is a new sacrificial exploit which, when it is perpetrated, makes it possible to create the essential but missing support which allows the subject to live, if only for a moment, before dying. This new sacrificial form begins with the sacrifice of victims who have been carefully, if randomly, selected and ends, after the brief but intense moment of intoxication with his own identity, with the sacrifice of the sacrificer, who determines and then carries out the sentence appropriate to his impossible exploit.[58]

Postmodern sacrifice thus introduces a new sacrificial form into the history of humanity. It is, of course, still a desperate appeal to the social bond. The actions of postmodernity's mad killers in fact raise political questions. Corporal Lortie entered the Quebec National Assembly on 8 May 1984 with the stated intention of opening fire on the province's elected representatives. In 1999, the two authors of the Littleton massacre chose to strike on 20 April, which is the day of Hitler's birthday. Friedrich Leibacher opened fire on the Cantonal Parliament of Zoug in Switzerland on 28 September 2001. Richard Durn attacked local councillors in Nanterre on 26 March 2002. Robert Steinhauser killed at his school in Erfurt on 26 April 2002, evoking memories of the Littleton massacre; and so on. But the type of

---

[58] This is stated quite clearly in two sentences from the diary of Richard Durn, who opened fire on Nanterre's town council on the night of 26–7 March 2002: 'I just want to kill in order to feel that I am alive for a few moments'; and 'I think that a madman like me should be killed on the spot and without any hesitation'. See *Le Monde*, 10 April 2002.

sacrifice performed in these acts is no longer intended to create a third party representing a social guarantor for the members of a community by successfully inverting abjection and turning it into something sacred. Because the blow struck at the other is motiveless and therefore untenable, it rebounds upon the one who strikes it, and immediately undoes what he is trying to do. It is immediately annulled and revealed to be the isolated act of an asocial madman.[59] As the appeal to the social bond implicit in these acts gets nowhere, this form of sacrifice simply takes us from symbolization to asymbolization.

When we think of the recent past and of how the modern subject looked then, we cannot fail to be struck by the differences between the modern and the postmodern subject. The modern subject was characterized by something resembling a passionate desire to be another, that is to say, a desire to create himself as subject to the Other. Modernity invented so many forms of that desire to be another! We can recall the flamboyant subjects of a recent modernity: we had to become the clairvoyant subject of the Poem, the subject of the proletariat, the subject of the pure intensity of the unconscious, the subject of other cultures that were far away or had been lost or forgotten . . . whereas the *Kulturarbeit* of the modern era supported a desire to be other, the postmodern subject now states that he wants only to be himself and no one else. That is why, whereas modern pathologies often revolved around a passion for being another, postmodern pathologies now revolve around the issue of having to be self-foundational. And they do indeed appear where the hysterological constraint is at its greatest. It has to be understood that hysterology is nothing more than an effect of what Lacan used to call *Verwerfung* or foreclosure (of the name of the father). And it is indeed true that, if I have no father, I must generate myself. This is why these hysterological pathologies, marked by *Verwerfung*, put on the agenda something which goes beyond neurosis and raise the question of the psychoneuroses. It seems to me that Lacan understood this perfectly well. After 1968, at the beginning of the 1970s, he spoke of the 'discourse

[59] Many commentators refuse to see these incidents as anything more than the isolated actions of madmen and refuse to attempt to supply any social, political or cultural aetiology. They forget that, far from relating to a purely organic form of madness, these acts are a perfect expression of the state of the postmodern social bond.

of the capitalist', which promotes *Verwerfung* (Lacan 1972b): 'The distinguishing feature of the discourse of the capitalist is this: *Verwerfung*, rejection, expulsion from all the fields of the symbolic, with the implications I have already mentioned. Rejection of what? Of castration.'[60] The rejection of castration, the desire for omnipotence, hysterology, *Verwerfung* and desymbolization are all closely bound up with capitalism. It is therefore not enough to cling, as we do so often, to the idea that capitalism and the desymbolization it brings about lead only to perversion. The main reason why perversion is now so common is that its imperative to enjoy objects is perfectly compatible with the status of the disposable and renewable objects of the commodity system, but also, and above all, because it represents the final defence against psychosis, which is closely bound up with capitalism. In a word, capitalism generates schizophrenia. Deleuze and Guattari understood this when they wrote their *Anti-Oedipus* of 1972, and the book is, after all, subtitled *Capitalism and Schizophrenia*. The only problem is that, like the Marx, who believed that the proletarian produced by capitalism was going to redeem the world, Deleuze and Guattari insisted on believing that the schizophrenic represented the new figure of the Saviour.[61] They were asking a lot of schizophrenia. Redeemers of Artaud's stature are few and far between, and it is beginning to be noticed that capitalism tends mainly to produce destroyed subjects and poor, desymbolized wretches.

From guilt to shame: the question of the superego

In postmodernity, we are no longer dealing with a neurotic subject characterized by a compulsive guilt bound up with the supposition that there is an Other whose expectations are always disappointed. What defines the subject in postmodernity is something resembling a feeling of omnipotence when we succeed and complete impotence when we fail. As Alain Ehrenberg has demonstrated, being ashamed (of oneself) has replaced guilt (vis-à-vis others). Witness an

[60] On Lacan's 'discourse of the capitalist', see in particular his seminar of 1969–70 (Lacan 1991); his closing speech to the 1970 Congress of the École Freudienne de Paris (Lacan 1970a); and in the lecture given in Milan in 1972 (Lacan 1972a).

[61] 'For what is the schizo, if not first of all the one who can no longer bear "all that": money, the stock market – the death forces, Nijinsky said – values, morals, homelands, religions and private certitudes [. . .] The schizophrenic process [. . .] is the potential for revolution' (Deleuze and Guattari 2004: 374). *Anti-Oedipus* contains many other expressions of this belief.

expression that has become extremely popular with young people: *'j'ai la honte'*, *'il m'a collé la honte'* ['I have shame', 'he's stuck shame on me'] (see Mathieu Kassovitz's film *La Haine*). Whereas I used to feel guilty vis-à-vis others, shame involves only me. Guilt came from the frustration I had to suffer, and I could not overcome it without a symbolic effort which involved a long period of introspection and a projection into a possible future. Thus guilt was the product of a frustration which involved the elaboration of a personal project. Such a project could take a lot of detours and could be pursued in one of the fields in which symbolic redemption seemed possible (modern culture ensured that there were a lot of them on offer). Shame, by constrast, requires a rapid remission. I am ashamed in the same way I am hungry or cold. In that sense, shame is an expression of a narcissistic intolerance of frustration. I must respond to shame immediately. Whereas I had to work on my guilt in order to try to give it a meaning, when I am in the grip of shame I am forced to make reparation as soon as possible and to respond immediately. Whereas guilt implied a relationship of meaning and a detour through the symbolic, shame imposes a relationship of force and a real and immediate confrontation.

What contemporary psychoanalysis sometimes has to say about postmodernity unfortunately does not lead to a good understanding of this mutation. Indeed, it is often said that postmodernity simply corresponds to a collapse of the ego-ideals.[62] Some analysts even go so far as to say that their collapse may be the source of a new freedom, because it will dissolve a collective transference onto old idols. In my view, this at least proves one thing: that Freud was quite right when he admitted, late in life, that he had little to say about the superego because 'we ourselves do not feel sure that we understand it completely' ([1933]: 63). How can anyone fail to see that the collapse of ego-ideals has much more serious implications? It affects the construction of what, to restrict the discussion to the Freudian subject, is known as the *superego*, which is an agency formed through the introjection of ego-ideals. When the subject has no ego-ideals, the sociogenesis of the superego breaks down because it has nothing to feed on, so to speak. The collapse of the ego-ideals therefore brings about the collapse of the symbolic side of the superego, and that is where the law is inscribed. In the absence of any agency that asks them to account for themselves, subjects sometimes become indifferent to the

---

[62] See for example the position of Gérard Pommier (2000).

meaning they ascribe to their own acts. It is as though they were absent from their own acts. Because they have been excluded from the feeling of guilt, it seems to them that they no longer have to explain any aspect of their behaviour. They then conclude that the way they act is inscribed in their nature, and that there is nothing more to be said about it. This calls into question the very meaning of analytic work. Strictly speaking, we are no longer dealing with symptoms which mean something to those who exhibit them, and which can therefore be elucidated, but with mere behaviours. Jean-Pierre Lebrun calls them a-symptoms.

We are therefore dealing with a *desymbolization* and we must make a close study of it (as I shall attempt to do). If we do not, we will lapse into an otherworldly belief in liberation. That, unfortunately, is not all, as the collapse of the symbolic aspect of the superego can easily lead to the exacerbation of its 'obscene and ferocious' aspect (Lacan [1958a]: 517).[63] That aspect of the superego demands order, and does not necessarily relate it to any law. This internal division of the superego runs through each subject as well as between subjects. In postmodernity, we therefore find as many subjects who have lost the symbolic side of the superego as subjects who have a superego with an obscene and ferocious aspect. Truth to tell, the fewer there are of the former, the more there are of the latter, which suggests that we are in for some very dark political times. The result of the first round of the presidential election of 21 April 2002 gave us a foretaste of them.

But this is not all. The contemporary collapse of the superego may presage nothing less than an irresistible weakening of the critical spirit. For Freud, who knew his Kant, the human capacity for morality and practical reason, which was revealed by Kant, has its origins in the superego. It is clear from the *New Introductory Lectures on Psychoanalysis* (Freud [1933]) that, in Freud's view, the birth of 'conscience' is impossible without the formation of the superego. Freud goes even further in the direction of what I would happily call a (meta-)psychological version of Kantian ethics when he remarks ([1924]: 167) that 'Kant's Categorical Imperative is thus the direct heir of the Oedipus complex'. In Freud, the 'father complex' repositions and justifies Kant's ethics by giving it a (meta-)psychological content. The theoretical collusion between the superego and the critical spirit is a further indication of the close link between the Kantian and Freudian subjects. The collapse of one will inevitably lead to the lability of the other.

---

[63] On the 'obscene and ferocious' aspect of the superego, see also Lacan (1992).

Be that as it may, the market is flooding into the empty space left by the contemporary collapse of the ego-ideals and the symbolic aspect of the superego. The advertisers have already realized that they can exploit the debacle of the superego and attempt to make brands our new symbolic markers. The market (and especially the market in images) has become a major supplier of new and volatile ego-ideals which are constantly being reshaped. It is all the easier to identify with certain of the ideals' features (the famous *einziger Zug* or 'unary feature') as the subject goes adrift, being without a symbolic superego. How many little foot-soldiers do the brands have these days marching through the streets? How many Loanas turned up in our schools after the real Loana won the first *Loft Story* reality show?

I think, therefore, that we should not be analysing postmodernity as the period when we lost all our illusions about our imaginary idols, but as the period that saw the disappearance of the agency within the subject that says: 'You do not have the right to . . .' We might say that, in postmodernity, the Father is killed, but that there is no feeling of guilt and no disavowal of the murder to allow some figure of the Other to come into being. Postmodernity therefore produces subjects who have no real consistency at the level of the superego. They are impervious to symbolic injunctions and extremely vulnerable to traumas of all kinds. Because they have become incapable of repression, they cannot feel guilt but they are subject to shame. The disappearance of guilt is now so widespread that it even affects political circles. One recalls the historic and appalling comments made by a Minister for Health during the contaminated blood scandal of the 1980s: he accepted 'responsibility but not blame'.

The symbolic world of the postmodern subject is no longer the world of the modern subject: in the absence of a Subject, in other words without markers which can be used to found a symbolic anteriority and exteriority, the subject cannot succeed in moving in a sufficiently ample spatiality and temporality. The subject is caught in a dilated present where everything is at stake. The subject's relationship with others becomes problematic because personal survival is always at stake. When everything is decided in the immediate, projects, anticipation and introspection become very problematic operations.[64] As a

---

[64] The studies of children and those they call the 'new *lycéens*' undertaken by Charlot, Bautier and Rochex show that many of them have yet to get beyond an ' "I" that is imbricated in personal experience', cannot decentre themselves and cannot establish any agency that exists independently of their actions. See Charlot, Bautier and Rochex (1992: 172–4); Bautier and Rochex (1988: 138f, 214f).

result, the entire critical world and what Kant called the (critical) power of the mind comes under attack.

What is to be done when there is no more Other? Can we construct ourselves on our own by using the numerous and effective resources that our societies provide for that purpose? By all means, but it is far from certain that autonomy is a demand to which all subjects can conform. Autonomy is a conquest that demands a real asceticism. Most of those who succeed in meeting the demand for autonomy were once 'alienated' and had to struggle to free themselves. In that sense, the apparent state of freedom promoted by neoliberalism is quite illusory. To that extent, we might say that there is no such thing as freedom, and that there are only liberations. And that is precisely why those who have never been alienated are not necessarily free. The new subject of the postmodern world seems to have been abandoned rather than freed: 'I am free, abandoned' (Beckett 2003: 316). These new subjects are so free that they have in reality been abandoned [*abandonné*], that is, 'banished' ['*mis au ban*']. Giorgio Agamben's comments (1998: 28–9) about *homo sacer* evoke the strange sovereignty of these new subjects:

> He who has been banned [*mis au ban*] is not, in fact, simply set outside the law and made indifferent to it but rather abandoned by it, that is, exposed and threatened on the threshold where life and law, outside and inside, become indistinguishable. It is literally not possible to say whether the one who has been banned is outside or inside the juridical order.[65]

This is also why young people who have been *à ban donnés* or *donnés au ban* [given the ban], and in many cases relegated to the *banlieues* [outskirts], are such easy prey for anything which appears to satisfy their immediate needs. This is why postmodernity's new subjects are such easy targets for an apparatus as powerful as the market, which can invade and take over their lives thanks to its ability to control our day-to-day time and space – I am thinking of the control exercised by images (TV, films, games, advertising . . .). The docility with which these new subjects allow themselves to be tempted by commercial brands and wear their logos (which obviously mention designer labels and brands)[66] is an accurate reflection of a new servitude, which is as

---

[65] Agamben indicates that 'abandoned' derives from 'given the ban' [*à van donné*] and that, in the Romance languages, '*mettre à bandon*', '*à ban donner*', originally meant 'to put in power' as well as 'to let free'.

[66] On the marking and scarification of the postmodern body, see the work of the psychoanalyst Jean-Louis Chassaing (2000).

voluntary and unconscious as those that went before it, and the previous – and critical – generation finds it very confusing. Far from being nomadic, as Deleuze wanted to believe, many of postmodernity's new subjects simply find themselves in the position of being orphaned by the Other. So that they try as they can to compensate for this absence of the Other. Abandoned by the subject, these populations are ready to fling themselves into every mass delusion, from the fanaticism of football supporters to fashions for conspicuous consumption and commercial logos,[67] and this is, it seems to me, related to one of the characteristics of postmodern political space – as studies of mass society (by Herbert Marcuse, amongst others) were already noting in the 1960s.

Postmodern forms of compensating for the absence of the Other

We can identify several ways of trying to compensate for the absence of the Other, and they are very 'logical'. Postmodern societies' new subjects are experimenting widely with them.

• The first tendency is exemplified by *the group*. When there is no Other and when we cannot deal with the autonomy and self-foundation that are demanded of us on our own, we can always try to do so in a group. All we have to do is become part of an individual with several distinct bodies; in other words a group. It is not the first time humanity has come up with this solution. The anthropologist Maurice Leenhardt long ago demonstrated that, amongst the Melanesians, for example, several bodies (maternal uncle and nephew) could come together to form a single social persona. Transitivity is a characteristic feature of gangs: given that we are all part of the same persona, you may be hurt if I fall. A gang has a collective name, which is used by everyone in it. It has its signature, its

---

[67] See the excellent article by Jean-Marie Brohm and Marc Perelman (2002), which demolishes the myth that football is an integrating force, and demonstrates that it functions as a 'vector for a generalized social disintegration: the acceptance, if not the incitement, of verbal and physical violence, support for non-democratic values (the warrior ethos, the spirit of revenge, easy money, the adulation of idols, turning a blind eye to drug use, and so on), exaggerated chauvinism, the inversion of all the values of solidarity for the sake of personal gain, hatred for opponents . . . In short, a new sporting order has been established and forced upon the whole population.'

initials or its tag, and it uses them to mark and delineate its territory. A short train journey is all it takes to see how widespread the phenomenon of what the initiated call 'burners' has become.[68] Should an individual become detached from the collective figure represented by the gang, because, for example, he develops an interest in something other than the gang's preoccupations, the gang, which cannot tolerate the loss of one of its members and is jealous of its integrity, has no option but to bring that individual back to the fold by all means possible. It can sometimes be very difficult for a schoolteacher to talk to a pupil who is a gang member, because the whole group comes along or responds to the slightest prompting by spelling out its prerogatives and goals. It is quite impossible to enter into any critical discourse. Groups, then, provide the subject with the complete antithesis to autonomy. All their members fuse into a single entity, preferably that of the group's leader.

Gangs are variations on groups. In a sense, one naturally evolves into the other. A gang is a group which has succeeded in imposing its expeditious methods ('taxing', assaults, revenge attacks). Schools in difficult areas are especially likely to see groups turning into gangs. It is interesting to note that the methods used by gangs can be very effective when it comes to economic competition. The rap industry is a perfect illustration. It has seen the emergence of production companies managed by gangs according to gang methods and capable of taking on the majors and of integrating themselves into the market where all the small independent firms failed.[69] Some gangs and mafia-style groups are well aware of this fact and use it to take control of certain sectors of the market.

• The second tendency has to do with the selection of an ersatz taken to compensate for the absence of the Other. *Cults* provide the model. When there is no Other, we can establish a sort of voluntaristic Other that gives the subject an absolute guarantee against any possibility of absence. This is what happens in the many cults that flourish in postmodern societies – a small group comes together and parades the effigy of a guru or some new absolute master; if need be, it will clash with other groups who have rallied

[68] See Gilles Boudinet's ethno-sociological study of the phenomenon (Boudinet 2001).

[69] An excellent dossier on this was published by the weekly *Télérama* in November 1999.

to the banner of another guru. In postmodern space, the collapse of the Other inevitably leads to the appearance of cults which draw on orientalism, syncreticism or charismatic religions (consider the rapid spread of the neo-pentecostalists). They can even become associated with extremely virulent fundamentalisms. Whilst groups and cults do fuse in some cases (one thinks, for instance, of 'Satanism'), it is not unusual to see them competing (the same family might, for example, include one child who belongs to a group and another who has joined a cult, as a way of resisting the attractions of the group).

• The third tendency also has to do with an ersatz taken to compensate for the absence of the Other. When there is no Other, we can inscribe the Other in the order of need rather than in that of desire. This is what is called *addiction*. Addiction is often, and rightly, described as a reaction to depression and as a flight into compulsive behaviour: products which are consumed so compulsively quickly become indispensable. When we speak of addiction, we immediately think of drugs, but it has to be remembered that drugs are no more than rather special commodities. I would therefore say that the postmodern subject can develop a habitual addiction to commodities, and that the market promotes and encourages this addiction because it sees it as a way of expanding the commodity cycle. Some subjects may also be addicted to drugs, which are the most expensive and addictive of commodities. This is what we see happening with the widespread phenomenon of drug addiction. The goal is no longer to turn a difficult existence into a symbolic quest in which a cleverly put together and expressed construct (poetry, dance, song, music, painting . . .) compensates for the normal imperfections of the Other. In drug addiction, that laborious quest is transformed into a mere dependency on an Other who has been expelled from the field of desire and somehow reinscribed in the reality of need. At least we know what the absent Other is: nothing but a chemical product, as addictive as possible, but which can be obtained, provided that we become its slave.

• The fourth tendency implies going still further and actually attempting to become, and take the place of, the Other. We adorn ourselves with the signs of the Other's characteristic omnipotence and grant ourselves the power of life and death over our fellow human beings by acquiring supposedly magical powers. We then have absolutely no qualms about committing the most terrible acts of violence, as in the Littleton case.[70]

The extreme acts committed by adolescents in all of today's postmodern societies appear to me to combine in variable proportions these possible substitutes for the Other: ultimately, it is possible to be a member of a group, to be addicted to some product or other, to be a cult member and at the same time to be subject to extreme violence. We constantly see the new subjects of our postmodern world, who suffer because there is no Other, suddenly switching from petty crime to addiction, religious fanaticism or hyper-violence.

Far from being explicable in terms of the media's thirst for sensation, and far from being erratic in the medical sense of the term and therefore inexplicable because they result from mysterious impulses that suddenly come over certain young people, these tendencies appear to me to be perfectly consistent with the decline of the Other in our societies. They are a direct result of it, and they affect those populations who are most vulnerable to its effects.

I am not saying that the extreme forms of behaviour engendered by the absence of the Other affect all young people, but they do represent a worrying and very widespread tendency, which is already mobilizing sequences of identifications, vague fascinations and scraps of stories and narratives. The market was very quick to understand this, and has developed a whole industry based on games, music and violent images that feed on the strong affects triggered by the absence of the Other.[71] It is, I repeat, true that few adolescents act out these

[70] On 20 April 1999, two boys aged eighteen and seventeen killed thirteen of their classmates in Littleton (USA). They then committed suicide. They were both obsessed with information technology, video games and certain cults. It is now believed that the two young authors of the Columbine High School massacre planned to hijack an aircraft and crash it into the World Trade Center once the massacre was over. The events of 11 September 2001 could therefore have taken place on 20 April 1999, with two American boys at the controls.

This highly significant event was followed by others of the same type in different countries. See the studies published in *Journal for the Psychoanalysis of Culture and Society* (Ohio University Press), including my 'Modernity, post-modernity and adolescence' (Dufour 2000).

[71] I am thinking of, amongst other things, the series of *Scream* feature-length films made by Wes Craven from 1997 onwards. The films appear in the mental landscapes of a number of adolescents who have committed murder. Some of them say that they received messages from the films and heard voices telling them to kill their father, mother or girlfriend . . . (see the dossier published in *Le Monde*, 22 June 2002).

tendencies, and that those who do so are probably very fragile individuals who receive little support from their families, or what remains of them, but the syndrome is by no means uncommon, as we can see from the 'petty criminality' ('taxing', theft, violence, assaults . . .) which is becoming the norm.

Rejecting the fiction of the Other may well have freed us from our tyrannical old idols, but it also brings us face to face with some 'impossible' questions. The 'Market' either leaves them wide open or rushes into them, making the situation worse. It was inevitable that the populations that are most vulnerable to this tendency of the Other to fade away should include adolescents, and in that sense adolescents are the exemplary representatives of postmodernity. But the fact that they are the first to be affected by this phenomenon – at an increasingly early age – by no means indicates that adolescents and young adults are the only ones to be affected by these problems. Let us be quite clear about this: they affect the social body in its entirety. We have to understand that the phenomena generated by this 'fading' of the Other do not correspond to some regrettable historical accident that can easily be resolved. They are warning signs about a structural state that is becoming established in our societies. It will have a deleterious effect on major aspects of the social bond.

These tendencies are already so powerful that they can take on major proportions. September 11, 2001 showed us the true extent of the phenomenon: the absence of the Other can lead members of cult-like organizations to become involved in extreme violence. In an age of globalization, there is no reason to think that violently fanatical groups will go on acting at a local level now that they are perfectly capable of operating at a global level, as we can see from the terrible attack on the World Trade Center carried out by those known as 'Allah's madmen'.

The strangest thing of all is that this devastating religiosity should have inspired a messianic rhetoric which uses and abuses extreme religious symbolism in the very heart of the political system of the victim of 9/11 – namely the United States, which is the world's most powerful state and greatest democracy. By promoting a worldview in which 'Good' fights the 'axis of evil', a small group of Christian fundamentalists and ultraconservative neo-Republicans used an ambiguous election to seize control of the White House. They, too, are

---

[72] According to the editorial in *Le Monde* on 29 March 2003, 'President George W. Bush is a born-again Christian. He was born again after a very misspent youth. He is

prepared to commit all sorts of extreme acts 'in the name of God'.[72] One sometimes wonders whether their response to the quasi-cult of Allah's madmen has not been the creation of a sort of violent Christian cult which, in the face of opposition from the churches themselves, has taken control of the most powerful country in the world.

We will soon see to what extent this gloomy hypothesis will be verified, but we can already conclude that the current desymbolization of the world can easily coexist alongside – or even provoke – the violent return of fanatical religiosity. This tends to prove that Marcel Gauchet's thesis (1985) about the 'exit of religion' – which I accept – by no means precludes the return of violent outbursts of religiosity. On the contrary.

---

not content to end his speeches with the famous "God bless America" used by all American Presidents. His speeches abound in references to God, and all cabinet meetings now begin with a prayer. Ministers take turns to lead prayers. And Congress has just proclaimed a "day of humility, prayer and fasting for the people of the United States". This will teach the American people to ask for God's advice "on how to meet the challenges the nation must face". The danger has been recognized by religious dignitaries, including representatives of the American Churches and even evangelical Methodists like the Bush family. They do not recognize themselves in the President's "fundamentalism", which they describe as an ideology that has nothing to do with the God of the Bible.'

The other component in the American ruling coalition, namely the neoconservative heirs to the philosopher Leo Strauss and to the strategist Albert Wohlstetter, has nothing to do with the Protestant fundamentalism of the Southern States, as many of its respresentatives are Jewish intellectuals from the East Coast. But, like Leo Strauss, they still think that religion is a useful way of sustaining the illusions of the majority, and that order cannot be maintained without those illusions. See the excellent dossier published on 'Le Stratège et le philosophe' in Le Monde, 15 April 2003.

2 *Homo Zappiens* Goes to School: The Denial of Generational Difference

The argument outlined in chapter 1 can be read as an attempt to reply to Pierre Bourdieu's article on 'The essence of neoliberalism', which was published in *Le Monde Diplomatique* in March 1998. In that article, Bourdieu suggested that neoliberalism should be seen as a programme for the 'destruction of collective structures' and for the promotion of a new order based upon the cult of 'a lonely, but free individual'. This conception is not mistaken, but it is patently inadequate, as if the argument broke off just when the important point was about to be made.

Neoliberalism certainly targets collective agencies (the family, trade unions, political forms, nation-states and, more generally, culture insofar as it is a site for generational transmission and collective representations), because they might hinder the free circulation of commodities. No one doubts that it targets them, and the defenders of neoliberalism openly admit to doing so. In their view, there must be no exceptions to the demand for the totally free circulation of commodities, which should not be accountable to any agency. Yet Bourdieu's analysis appears to me to have a serious limitation that it is difficult to hold against the eminent sociologist . . . because it is a limitation of sociology, Bourdieu stops where sociology stops, or, in other words, at the point where, in my view, it is essential to start thinking again. 'What subject-form is now coming into being?' That is the big question we have to deal with. It is inconceivable that neoliberalism, which destroys collective agencies, should leave intact a subject-form that is heir to a long historical, philosophical and theologico-political process of individuation.

Aside from Bourdieu, this criticism is addressed to the many analyses which simplistically characterize the contemporary period as that of the triumph of individualism. These studies simply forget that we are not dealing with the appearance of a supposed individual who has always existed, but with a specific and previously unknown subject-form, which in consequence must be carefully defined.

This is why we have to begin our analysis again. We should no longer limit it to the strictly sociological data but open it up by introducing a specifically philosophical dimension. What is happening to the subject-form in this period of neoliberalism?

In the previous chapter, I attempted to show how the two great processes of intellection which constitute subjectivity are coming under attack. Where reflective consciousness (the 'secondary' processes) is concerned, neoliberalism wants at all cost to do away with the *critical* subject, whose apotheosis is signalled by Kantianism. Where the unconscious (the 'primary' processes) is concerned, neoliberalism wants to have nothing more to do with the old subject it inherited from modernity. That subject was revealed by Freud and it was, in its classic form, *neurotic* and haunted by guilt. Neoliberalism wishes to replace this doubly determined subject with an *acritical* subject with, insofar as that is possible, *psychotic tendencies*. This is, in other words, a subject who can be plugged into anything, a floating subject who is always receptive to commodity flows and communication flows, and permanently in search of commodities to consume. It is, basically, a precarious subject. Its very precariousness is auctioned off by the Market, which finds new outlets by becoming a major supplier of identity kits and images for the subject to identify with. As Foucault prophesied twenty years ago, the world has become Deleuzean. The contemporary subject-form tends towards the schizo, as that is the only form which can navigate these shifting and multiple flows. But the world has become Deleuzean in a way that would probably have surprised or even horrified Deleuze himself: as I have already pointed out, Deleuze in a sense thought that he could outstrip capitalism by deterritorializing faster than it could. But there is now every indication that he underestimated both the amazing speed with which capitalism can absorb things and its uncanny ability to recuperate criticism. He never suspected that it was in a sense capitalism itself that would implement the Deleuzean programme – which, once again, confirms the adage to the effect that, when the political dreams of philosophers come true, they do so in the form of nightmares.

It remains for me to demonstrate in this chapter that the manufacture of this new non-critical and near-psychotic subject (or schizoid, if we prefer to put it that way) owes nothing to chance. Various currents (from Christopher Lasch to Lyotard, via Dumont and Lipovetsky) have been looking at the emergence of this subject for over twenty years now. This is a subject who has been freed from the grip of the grand soteriological narratives (be they political or religious). The 'postmodern' subject has been left to her own devices, knows no anteriority or finality, recognizes only the here and now, and plugs the parts of her little desiring machines into the flows that run through them as best she can.

This 'postmodern' subject is not emerging as the result of some inexplicable twist of history. This is the product of a terrifyingly effective undertaking. At its centre we find two major institutions, and they are dedicated to the manufacture of the postmodern subject: television and a new educational system[1] which has been greatly transformed by thirty years of reforms.[2] Those reforms are described as 'democratic', but they are all designed to do the same thing: to enfeeble the critical function.

Television

Given that human beings are the creatures of language, it is highly probable that any new language practice will have a profound effect on the individuals who have to come to terms with it. The book, which was the great medialogical invention of the Renaissance, had major effects on forms of symbolization at both the cultural and the individual level. Anyone who doubts this has only to consider the philosophical and ontological questions which have been asked of writing and literature since then (they reached a paroxysm in the twentieth century, which was probably the moment when literature reached its apotheosis). A brief quotation from Maurice Blanchot may give a synthetic but very cogent description of these questions: 'The experience that is literature is a total experience, a matter that does not tolerate any limitations, will not accept any stabilization or reduction. [It might be] the experience of what has always been said, of what cannot cease to be said and cannot be understood' (Blanchot 1959: 322). The experience of literature seems therefore to be very powerful because

---

[1] Mauss regarded magic as a *total social fact that made use of several institutions*, and I see education in the same terms. Three institutions (the family, television and schools) are certainly involved in education, and I look here at two of them but not at the role of the family. On the role of the family, see Roussel (1992) and Théry (1998).

[2] The stages of its transformation have been reconstructed by Liliane Lurçat (1998).

it can bring speaking subjects face to face with the mystery of their being. It is not unreasonable to take the view that, in the same way, new communication technologies, as they are now known, have already had an effect on the symbolic function and forms of symbolization.

What effect does television, which is the most widely used of these means of communication, have on children? The question is worth asking all the more as television begins to erode children's minds at a very early age. When they start school, many of today's children have been fed a non-stop diet of television from their very earliest years. This is a new anthropological fact, and we have yet to come to terms with all its implications: human children begin to watch television before they can talk. We have an intuitive understanding of why this should be the case: television is the only instrument that keeps children quiet without anyone having to look after them. As all the studies show, children spend several hours per day consuming images. According to a UNESCO study, 'children around the world have . . . regular access to television and watch it for an average of 3 hours per day. This represents at least 50 per cent more than the time they spend on any other activity, including homework, being with friends or reading.'[3] Although this figure is high, it is no more than an average: almost one third of children spend four or more hours per day watching television (and most of them are the children of underprivileged classes and minorities).

The way in which the space of the family is being inundated by an uninterrupted flow of images from a tap always turned on obviously has major effects on the formation of the future speaking subject. Not least because of the preponderant role played by ubiquitous and aggressive advertising. Television provides a veritable apprenticeship in consumerism and encourages a monocultural approach to commodities.[4] This outrageous incitement is not without its ideological purpose. The most aggressive advertisers are well aware of how they can profit from the postmodern collapse of all the figures of the Other, and therefore they have no scruples about advocating the exploitation of 'the fragility of the family and of authority in order to establish

[3] Groebel (1998), also available online via scholar.google.com.
[4] See Moreira (1995). According to *Consumer Report* magazine, an American child sees an average of 40,000 adverts per year. American kids' purchasing power is of great interest to the marketing people, as it is estimated to reach almost $15 billion – to say nothing of the influence they have on their parents' spending, which is estimated to be almost $130 billion (1991 figures).

brands as new points of reference'.[5] Brands as new points of reference: this brings us to the heart of a novel ideological operation which has a major clinical effect in our postmodern societies. Just as the Indians of Amazonia were thrust into a regime of commodity exchanges when 'gifts' were hung up in *tapini* (shelters made from leaves; above, p. 3 n2), children are now being projected into the world of commodities as television screens are used as virtual *tapini* displaying potentially desirable products.

On top of the advertising, there is the violence of the imagery: by the time he or she reaches the age of about eleven, the 'average' child will have seen some 100,000 acts of violence on television and will have witnessed some 12,000 murders (Josephson 1995). Of course the stories told by the supposedly kind grandmothers of yesterday included a fair number of horror stories about child-eating ogres, and those stories were quite literally just as gruesome as today's banal images of gore. It should, however, be remembered that there are two crucial differences: (1) the grandmothers mediated the horror by integrating it into the enunciatory circuit; (2) there is an obvious difference between the obviously *imaginary* world of fairy-tale ogres, which forces children to evaluate it as an *other* world (a world of fiction), and the *very realistic* world of the serials, with their fights, violence, rapes and murders: they are not distanced from the real world.[6] Child psychiatrists are already reporting cases of children who believe they can jump unharmed from an upstairs window 'like they do on telly'. It is no longer a symbolic injunction that stops them from doing so; it is trauma, in other words the real.[7]

Even if the picture is already gloomy as it stands, it is not enough to consider just the *content* of the images: the very form of the medium itself can be dangerous, *no matter what it shows*. This is a crucial point, as it raises the real question about the role television plays in what I

[5] Brochure distributed at a colloquium organized in Paris on 26–7 February 2002 by the Institute for International Research. The colloquium's theme was 'Targeting communications so as to reach children at the heart of their world'.

[6] A study carried out by Columbia University's psychologist Jeffrey Johnson and colleagues and published in *Science* (vol. 295, 29 March 2002) found a clear correlation between violent adolescent behaviour and the length of time spent watching television

[7] Paper presented at Marcel Gauchet's seminar on the philosophy of education on 13 February 2002 by Michèle Brian. She explained that child psychiatrists were seeing children who escaped symbolic prohibitions (such as a parental 'No') only to suffer traumas. For children like there, it is now trauma that sets the limits.

call a diffuse but very effective desire to manufacture subjects with psychotic tendencies. Yet this question is almost never raised. At best, we denounce the harmful role of advertising and violence.[8] At worst, it is argued that the only problem with television is that there are not enough 'attractive' programmes.[9] But as a rule no one looks at the very serious issue of the semantic disturbances that are caused by televisual images. It is as though there was an a priori belief that massive exposure to such images had no effect on the psycho-semio-genesis of speaking subjects and on their socialization.

We therefore often forget to mention the fact that, the more time we spend watching television, the less time we have for our families. The family's role in general and in cultural transmission is greatly reduced as a result. In that sense, the expression 'the children of television' should be taken literally and, far from raising a smile, should be seen as a rather pathetic admission that television has effectively taken over the parental role of educating children.[10] Television has become what studies carried out in Quebec call a 'third parent'. It is a very active parent and increasingly tends to oust children's 'real parents'.

[8] See, for example, the report on 'Les Enfants, acteurs courtisés de l'économie marchande', commissioned by Jack Lang when he was Minister for Education and submitted by the sociologist Monique Dagnaud in late February 2002. She proposed establishing a non-commercial children's channel and lessons about consumerism at school. See also the report commissioned by Minister for Culture Jean-Jacques Aillagon and submitted by the philosopher Blandine Kriegel on 14 November 2002. The report stressed the effects which televised violence had on children and young adults, including 'the lowering of inhibitions and guilt, the acquisition of stereotypes, over-stimulation and imitation pure et simple'. The effect was 'clear and proportional to the amount of time spent in front of the screen', said the report, which recommended stricter controls on the broadcasting of violent images. It is noteworthy that neither of these recent reports looks at how the medium itself distorted access to the symbolic.

[9] This was the position taken by former Minister for Education Luc Ferry, even though he is a philosopher. He recommended that 'boring intellectual programmes should not be shown at 8.30 in the evening', and took the view that, all things considered, there were 'almost too many interesting programmes to watch' on television. The minister, who is not one of those 'anti-telly' intellectuals' was, in any case, quite unperturbed: even when television 'scrapes the bottom of the barrel' (dixit), there is no need to worry: 'Being a democrat, I think that the public is on the whole intelligent enough to realize that "Big Brother" is not all that interesting.' Interview in *Le Monde*, 9 August 2002: 'Luc Ferry: Television invites us to go further'.

[10] Shortly before he died, the great philosopher Karl Popper drew attention to this problem in an interview (in Italian) with Giancarlo Bosetti; 'Against television' can now be found in Popper (1996).

But what happens to the 'less and less time' that is devoted to generational transmission? What happens when children are put in front of a television set which talks to everyone and to no one in particular even before they can talk? I will try to demonstrate that this has very specific effects and that it may even bring about the collapse of the symbolic and psychic world.

Text and image

Let us note, first of all, that massive exposure to televisual images distorts the centuries-old relationship between text and image. Of course images existed before intergenerational relations were invaded by television, but our initiation into symbolic practice began with texts from which we inferred images. I use 'text' to mean oral statements – ordinary speech, tales, versions of myths or legends – as well as scriptural statements (sacred texts, serialized stories, novels . . .). Even simple situations provide a clear illustration of the primacy of the text. Listening to a story-teller or reading a novel triggers psychic activity: the listener or reader creates mental images and is, in a sense, the first person to see them. The Phaeacians who gathered around the *aoidos* as he recounted the exploits of Ulysses witnessed them and 'saw' them 'live' in their minds' eyes. This ability to make present that which is absent is obviously a key issue in symbolization. Besides, it was listening to the story of his own exploits that allowed Ulysses to 'come home' when he reached Alcinous's island. His 'homecoming' was so intense that he had to 'cover his face', probably so that he could weep with emotion, as Heidegger speculates in his 'Aletheia' (Heidegger 1975). I read a passage from *Le Côté de Guermantes*: 'We left Paris, where, although its was the beginning of spring, the trees on the boulevards had scarcely put out their first leaves. When the train deposited Saint-Loup and myself in the suburban village where his mistress lived, it was a source of wonder to see that every little garden was filled with a huge white altar of the blossom on the fruit trees.' As I read, I 'see' a train that disappeared fifty years ago, a suburb that no longer exists, a late spring, two friends, a date . . .

The Greek story-teller introduced his listeners to the world of the living forces of *physis* by opening a window on to a primal world, a divine world that was normally hidden from the gaze of mortals – a world in which were plotted the events of the second world, where they lived. The story-teller worked the miracle of showing the inhabitants of this world of appearance a supposedly *true* world, a real world where things were organized. The reader, for her part, imagines something of the world the author created.

We see here the status of the archaic image, which has been rendered so intelligible by Jean-Pierre Vernant (see chapter 8 in Vernant 1979), and the status of the fabula into which the reader is, according to Umberto Eco (1979), invited by his interpretation of the text and what it leaves unsaid.

Not all listeners or readers see the same images. Obviously not. We are familiar with the controversies that arise when a film-maker tries to adapt a literary work on the big screen: as no two readers 'saw' the same thing, everyone claims that the picture is 'not true' to the original. This objection is so widespread that the only possible solution seems to be not to be faithful to the original (the least said about that, the better), but to transpose it into a different creative world. Of course we 'see' when we read a text or listen to words, but we see what no image can really show. How can an image capture the unpredictable trajectory of one of Proust's sentences? How can an image capture the concomitant use of an imperfect and a past historic tense? The fiction produced by a text is irreducible to an image.

This predisposition for *fiction* and *fabulation* must obviously be seen in terms of a general anthropology: it is a disposition of the species. The use of the signifier (which is the constituent element of the symbolic at the levels of articulated phonation, writing and sign language alike) generates signifieds and is, therefore, meaningful only when it is combined with our species' characteristic ability to create images.

An image is not, however, just a reflection of a text. The image has its own efficacy and power: it can quite simply put the text into abeyance. There is a good reason for this: an image is not articulated in the way a text can be said to be articulated. We can even list, in no particular order, the text's four levels of signifying articulation: (1) a level of elementary units at the sonic level of *phonemes*;[11] (2) a semiotic level of signification that introduces *morphemes*; (3) a level of significance which introduces *sentences* (Benveniste describes this level as 'semantic' so as to distinguish it from the 'semiotic' level; (4) a mythological level relating to narrative, and which introduces what Lévi-Strauss identifies as *mythemes* (minimal narrative units). But

[11] This is the object of phonology: there is a finite number of phonemes in any given language and each phoneme is defined by its differential relationship with the others.

whilst texts are highly articulated, all attempts to give images the same status have ended in failure. No matter whether we look at the level of the mental image or signified, or at the level of the physical (pictorial, filmic . . .) image or signified, these attempts have at best produced very useful taximonies, but they have never succeeded in defining the intrinsic nature or internal organization of the image – there will never be any need to 'read' an image from top to bottom, from left to right, from centre to edge or from one particular viewpoint, rather than attempting to grasp it as a whole.

It is probably its non-articulated nature that gives the image its ability to interrupt the text: a single image can call into question very dense networks of meanings and significations that have been duly organized into a text. This is also the source of aesthetic emotion: a single image or a sequence of images appears – it might be a dazzling dance step, the sight of the pediment of a Greek temple, the capital of a Romanesque pillar, the tympanum of the central porch of a Gothic cathedral, a painting by Bacon or a film by Welles – and what was a 'textual' system of organized representations is suddenly disrupted. A mere image obliges us to create another text, which takes into account and integrates the disruption we experience. This is obviously not a matter of trying literally to translate an image into a text, but of repairing the tear that has been made in the fabric of the text by what Barthes (1982: 96), speaking of photography, calls the *punctum*: 'A photograph's *punctum* is that accident which pricks me (but also bruises me, in poignant terms).' I am obviously not saying that we have to find the text that corresponds to the image; what we need is a text that can suture the rent which has appeared in the networks of meaning, a text that does not preclude another text (or other texts). The image can thus be situated in a relationship of 'before and after' with the text (or at least a pre-textual relationship), and can then acquire the ability to represent something that cannot be said.

The 'punctiform' aesthetic image is not the only type of image not to be articulated with the text. The other is internal to the subject and is known, after Freud, as a *fantasy*. This may be a matter of 'unconscious representation'. Such images can indeed be unconscious in the sense Freud had in mind when he was distinguishing between 'the presentation of the thing' (in other words, the signified) and 'the conscious presentation . . . the presentation of the thing plus the presentation of the word belonging to it' (the signifier) (Freud [1915]: 201). Fantasies therefore have to do with the wandering images – conscious or unconscious – that haunt the psychical apparatus. The characteristic feature of these images is that they have become detached from a text which can be represented only as a 'lost' or 'censored' text (one recalls Lacan's definition of the repressed as this 'censored *chapter*' in my story). As the 'text' of the fantasy eludes the very person who acts as its carrier, these images come back to the subject in repetitive or intrusive ways, and cannot be stabilized or linked together in a cumulative process. Any external image can therefore sustain the fantasy by compulsively attaching itself to it, in a sequence that has no text.

The only way to prevent the tear made by the *punctum*, or the unbinding of the fantasy, is to find the corresponding text. As a result of Freud's influence, we often attempt to find the text of the fantasy in the very special discursive structure known as psychoanalysis. And we attempt to find the aesthetic image which, like the *punctum*, interrupted the networks of signification in the critical processes which question the image: we induce text from image, and can then move to and fro between the heterogeneous worlds of text and image in all kinds of ways . . . if, at least, we want the image to lead towards something different from its simple invasion by the fantasy – this 'something' being, in the case of both fantasy and aesthetic image, a knowing, or at least something which escapes the compulsion and becomes part of a cumulative discursive process.

The educational value of the image must not be restricted to the classroom: the reason why the film-maker Jean-Luc Godard can be said to be a great teacher is that he was able to demonstrate the unrelenting work that has to be done if we are to make the transition from image to text in a period which, increasingly openly, scorns that work and is content with bare images that give on to the never-ending and pointless repetition of the fantasy.[12]

The symbolic function

Having established the text–image relationship, we can go on to look at the symbolic function: how is it transmitted and how is it acquired? Once again, the text takes priority and the symbolic function is transmitted primarily through discourse, which brings with it a whole imaginary world. We know that generations of parents have always educated the next generation by passing on narratives. Passing

---

[12] Remember the famous 'Ceci n'est pas une image juste, c'est juste une image' ['This is not a just image, but just an image'].

on a narrative actually means transmitting contents, beliefs, names, genealogies, rites, obligations, knowledge, social relations . . . but, above all, it means passing on the gift of speech. It is a way of passing on to the next generation the human ability to speak, so that the narrative's addressee can identify herself as a self and situate herself in relation to the others who are around her, who came before her and who will come after her. The speaking subject must be instituted; if that anthropofacture does not take place, the symbolic function simply cannot be transmitted.

Basically, it has always been the oldest human activity – talking face to face – that provides access to symbolization. As a result, we transmit the gift of speech without even realizing that we are doing so; it is rather like the invisible miracle performed by the members of Borges's Sect of the Phoenix, who passed on a secret from generation to generation without realizing it. Well, it is possible that, with the advent of television, we suddenly no longer know how to pass on this gift.

To simplify things greatly, we might say that, because they have spent time with their parents and because verbalization plays an essential role in that relationship, as the baby is 'talked' into the other's discourse even before it is born, children acquire a set of symbolic markers as they respond to that interpellation.[13] These markers consist of special signifiers known as deictics, such as 'I', 'here' and 'now' (see chapter 5 in Benveniste 1971). Deictics are 'empty' signs which make no reference to 'reality'. They are pure signifiers, which are always available and become 'full' when a speaker uses them discursively. They include personal indicators (both subjective – 'I', 'you' – and non-subjective – 'it'), spatial indicators ('this', 'that', 'here') and temporal indicators ('now', 'today', 'yesterday'). Thanks to these indicators, the speaker can index herself as she *who* speaks; at the same time, she establishes a *where* and *when* she is speaking. This process signals that the speaking subject is located within an enunciatory scenario that allows the external world to be represented in a discourse. Access to the symbolic, therefore, requires the use of these personal markers ('I', 'you', 'he/she'), temporal markers (of presence, co-presence or absence) and spatial markers ('here' and elsewhere).

---

[13] Verbal intercourse is itself inserted into a broader organic intercourse: the exchange of glances (seeing oneself, seeing and being seen by the other), vocal exchanges (hearing and being heard by the other), the exchange of bodily substances (the breast, the faeces) . . .

Access to the symbolic world is of vital importance, as it relates to the essential ability that marks the difference between human beings and animals: the ability to speak, to designate oneself as a speaking subject by addressing one's fellow human beings from this stance and by sending them signs supposed to represent things – I say 'supposed' as there is nothing to indicate that the signs do actually refer to real things or facts. Human beings constantly 'invent' what they call reality. It is therefore very easy to represent the symbolic function: integration into a system in which 'I' (present) speak to 'you' (co-present) about 'him/her' (absent, that is, the one who must be re-presented).[14]

Therefore I say it once again: the system which guarantees access to the symbolic function, and hence to a certain minimal psychic integrity, is acquired essentially through discourse: parents and close relations talk to their children, and the symbolic function is gradually established. The gift of speech is passed on from one generation to the next. The human aptitude for speech is passed on in such a way that the person we talk to can in turn identify herself – in time ('now'), space ('here') and as a self ('I'). She can then use these markers to invite everyone else into her discourse.

Television can, in some cases, pose a serious threat to the essential transgenerational transmission of the most precious human gift of all: discourse. Which cases are these?

Massive exposure to televisual images and its effects on the symbolic function

We will look first at what happens when the symbolic markers of time, space and person have been more or less solidly established through normal discursive intercourse. In this case, the only problem, apart from the violence of the images and the apprenticeship in consumerism we mentioned earlier, is that the time devoted to learning has to compete with the time spent watching television. A French study published a few years ago after an epidemiological survey on children and television showed that the children who got the best marks at school watched television for less than fifty minutes a day. The incidence of memory loss, difficulty in concentrating, hyperactivity, excitability, aggression and insomnia proved to be proportional to the

---

[14] I suggest elsewhere (Dufour 1990) that the triangle of 'I/you/he or she' should be regarded as the basic configuration of symbolization.

amount of time spent in front of the television.[15] Moderate use of television was the only way to escape this inevitable outcome. This is not difficult to understand: symbolic markers that have at least some stability can take control of televisual images and, if required to do so, the subject can retranscribe those images as discourse. If the subject's discursive markers have been established, he can take control of images and come and go between image and text. This interplay can even be both ludic and educational: the only requirement is that the impersonal medium must enter into discourse and its interpellating system.

We can go further. Once the basic symbolic markers are in place, the subject can use every sensory prosthesis imaginable: those which broadcast *sound* across distances (the telephone, the radio); the *written word* which brings the elsewhere here; *images* which introduce an elsewhere into the subject's here (a *narrative* elsewhere, thanks to icons, statues or films; a *physical* elsewhere, which exists thanks to microscopes and telescopes . . .); the *telepresence* which transports the subject's here into the elsewhere of a virtual space . . . These sensory prostheses provide access to new *jouissances* because they use the subject's ability to play with the symbolic categories of here and elsewhere, now and before, and because it is these categories that constitute him as a subject. When I say '*jouissance*', I mean the 'vertigo' that comes from transporting a sonic 'here' or a visual 'elsewhere', or of bringing an 'elsewhere' right 'here'. These technologies introduce the subject to new ludic dimensions to the extent that he can play – in the true sense of the term – on the symbolic markers that make him a self-evident reality (an 'I' that exists at the point where 'here' and 'now' intersect). There is obviously nothing to prevent the subject from targeting this *jouissance* and setting himself epistemological or creative goals . . . apart from the fact that we can only play with categories that actually exist.

If the child's symbolic markers have not been properly established or prove to be fragile, the consequences can be very serious indeed: the external image becomes a sort of extension of the internal images and fantasies that haunt the psychic apparatus (these are often images of omnipotence or complete impotence). The individual who acts as their carrier does not have the key to these fantasies. These images can therefore assault the individual who sees them, without ever getting anchored or forming a cumulative process that can be mastered, and

[15] The study was carried out by Marcel Rufo, who teaches child psychiatry at the Université de Médecine de Marseille.

this causes more suffering. They simply return in repetitive fashion and force the subject to become dependent upon them. On the one hand, they cannot be objectified, which means that they do not open on to any procedure that leads to knowledge; on the other, they cathect any external image they are given and come to form a kind of screen, one must say – which stands between the subject and the reality that filters through to him.

In this case, which is becoming increasingly common, the use of television is very pernicious, because it makes the subject's mastery of the symbolic categories of space, time and person a still more distant prospect. The multiplicity of dimensions on offer can become a further obstacle to mastering these basic categories; it blurs their perception and adds to the symbolic confusion and to the unbridled fantasies. The subject's very discursive and symbolic capacities are undermined.

Because it cannot transmit the gift of speech by itself, television burdens the symbolic anthropofacture of new subjects with debt and makes it more difficult to pass on the most precious heritage of all: culture.

We cannot say that we did not know. We were warned about the current civilizational disaster. In the 1980s, Fellini, a visual artist and one of high culture's heirs, drew up the likely balance sheet of the catastrophe that was occurring in *Ginger and Fred*, a film that is at once funny, nostalgic and visionary. It showed that, thanks to television, centuries of art and culture were going down the drain, in a trashy environment of commercial nihilism. I am not saying that this diagnosis is inevitable: television can, as we have said, be a window on to a wider world, provided that a minimal symbolic already exists. But the use of television cannot compensate for the breakdown in symbolization, as we might be tempted to believe in our naivety. Worse still, there is a danger that it will place further obstacles on the road that leads to the symbolic world.[16]

This remark obviously applies to all sensory prosthetics, and not only to television. It applies to all the tele-matic devices that rely upon

---

[16] Michael Haneke's film *Benny's Video* (1993) gives a convincing and quite terrifying idea of what effects this situation may have if it is taken to extremes. It is about a teenager whose relationship with his parents is purely functional and whose only contact with the world is through the mediation of video screens. When a tiny part of that world (a girl) impinges upon him, his reactions are totally inappropriate (in fact he kills her). Haneke has subsequently pursued his analysis in still more terrifying films, including *Funny Games*.

tele-presence, in other words to everything which transforms the 'over there' into an 'over here' (video games, the mobile phones that we all have with us twenty-four hours a day, the internet . . .).

We can therefore say that the use of these sensory prosthetics will allow us to develop a new aptitude for *jouissance* only if the symbolic function has been more or less established. If that is not the case, it can only lead to more suffering.

The most likely outcome is that some will become much more competent whilst others will become increasingly confused as they lose control of even a minimal symbolic. In a period which promises the development of sensory and communicational prosthetics on a huge scale, we risk heading towards a world divided between, on the one hand, those who have satisfied their basic symbolic needs and, on the other, those who have failed to do so. The new 'communications technologies' can, in a word, lead to a new symbolic mastery of time and space, but they can also inhibit it.

We live in a world where some subjects are in the process of becoming ubiquitous and practically free from all spatio-temporal restraints, whilst others are losing the ability to inhabit any space at all.

Education

Most young pupils in our schools are now 'television children' whose symbolic markers are not well established. We can therefore understand why many teachers are forced to reach the bitter conclusion that the children they have to deal with 'are no longer pupils'.[17] Adrien Barrot's remarkable little book (2000) gives a succinct account of how things stand: 'They no longer listen.' One might add that it is probably because they can no longer talk that they can no longer listen. Not in the sense that they have been struck dumb – far from it – but in the sense that they now find it very difficult to become part of the discursive sequence that allows everyone to alternate between the role of speaker and that of listener.

The discursive sequence and the authority of speech

The question of how speaking parts are distributed in discourse is not as trivial as it might seem. It means in fact that speech itself has

[17] Adrien Barrot's little book (2000) is only one of the many accounts and analyses to reach the same conclusion.

its own authority. It has the authority to give everyone a role in the discursive sequence. Maurice Blanchot describes this very well in his *Pas au-delà*, which is one of his greatest books: 'Speaking always means speaking in accordance with the authority of the word' (Blanchot 1973: 67). Which means that authority (the authority whose loss we deplore so much today) is never, whatever anyone might say, *someone's* authority. When it is *someone's* authority, it rapidly shows itself for what it is: something so cruel and grotesque that we can scarcely subscribe to it. Authority is that which is implied by access to the symbolic function itself, that which makes us become speaking subjects at the very moment when we become language's objects, or even its serfs. Thanks to a strange quirk of destiny, the speaking animal discovers herself just as she loses herself – which inevitably leads to asking the most searching of questions. We know how Blanchot suggests we approach this mystery (1973: 80): when we have spoken, we must fall silent and write because 'writing removes . . . all horizons and all foundations'. To put it in Heideggerian terms, writing brings us closer to being. There is therefore a link between speech and writing: speaking encourages us to write, and writing takes us to the edge of the enigmatic centre of language.

To escape the authority of speech is therefore to escape the writing that takes speaking beings closer to the multiple aspects of the enigma surrounding their condition. A sad fate awaits these new pupils who are ill at ease with the symbolic function: they have, so to speak, been deprived of an enigma. Being unable to speak in accordance with the authority of speech, they can neither write nor read.

How, in these conditions, can they enter the discursive sequence which, at school, allows one party (the teacher) to put forward rationally based propositions (a multiple body of knowledge which was accumulated by earlier generations and is constantly updated), and then allows the other party (the pupil) to discuss them for as long as is necessary? We might of course conclude that, given that they cannot, we should stop asking them to do it. This is why so many pedagogues have, with the best intentions in the world, stopped setting all the exercises that these new pupils are incapable of doing. This is a strange response, if we think about it for a moment: it is rather like a doctor breaking a thermometer in order to treat a patient.

It is, however, quite obvious that many teachers spare no effort and often wear themselves out in the attempt to get their young charges to adopt the 'pupil' function,[18] and simply to do their jobs as teachers. What is new is that, just as pupils have been prevented from becoming pupils, more and more teachers are being prevented from doing their jobs. For thirty years now, we have had one 'democratic' reform after another, and politicians and their advisers, as well as education experts, have never stopped telling teachers that they should abandon their old presumption that they should teach. Former minister Allègre at least had the courtesy to say openly what others say in much more roundabout ways. In an interview published in *Le Monde* on 24 November 1999, he admonished teachers by telling them to overcome their 'archaic tendencies', which he caricatured in these terms: 'All they have to do is listen to me: I'm the one who knows.' And he replaced the term 'pupil' with the new category of 'the young', saying that: 'What young people want . . . is to inter-act.' His comments rightly provoked a lot of responses.[19] He was in fact confirming the fact that democracy in schools means that there are no more pupils in them. And if there are no more pupils, why do we still need teachers and, with them, something to teach?[20]

Generational denial

Do we have to recall the premonitory studies Hannah Arendt made of the United States, which is, of course, where the movement started? Over thirty years ago, she was already warning us about the devastating effects on children's education of the unconditional and uncritical

[18] I allude to the numerous cases of 'teacher depression', which former minister Allègre seemed to regard as a form of malingering.

[19] From Alain Finkielkraut, amongst others. It seems to me, however, that whilst Finkielkraut rightly identifies the symptoms of the current decline in education standards, he forgets to look its aetiology. There is a very simple explanation for this blind spot: he refuses to relate these symptoms to the extension of the market model and its pernicious effects on the cultural and symbolic field. According to Finkielkraut, 'the current frenzy for reform should not be imputed to a cynical desire to subordinate the educational system to the laws of the market and the needs of industry. Educationalists are inspired by the spirit of friendliness rather than the spirit of capitalism' (Finkielkraut 2000). Now it so happens that there is no contradiction between 'the spirit of friendliness', with its ideals of 'autonomy' and 'transparency', and the new spirit of capitalism. On the contrary. On this point, see Jean-Pierre Le Goff's remarkable analysis (1999).

[20] In the title of the final report of the organizing committee on consultation in secondary schools, teachers became 'adults who accompany young people as they learn' (Ministère de l'Éducation Nationale 1998).

acceptance of 'modern' pedagogic theories that challenged all forms of authority (including that of the schoolmaster who, as we have seen, is no more than the visible embodiment of the real problem of authority amongst speaking beings). We tend to laugh at the idea of authority these days, but we are wrong to do so. Hannah Arendt knew perfectly well what she was talking about (Arendt 1961). It is no coincidence that she did so much work on totalitarianism and that her work is still, as they so rightly put it, authoritative. It teaches us, amongst other things, that, without a proper understanding of authority, we are heading straight for totalitarianism.

According to Arendt, authority is not compatible with persuasion (which presupposes equality) and it categorically precludes all external means of coercion (coercion is a characteristic of totalitarianism). Being the third term that mediates between equality and coercion, authority answers a very specific need: 'those who are born as newcomers [must be] guided through a pre-established world into which they are born as strangers' (Arendt 1961: 91). She also explains that someone must take the responsibility for doing this. Otherwise, 'authority has been discarded by the adults, and this can mean only one thing: that the adults refuse to assume responsibility for the world into which they have brought the children' (1961: 190). It follows that any discourse that challenges the authority of those who have a generational responsibility for introducing these newcomers into the world also fails to institute children and 'young people' as pupils.[21] This in fact corresponds to a refusal on the part of adults to accept their responsibilities as co-authors of the world into which they nevertheless introduce the new subjects who come along – simply because another generation arrives to replace the last. Just as there was once a discursive sequence which was authoritative because it allowed subjects to speak in turn, so there is a generational sequence which must have the authority to give every generation its place. Instituting [*instituter*] young people as pupils: that is the task of those we used to call *instituteurs* ['primary schoolteachers'] – and how can we fail to see the official rejection of the term as a real symptom? Unless we position ourselves as adults, we cannot position the other, or the newcomer . . . unless we put him or her in an impossible position and say: 'I am putting you in a situation which I have helped to create and for which I refuse to take any responsibility, even in a critical sense.' This type of discourse is basically a denial of generational difference:

---

[21] Marcel Gauchet sums this up nicely when he remarks (2002: 18f) that the school system leads to democracy, but cannot be democratic itself.

this is a generation that no longer accepts its responsibilities towards newcomers. It is not so much the master and his authority that are at stake as the refusal of one generation (roughly speaking, the generation of 1968) to take on the responsibility which is incumbent upon it, just as it was on all previous generations: that of inducting those who are born as newcomers into the world. It is as though that generation completely refused to grow old . . .

We are, then, faced with a complete denial of generational difference. As this denial has become one of the postmodern era's characteristic dogmas, we find ourselves faced with an absurdity – children with no forebears – that has been elevated to the status of an absolute truth which literally prevents the educational system from working. The question is how to overturn this dogma, in the full knowledge that everything and everyone confirms it: public opinion and parents who no longer know how to be parents; scientific opinion with its educationalists and psychologists who, by constructing the theoretical object known as the child as a specific and isolated entity, have helped to justify this denial of generational difference;[22] the philosophers of law and the jurists who celebrate children's liberation and children's rights;[23] even the political authorities who recognized, in (the preamble to) the 1989 *loi d'orientation*, the fact that the 'educational system must be pupil-centred' (1989 was also the year of the Geneva 'International Convention on Children's Rights'), and overlooked the fact that the pupil has first to be instituted. It is as though our era could not make a clear distinction between the legal need to protect children (from all forms of abuse) and the idea that there is no difference between the generations.

Some wits have even attempted to find a Freudian justification for this denial of generational difference.[24] And 'The claims of

[22] For a very detailed account of the scientific origins of this extreme valorization of childhood, see Ottavi (2001).

[23] See Renaut (2002). I have to admit that I do not understand how someone with such a detailed knowledge of Kant (cf. Renaut 2001) and who has translated some of the Königsberg master's key works can ignore what Kant has to say about education: only a few lines are devoted to Kant. It seems to me to be difficult to subscribe to the idea of the long march of history to a necessary and unavoidable children's liberation, and at the same time to claim to be inspired by Kant's theses on education. Kant's central thesis is that 'one generation must educate the next', and this seems to me to be quite incompatible with the 'child-citizen' thesis.

[24] I am thinking of the psychoanalyst Maud Manonni's preface to the French translation of A. S. Neil's famous *Summerhill* (1960) (Neil himself was a psychoanalyst). Manonni celebrates 'children's autonomy, in other words the baby's right to live freely'.

psychoanalysis to scientific interest' (Freud [1913]: 189–90) does contain certain remarks that seem to be arguing along these lines:

> The forcible suppression of strong instincts by external means never has the effect in the child of these instincts being extinguished or brought under control; it leads to repression, which establishes a predisposition to later nervous illness. Psychoanalysis has frequent opportunities of observing the part played by inopportune and undiscerning severity of upbringing in the production of neuroses, or the price, in loss of efficiency and of capacity for enjoyment, which has to be paid for the normality upon which the educator insists.

Yet, whilst Freud is opposed to coercion (as was Hannah Arendt), that never leads him to preach the doctrine of laisser-faire, or to endorse an exclusive focus on the child. On the contrary, Freud was the first person to question assumptions about the innocence of children – remember the famous discussion of the child's 'polymorphous perversity' in the 'Three essays on the theory of sexuality' (Freud [1905]). Elsewhere ([1913]: 190), he notes 'the importance of socially unserviceable or perverse instinctual impulses which emerge in children'. He suggests that, if they are forcibily repressed, they will 'simply emerge elsewhere'. But he does not recommend giving a free rein to what he has no hesitation in calling 'children's naughtiness'. Freud's ideal is 'civilization'. Our impulses must be channelled in the direction of civilization: 'Our highest virtues have grown up, as reaction formations and sublimations, out of our worst dispositions' ([1913]: 190).

In that sense, Freud was a true Kantian, as was Hannah Arendt. According to Kant, forming a critical subject meant preventing the possibility that freedom might be misused. In his *On Education*, he remarks that 'children should not be educated on the basis of the present state of the species, but in accordance with its possible and improved future state, or in other words in accordance with the ideal of Humanity'. The precondition for an apprenticeship in critical philosophy is the human ability to move from a state of savagery – an actual state – to a state which does not exist yet, but which must come into existence. We cannot make that transition without *discipline* (Kant 2003: 2–3, 3, 7):

> Discipline changes animal nature into human nature. Animals are by their instinct all that they ever can be: some other reason has provided everything for them at the outset. But man needs a reason of his own. Having no instinct, he has to work out a plan of conduct for himself. Since, however, he is not able to do this all at once, but comes into the world

undeveloped, others have to do it for him. All the natural endowments of mankind must be developed little by little out of man himself through his own efforts. One generation educates the next [. . .] It is discipline which prevents man from being turned aside by his animal impulses from humanity, his appointed end. Discipline, for instance, must restrain him from venturing wildly and rashly into danger [. . .] discipline, thus, is merely negative, its action being to counteract man's natural unruliness. The positive part of education is instruction. Unruliness consists in independence of law. By discipline men are placed in subjection to the laws of mankind, and brought to feel their constraint. This, however, must be accomplished early [. . .] there is no one who, having been neglected in his youth, can later come to years of discretion without knowing whether the defect lies in discipline or culture (for so we may call instruction). The uncultivated man is crude, the undisciplined is unruly. Neglect of discipline is a greater evil than neglect of culture, for this last can be remedied later in life, but unruliness cannot be done away with, and a mistake in discipline can never be repaired.

From the educational point of view, the break between modernity and postmodernity is striking: one generation ceases to educate the next. As the generational motif disappears, there is no more discipline and, because there is no more discipline, there is no such thing as education. The postmodern educational apparatus therefore has one astonishing feature: even though compulsory education is (for the first time in history) almost universal, there is less and less education.[25]

What is a pedagogue?

If we fail to make a distinction between two types of pedagogue, we will not be in a position to understand anything:

1   for the sake of his pupils, the *postmodern pedagogue* no longer sets them tasks they have become unable to perform. Our answer to this has to be the old adage that we should never trust anyone who does something for the good of others;

2   the *ordinary pedagogue* tries by every means possible to introduce his pupils into the discourse of knowledge by adopting the role of the proponent, giving his pupils the critical role.[26]

[25] There is one obvious symptom of the disappearance of the generational principle: the development of the so-called 'older brother' policy ('equals', who are just a few years older, are given responsibility for enforcing discipline in playgrounds, on housing estates and on the bus).

[26] On the construction of this specific discursive space, see Berthier and Dufour (1996).

Having established this crucial distinction, it only remains for me to add that the principles of postmodern pedagogy (the assertion of the child's autonomy; the promotion of pedagogic techniques which make no reference to what is being taught; the replacement of 'learning' by 'doing') were clearly identified by Hannah Arendt as early as 1961.[27] Forty years later, we find postmodern pedagogues saying precisely the same thing. The educational model that is now prevailing over 'archaism' incorporates the famous 'audiovisual revolution', which coincided with the 'revolution in education'. As a result, what now goes on in schools is modelled on the televised 'chat shows' model: everyone can give their opinion 'democratically'.

As a result, everything to do with knowledge becomes an intersubjective issue. We no longer need to make the critical effort to abandon *sans cesse* our own point of view in order to put forward propositions that are less narrow, less specious and better constructed. This discourse can no longer tolerate the teachers who once constantly encouraged and urged their pupils to adopt a critical stance. They are the enemy because they do not respect 'young people's' points of view. This is the explanation that many postmodern pedagogues give for violence in schools: the 'young people' are reacting against their teachers' overbearing authority – some militant postmodern pedagogues go so far as to compare the way the worker class resists the bosses to the way 'young people' resist education![28] Without further ado, they compare the lack of symmetry between the teacher's knowledge and that of the pupil with the violence of social domination. In fact they fail to see that the reason why so many young people find themselves forced to use violence is that the system they themselves have established leaves them no other way out: they have been 'produced' to escape the relationship of meaning and to avoid the slow, patient elaboration of a discursive and critical position. It is therefore quite predictable that, the certainties of postmodern

[27] See Arendt (1961). Arendt explains that, whilst these three ideas free children from the authority of adults, in fact they subject them to an even more frightening and truly tyrannical authority: the tyranny of the majority. It should be noted that the second idea (the promotion of teaching skills that make no reference to the subject-matter being taught) has been broadly picked up by Jean-Claude Milner in his resounding attacks on educational theorists (Milner 1984).

[28] In an interview given to the *Journal de Saint-Denis* (no. 344, 2000), the sociologist B. Charlot compares, without further ado, the pupil who is called a 'clown' by his classmates (because he works in class and talks to the teachers) to those called 'collaborators' in the logic of the Resistance!

pedagogues notwithstanding, the less they are involved in the teacher–pupil relationship, the more likely it is that they will turn to violence.

If we do in fact leave behind the relationship of meaning, we inevitably move in the direction of power relations and of an era of generalized violence: I allude to the tens of tragic events which have occurred in the developed countries and which conceal thousands of other more mundane acts of violence (extortion, theft, rape, aggression, anti-social behaviour, disrupted classes). This phenomenon now affects all the developed countries. I have already mentioned the Littleton massacre in the United States and the Erfurt massacre. I might also mention those which have taken place in Japan. In June 1997, a fourteen-year-old boy from Kobe killed two little girls and then a boy of eleven; he decapitated him and left his head outside his school. On 28 January 1998, a thirteen-year-old boy in a medium-sized school 100 kilometres north of Tokyo stabbed his English teacher to death because the latter had criticized him for being late for school so often. On 10 February 1998, fourteen-year-old twins in Tottori, which is 120 kilometres north-west of Kobe, went out into the street, picked out an old lady at random, stabbed her to death and explained (and I quote) that they 'wouldn't have to go to school any more'. In 1999, two French *lycéens* threw one of their classmates down a stairwell, to punish him for being a good student. Since then, several murders or attempted murders have been committed by *lycéens* in or near schools in various regions. In the year 2000 alone, numerous incidents of extortion were reported in France (there were demonstrations by parents in Montpellier, Vénissieux, Beauvais . . .), together with incidents of pupil-to-pupil violence (Mantes, Longwy . . .) and assaults on teachers (Strasbourg, Brive). Some schools were fire-bombed (Bondy . . .).

Many postmodern experts on education have, as usual, reacted to these events by trying to convince us that they were dreamed up by the media. It was only when events took a tragic turn that there was any public recognition of how serious things had become. The first international conference on 'Violence in schools and public policy' was held at UNESCO's headquarters in Paris.[29] The Prime Minister attended. The question of the symbolic destructuration typical of the postmodern period was, of course, never raised, as the researchers

[29] The conference took place on 5–7 March 2001 and was attended by 600 participants from twenty-five countries.

were primarily concerned with finding a sociological explanation for the violence (we know what that is: compensating for social inequalities will put an end to the violence),[30] whilst the politicians were interested only in reducing media interest in it.

'If we can't educate them let's anaesthetize them!'

The United States has come up with a very American 'answer' in its attempt to contain the damaging effects of the wave of violence in which 'young people' have become involved. It is assumed that it is the nature of the individuals concerned that is the problem, and it is forgotten that they were made to act like this. Rather than trying to listen to what these children are acting out because they cannot manage to put it into words, they diagnose them as 'giddy' or 'hyperactive' and leave them to their own devices by medicating them at an increasingly early age. It is estimated that between five and ten million junior and high school students are now on 'Ritalin'. The drug (which is related to the amphetamines) has a sedative effect on hyperactive children by way of improving their concentration, but it also has the same addictive effects as cocaine and the opiates.[31] The use of this chemical straitjacket finally perfects the manufacture and monitoring of near-psychotic subjects.

France and the other developed countries have not got so far yet in using chemicals to control their young people,[32] but they are making progress: the prescribing of anti-depressants for children and teenagers is even beginning to attract media attention.[33]

For the moment, we are actively encouraging children to abandon the relationship of meaning, and we are transforming the school system into what Jean-Claude Michéa (1999) calls 'the school of total capitalism'. He means by this a school system which trains pupils to

[30] The Left often makes this mistake. When he was a minister, Lionel Jospin also believed that a return to full employment would put an end to violence.

[31] See Gavarini (2001: 347f). The serious addictions and deaths attributed to Ritalin are now the subject of several court cases in the United States (see Charles 2000). That is not all: in 2001, American doctors wrote almost 2.5 million prescriptions for anti-depressants for children and teenagers.

[32] On the other hand, this is not too certain. In the 1990 survey cited earlier (above, p. 104 n15), Professor Rufo estimated that, in France, one in three children is taking or has taken 'something' to get them to sleep. It should not be forgotten that France, sadly, holds the world record for the consumption of psychotropics.

[33] See the *90 Minutes* programme on 'Antidepressants for children?' (Canal +, 16 March 2002).

lose their critical sense in order to produce individuals who are open to every consumerist pressure. In this system, which is counted good enough for most pupils, 'ignorance must be taught in every conceivable fashion'. Teachers therefore have to be re-educated under the guidance of experts who can demonstrate that they should no longer be teaching anything and should be relying on their impulses of the moment and their ability to control them. According to Michéa, the point is to establish the preconditions for the 'dissolution of logic': make no distinction between what is important and what is secondary, accept everything and its opposite without a murmur. The targets are nothing less than the Kantian categories of intellectual judgement, which allow us to unify the field of experience. A whole current within postmodern educational research, even in the universities, now argues that the last thing we should be doing is asking 'young people' to think. The important thing is to keep them entertained and amused. We must not bore them to death with lectures, and should let them zap 'democratically' from one subject to another while they interact as they please. We must simply let them talk about their own lives, and show them that the power of logic is no more than an abuse of the power of 'intellectuals' or 'Western' thought. Above all, we have to show them there is nothing to think about, that there is no object of thought: all that matters is self-affirmation and the relational management of that self-affirmation – and any self-respecting consumer should be able to do that. In short, education is at best a matter of turning out nit-picking cretins who are also good consumers.

It is of course probable that many pedagogues are not happy with this. They simply want to adapt to the way 'young people' are at school these days. But when they adapt to it on compassionate grounds, they help to trivialize a catastrophic situation, in which education is increasingly seen as a form of humanitarian action. The way pedagogues are being used is a further example of neoliberalism's remarkable ability to recuperate and exploit the libertarian schemata of the 1960s (Boltanski and Chiapello 1999).

It is true that, when he was Minister for Education [between 2002 and 2004], Luc Ferry, who makes no secret of his Kantian leanings, did try to undo some of the damage that had been done by 'child-centred education' (Ferry 2003). And yet it is quite obvious that, in his first year in office, Ferry the minister did not implement any of the recommendations made by Ferry the philosopher. Besides, both the old teams and the old pedagogic dogmas (such as 'whole word recognition') remained intact.[34] It is often said that the minister had little room for manoeuvre in that he had to discharge his duties in a difficult context, characterized by far-reaching pension reforms, by severe budgetary restrictions on spending on education (thousands of supervisory posts were cut at the very time when everyone was deploring the rise of violence in schools), by the decentralization of some of his staff and by strong ultraliberal pressure to cut state involvement in education. In my view, the unfavourable conjuncture does not really explain why the minister became so bogged down. That had much more to do with the lack of analysis behind his actions. He was stubbornly of the belief that it was May '68 as a whole (or what he indiscriminatingly called 'the '68 thought') that was behind these pedagogic aberrations, and not an individualism that had adapted to the new spirit of capitalism. Because he could not see the real reasons for the deep discontent in our schools, the minister could obviously not take the measures that might have made it possible to advance the goal of promoting the critical spirit in schools. All that remained of his arguments were purely verbal protests about earlier aberrations, and they looked very much like a political smokescreen. Of course the great principles were reasserted, but his declarations were really eyewash and could not conceal his real desire for a creeping privatization of education. Even as the Minister reassured us, the liberalization of education went ahead.[35]

It has to be recognized in passing that the government pulled off a major coup, which was perfectly in keeping with their communications policy, by appointing a Kantian to carry out this task. As it happens, the minister did not remain in post for very long.

The mission of educational institutions (including the universities) is now to absorb floating populations whose relationship with knowledge is no more than a secondary and sporadic issue. As for education, the important thing is to keep the unemployed of the future in school for as long as possible and at the lowest possible cost. A new type of soft institution – and postmodernity is very good at creating such things – is taking shape before our very eyes. Halfway between

[34] See the indictment made by the Sauver les Lettres collective: 'Luc Ferry: quand dire, ce n'est pas faire'. The document can be consulted as www.sauv.net.

[35] The first stage in the privatization of higher education was to grant the universities their independence and autonomy, which they were duly granted by the Joint Declaration of European Ministers for Education (Bologna, 19 June 1999).

a youth club, a cultural centre, a day hospital and a social asylum, it looks rather like an educational amusement park.

This principal mission obviously has not eradicated the few residual zones where knowledge is produced and reproduced, but they are likely to be dominated by the new technologies (in his interview with *Le Monde*, the former minister cheerfully promised that 'all the teacher's repetitive tasks will be recorded and saved'). Under the influence of international organizations (OECD, UNESCO, the World Bank and the European Union), this second network has, over the last few years, been reconfigured so as to adapt education to the needs of industry.[36] It must, of course, be open to competition – which presupposes that the universities will no longer have a monopoly on education. There is therefore a huge potential educational market, where the new information and communications technologies that support the teachers' repetitive tasks can be linked to 'differentiated teaching'.[37] In the meantime, the formation and reproduction of elites (which is another decisive function of the school of total capitalism) will, at the level of higher education, increasingly be a task for the Grandes Écoles and the like – or preferably, and when possible, for expensive elite schools and universities in the United States, at an annual cost of 25,000 dollars. And it has to be said that these institutions do function in accordance with a strictly critical model and are in no way affected by the educational drives designed to keep the majority happy.

There is nothing accidental about the manufacture of individuals who know nothing about the critical function and who are susceptible to floating identities. Today's television and schools accomplish this task to perfection, and the process follows a new non-egalitarian logic that serves the interests of the neoliberal system (see chapter 4 below). The implementation of this logic presupposes that one generation is no longer capable of educating the next. Thanks to this break in transmission, which is a very worrying feature of our advanced societies, the postmodern subject sees himself as non-generated, in the sense that he sees himself as owing nothing to the previous generation. On the contrary, it is as though society owed him a living, because no one

---

[36] See, for example, Millot (2003). The great thing about OECD studies is that they state their objectives openly and unashamedly. Sceptics should consult the 'education' page at www.oecd.org/.

[37] The basic principle behind differentiated teaching is to respond appropriately to the educational difficulties encountered by individual students.

asked his opinion before bringing him into the world. Perhaps we are witnessing the invention of the first non-generated generation. If that is indeed the case, we have yet to see the full effect of the inversion of the ancient symbolic debt.

3 The Denial of 'Sexion'

I have put forward the idea that postmodernity is based upon a denial of generational difference. We can now add that this denial has to do with the real: it is not a historical event that is being denied here (as in the various negationisms, for example), but an organic fact over which, whether we like it or not, we have no influence. Death, for example, is beyond our control. It does not result from some decision on our part: we are governed by the real and it is the real that insists that, as a rule, members of the previous generation die before members of the next. All that speaking subjects can do, then, is to attempt to inscribe in their symbolic organization a real fact they have to cope with as best they can. And, until recently, that is what they did. The fact that, in many languages, the patronymic of the son is the patronymic of the father with an additional 'son of . . .' is one example of this symbolic inscription. In other cases, the son is given the forename of an ancestor. And so, as Kant says, one generation finds that it has a duty to educate the next. In that sense, we can say that any denial of generational differences inevitably leads to desymbolization, as I have tried to demonstrate with reference to education. When we deny that there is a difference between the generations, the speaking subject has to respond to an impossible injunction and found himself.

There is a second difference of the same kind: sexual difference. It has as much to do with the real as generational difference: whether I like it or not, I am in the body of either a girl or a boy, and I have to come to terms with that fact as best I can by cobbling together the requisite symbolic or imaginary structures.

With both these differences, we are dealing with real and basic determinations that affect all subjects. We all have to come to terms with these two facts of nature – being born of the previous generation, and being born boys or girls – if we are to find our place in the human adventure and to accept our destiny.

Now this sexual difference is also the object of a serious postmodern denial. We know perfectly well that there are two sexes – but we still promote the *unisex* idea. This is obvious from many social phenomena, and especially anything to do with the fluidity of sexual identity – which receives a great deal of media attention – and with the pressing demand to allow homosexual couples to adopt – or even to have – children. All these attitudes actually presume that sexual difference is over and done with. Rather than commenting on these phenomena, I will look at what seems me to be much more significant: the disappearance of sexual difference from within the body of thought that once defined it most rigorously – psychoanalysis. We hear, for instance, the well-known and influential psychoanalyst Jean Allouch denouncing those 'psychoanalysts who have taken to defending sexual difference and to saying that it takes a mum and a dad to make a baby. In the name of Lacan!'[1] It is of course true that not all the psychoanalysts have jettisoned the category of sexual difference. But it does seems to me that the fact that even psychoanalysis – a modern discovery if ever there was one – has been affected by postmodernity is worthy of examination.

Surprise . . .

Jean Allouch's remarks were posted on the *Oedipe* website, which is described as 'The French-speaking psychoanalysts' portal'. Now if there is one concept in psychoanalysis that organizes sexual and generational difference, it is the Oedipus complex. What is surprising is that it is possible to live under the flag of 'the Oedipus' *and at the same time* express surprise when reference is made to sexual difference. But this is the way it is: sexual difference is now denied by at least one current within psychoanalytic thought, even though it is central to both Freudian and Lacanian thought. It will be recalled that, in Freud, the Oedipus complex takes the form of a prohibition: relations of alliance and relations of filiation must not coincide. In Freud's view, this prohibition is essential: it is this that shapes the formation of the social bond and of the speaking subject. As we have said, the Oedipus is explicitly bound up with an articulation of the difference between the sexes and of the difference between the generations. It is quite simple: if we deny the existence of sexual difference, this articulation is no longer possible.

---

[1] The interview with Jean Allouch appeared on the website www.oedipe.org.

There are postmodern psychoanalysts who 'forget' that the Oedipus myth is a constant reference in Freud. It first appears in 1897, in what was to become a famous letter to Wilhelm Fliess: 'I have found, in my own case too, [the phenomenon of] being in love with my mother and jealous of my father, and I now consider it a universal event in early childhood [. . .] If this is so, we can understand the gripping power of *Oedipus Rex* [. . .] Everyone in the audience was once a budding Oedipus' (Freud 1985: 272).

It will be recalled that Freud made his discovery in the months following the death of his father. The end of a period of intense relations with Fliess had reached the point of no return.[2] Freud referred (for only a few weeks) to this period as that of his 'self-analysis'. His recognition of his own feelings and the realization that they were a 'universal event' signalled the start of the process which, in ten years or so, was to transform Freud's symptom related to the myth of Oedipus into the concept of a 'complex'.[3] The sudden appearance of the complex was to become the theoretical cornerstone of psychoanalysis and it allowed Freud to put together the other pieces, which were already there at the end of the 1890s: the mechanism of transference (which Freud discovered through his analysis of his relationship with Fliess), daily clinical work with his patients, the role of the father, the analysis of dreams, the abandoning of the trauma theory in favour of a theory of fantasy, seen as an imaginary creation of libidinal desire rather than as a mnemic reproduction of a real event . . .

The reference to the 'gripping power' of *Oedipus Rex* remains a constant element and is mentioned in almost everything Freud wrote. Indeed, it would save time if we mentioned those works in which he makes no reference to it. I will mention here only those works in which the reference is developed at some length: *The Interpretation of Dreams* (1899), 'Three essays on the theory of sexuality' (1905), 'On the sexual theories of children' (1908), 'Five lectures on psychoanalysis' (1909), 'A special type of choice of object made by men' (1910), *Totem and Taboo* (1912), *Introductory Lectures on Psychoanalysis* (1916–17), 'Group psychology and the analysis of the ego' (1921), 'The ego and the id' (1923),

[2] It was primarily an epistolary relationship, as Fliess lived in Berlin. See Érik Porge's excellent studies (1994; 1996).

[3] The expression 'the Oedipus complex' first appears in 'A special type of choice of object made by men' (Freud [1910]: 171). The term was borrowed from Bleuler, a psychiatrist working in Zurich, and his pupil Jung. It refers to a system of representations which, without the subject realizing it, has a decisive influence on his behaviour.

'The dissolution of the Oedipus complex' (1923), 'Some psychical consequences of the anatomical distinction between the sexes' (1925), 'Inhibitions, symptoms and anxiety' (1926), 'Female sexuality' (1931), *New Introductory Lectures on Psychoanalysis* (1933; see in particular Lecture 31 on 'The dissection of the psychical personality'), *An Outline of Psychoanalysis* (1938) and *Moses and Monotheism* (1939). We may as well say that the conceptual network that Freud so patiently built up for psychoanalysis is articulated around the pivot, or centre of gravity, provided by the Oedipus complex. Besides, Freud does not hesitate to a recognize that the Oedipus complex is the touchstone of psychoanalysis: 'With the progress of psychoanalytic studies the importance of the Oedipus has become more and more clearly identified; its recognition has become the shibboleth that distinguishes the adherents of psychoanalysis from its opponents' (Freud [1905]: 226, footnote added in 1920).

The balance sheet drawn up in *An Outline of Psychoanalysis*, which Freud wrote shortly before he died, is quite unambiguous about the importance of the Oedipus complex to the psychoanalytic edifice: 'I venture to say that if psychoanalysis could boast of no other achievement than the discovery of the repressed Oedipus complex, that alone would give it a claim to be included among the precious new acquisitions of mankind' (Freud [1940]: 192–3).

It is true that, if we look more closely at Freud's references – many of them allusive – to Sophocles' play, we do find some omissions and a few inaccurate statements:[4] he does not mention Jocasta's suicide, even though this is what reverses the situation; he does not comment on the Sphinx's physical appearance; he writes that Oedipus receives from the oracle the advice to stay away from his country because he will become his father's killer and his mother's husband, but this advice does not feature in the account Oedipus gives Jocasta of his consultation of the Delphic oracle. And nothing of the legendary events that took place before the tragedy itself inspires any comment from Freud. His interpretations (of the Sphinx as father substitute, of the riddle, which he always relates solely to children's questions about where they come from, of the fact that blinding is an equivalent to castration . . .) do not really stand up to a detailed study of the legend itself.[5]

---

[4] See the comments made by Conrad Stein in his preface to the new edition of Marie Delcourt's book (1981), which was originally published in 1944.

[5] On this point, see the critical analysis made by Vernant (1972).

What conclusions should we draw from the fact that Freud treats his central reference in such a cavalier way? None, except to note that these elements do not appear in Freud's text because he was simply not interested in them. He was interested in something else, which we might formulate thus: Freud uses the Greek myth and the name of Oedipus to reveal, signify and open up a field of knowledge about humanity that had previously been touched upon only in fictional form. Sophocles' tragedy is the most famous example. By applying the name of Oedipus to disparate phenomena, Freud converts his own 'symptom' into an implicit field of investigation characterized by the constant cultural return of religious, literary, mythological, romantic or theatrical figures, and ultimately transforms this field into an explicit area of research. Freud's goal is to capture a modality that functions in all of us, that affects all our individual and social acts, and that remains deeply alien to our usual modes of thought. This modality clearly brings sexual difference into play: as a little boy, I am especially interested in someone who belongs to a different sex and to a different generation; she is forbidden because she is the possession of another man, namely my father. Things are more complicated for the girl, as the female Oedipus is 'a secondary formation' (Freud [1925]: 256), but this does nothing to change Freud's assertion that there is a difference between the sexes, except to say that it is secondary in girls. For both boys and girls, the figure of the father acts as a marker that can establish sexual and generational differences.

If it is true to say, as Lévi-Strauss has argued, that Freud's account, like that of Sophocles (and the Pueblo Indians and many others), should be viewed as one of many versions of the Oedipus myth, we must immediately add that Freud's version has a claim to having an exceptional status. It does not have a special status because it is the most recent version – all the versions that came before it were, in their own day, the 'most recent' and others will be in the same position. It is unusual because, unlike all the others, its ambition is to discover nothing less than the logic of the series into which it is inserted. Whether or not Freud is fully successful is a different issue, but there is no denying that this is what he is trying to do: why else would he explicitly relate the Oedipus myth to great stories like Shakespeare's *Hamlet* (Freud 1985: 272–3) or the story of the biblical Moses (Freud [1939])? – to say nothing of all the minor stories, or all the versions produced by all the family romances of all neurotics? From the start, the terminological change which turns 'the legend of Oedipus Rex' (1897) into the 'Oedipus complex' (1910) signals that a certain number of versions are being subsumed under the Oedipal law.

We know that it is Otto Rank who justifies the inclusion of a certain number of narrative figures in the Oedipal epic by outlining a single structure for all these narratives (Rank 2004). By combining several legends, including that of Lohengrin, Rank outlines a structure for hero myths which corresponds to the inevitable unfolding of the Oedipal drama: the child has high-ranking parents and his birth poses a threat to the position of his father, who exposes him and leaves him to die. The child is saved and adopted by humble people or animals, finds his real parents again, avenges himself on his father and achieves glory. Rank got his deserved reward, as this is the structure that Freud refers to in *Moses and Monotheism*.

When we look at the successive stages of the construction of 'Freud's version', from his first mentioning of the myth of Oedipus to the version he gave towards the end of his life in 1939, we find that references to Oedipus always have a heuristic effect on Freud's discourse. The chronology is easily established. It is immediately obvious that the 'gripping power' of *Oedipus Rex* stems from the recognition that we were all 'a budding Oedipus' (1985: 272). It then transpires that the legend is an expression of 'the nuclear complex of a neurosis' ([1908a]: 214), and then that the nucleus is a complex, in other words, a form that governs the subject's behaviour without him realizing it. Once Freud has established the complex's role in 'individual psychology', he next gives it a role in understanding 'group psychology', and thereby makes it the key factor in his opposition to Jung's ideas: '[In] *Totem and Taboo*] I put forward a suggestion that mankind as a whole may have acquired its sense of guilt, the ultimate source of religion and morality, at the beginning of its history, in connection with the Oedipus complex' (Freud [1916–17]: 375). After having discovered the *Urhorde*, Freud, who is still using the Oedipus complex as his principal weapon, reconstructs another key period in human history: the birth of monotheism, the 'dematerialization of God'[6] in favour of 'the idea of God' (Freud [1939]: 115) (the term can be seen as the ancestor of the Lacanian Name-of-the-Father). This

[6] This is the key passage (Freud [1939]: 115): 'Moses, as we know, conveyed to the Jews an exalted sense of being a chosen people. The dematerialization of God brought a fresh and valuable contribution to their secret treasure. The Jews retained their inclination to intellectual interest. The nation's political misfortune taught it to value at its true worth the one possession that remained to it – its literature.'

marks a 'victory of intellectuality over sensuality' ([1939]: 114). The father is thus linked to the cultural forms which dramatize paternity (in other words, to what we evoke by speaking of the Subject).

We can therefore say that Freud succeeded in transforming his 'symptom', which he discovered indirectly *and* with no outside help in 1897, into an immense field of knowledge which ultimately changed modern thinking about subjectivation. The Oedipus complex is in fact based upon a broad conceptual framework in which sexual difference is articulated with the notions of castration, guilt, the phallus, the superego, identification, the inverted Oedipus, bisexuality, the aetiology and 'choice' of neurosis, sublimation . . . The terminological unity is unequivocal: it refers to ontogenetic and psychogenetic processes, in other words, to the *symbolic inscription of the drives*. When I say 'drive', I am referring to a Janus-faced reality that is part organic and part psychical, and which forces every subject to come face to face with the most radical aspect of desire: incestuous desire. It is in the nature of desire to want the impossible. And when I say 'symbolic inscription', I refer to that which positions everyone with respect to the two differences that preserve and perpetuate the human race: sexual difference and generational difference. This first conceptual network is both ontogenetic and psychogenetic, and it is immediately reduplicated by a second network in which this inscription must, insofar as it is symbolic, be viewed as a civilizational phenomenon which is itself grounded in the phylogenetic process. To put it another way, all the conflicts in which the subject becomes involved as a result of the Oedipus complex – the crises and resolutions that occur during the dialectic that leads to its emergence – have to be seen as the verso of a process whose recto relates to anthropogenesis, phylogenesis and, ultimately, the mechanism of civilization. This second network, which is articulated with the first, brings out the implications of the Oedipus complex in the field of the foundation of societies and civilization, of social and political organization, and of law, ethics and religion. It is particularly obvious in texts like *Totem and Taboo*, 'Group psychology and the analysis of the ego', *Civilization and its Discontents* and *Moses and Monotheism*. The temporal dynamic of the Oedipus complex is thus extended to 'group psychology', as Freud borrows his anthropological raw material and theses from Frazer, Robertson and Darwin. The sequence is as follows: (1) a violent and jealous father wants to keep all women for himself; (2) the brothers band together to kill the father and eat him in the course of a festive totemic meal; (3) after they have murdered the father, the brothers become rivals; (4) the sons begin to feel guilty and disown what they have done; (5) they establish a totem corresponding to the cult of the dead father, and promulgate the law prohibiting incest.

Whereas the first network brings out the implications of the Oedipus complex at the level of personal and family ties, the second inscribes the Oedipus in a theory of *Kultur* (civilization) and social bonds. This second network has given rise to some particularly rich developments: we need only mention the work of Otto Rank, which we have already cited, Karl Abraham, Theodor Reik, Geza Roheim, Erich Fromm, and, in France and closer to us in time, Guy Rosolato and J.-P. Valabrega.

We know that Freud was quite disconcerted to discover this second network so late in his intellectual life. As he wrote to Ferenczi on 30 November 1911: 'Sometimes I feel as though I only wanted to start a little liaison and at my age discovered that I had to marry a new wife' (Freud 1993: 317). He in fact quickly realized that his new wife (social psychology) was the old one (individual psychology) seen in a different light.[7] The two are related because 'ontogeny is a repetition of phylogeny' (Freud [1913]: 184). This theory, which has enjoyed great philosophical success,[8] allows Freud to describe the Oedipus complex as the mainspring that brings about the transition from individual psychology to social psychology. According to Freud, relations between the individual and the history of humanity should be seen as a sort of complex dramaturgy: on the one hand, the individual can become a subject thanks only to a short and rapid repetition of history; on the other, the subject who emerges does so only in order to become an agent of the ongoing historical and civilizational process.[9] Quite apart from the theoretical implications of the proposition – notably the thesis that ontogenesis and phylogenesis are intertwined – this

[7] Cf. the beginning of 'Group psychology and the analysis of the ego': 'And so from the very first individual psychology, in this extended but entirely justifiable sense of the word, is at the same time social psychology as well' (Freud [1921]: 65).

[8] The principle was formulated in 1868 by the zoologist Haeckel, who popularized Darwin's theories. It was very widely used at the end of the nineteenth century: one has only to think of Husserl, another great Viennese contemporary of Freud's.

[9] Freud never abandons this idea and returns to it in the preface to the third edition, of 1914, of the 'Three essays on the theory of sexuality' ([1905]: 65): 'Ontogenesis can be regarded as a recapitulation of phylogenesis, in so far as the latter has not been modified by more recent experience. The phylogenetic disposition can be seen at work behind the ontogenetic process. But disposition is ultimately the precipitate of earlier experience of the species to which the more recent experience of the individual, as the sum of the accidental factors, is super-added.'

claim is not without its practical effects. Freud is not trying to find the 'primal scene' only in the history of individuals; he also finds it in the immemorial memory of the human race, which is transmitted via the individual psyche (Freud [1913]: 185–6; cf. the commentary in Assoun 1995: 164–5).

The only problem is that the recapitulation thesis is now untenable (Dufour 1999). Freud resorts to the recapitulation model to give psychoanalysis the irreproachable veneer of a science and to break, in scientistic fashion, with both philosophy and psychology. In fact he goes beyond this, as his model includes cultural as well as natural data, and the cultural data are in fact the more important of the two. Freud therefore describes the Oedipus complex as an event in the development of the individual that repeats humanity's primal drama: the murder of the father.

The recapitulation thesis has now been replaced by the theory of neoteny, which holds that, far from being the crowning glory of creation, human beings are in a sense born as 'unfinished' individuals and so regressive forms of the primates from which they are descended. According to this theory, which Lacan adopted when he was elaborating his mirror phase in the late 1930s, human beings start as degenerate apes who then evolve along different lines, mainly because they can compensate for their inadequacies. They represent, that is, the creation of a second nature, populated by symbolic epirealities. The neoteny thesis provides, in short, a support in the real which Freud did not have, and which makes it possible to take up the challenge of articulating individual psychology with group psychology. Thanks to the neoteny thesis, we are no longer obliged to invent a scientific myth such as that of the primal horde in order to attempt certain articulations of the two psychologies. The notion of a 'Subject' means that they can be conceptualized together as we rethink the question of how the ideals of the ego result in the formation of the 'superego'. Besides, Freud himself always held that the concept of the superego was not fully worked out.

If we look at recapitulation and neoteny, we can see that the hard kernel present there in both theories contains the Oedipus complex: a proposition about the symbolic inscription of the drives in the differences between the sexes and the generations. The fact remains that, whilst we can easily divorce the Oedipus complex from the recapitulation thesis, we cannot jettison the Oedipus complex without at the same time abandoning Freudianism in its entirety.

How to get rid of Freud's symptom

The above remarks immediately raise the issue of whether or not we are doomed to exhibit for ever the 'symptom' Freud happened to discover during his (self-)analysis of 1897, namely the Oedipus complex.

Before we attempt to answer that question, let us look for a moment at what I see as two current mistaken ways of going about getting rid of the specifically Freudian symptom.

The first is simply to jettison the Oedipus complex. If we do that, we also jettison the hard kernel of Freudianism – the symbolic inscription of the drives in sexual difference and generational difference – and find ourselves in the very difficult position of trying to discover, in the name of Lacanianism, the foundations of a Freudianism that is based upon precisely those two differences.

The second debatable way to get around this problem is to abandon the 'scientific myth' of the primal horde invented by Freud, and to try to give the father a juridical and normative form. This is the other tendency within contemporary Lacanian thought, as exemplified by Pierre Legendre. The two are mutually reinforcing and complementary: the more we try to do away with sexual and generational differences, the more we emphasize the normativity of the father.

I will begin by looking at normativity, and then return to the first issue.

It should be stated from the outset that the thesis of the normativity of the father, which has been put forward by Pierre Legendre, delights those psychoanalysts who are worried about the decline of the symbolic but irritates others, who are quick to denounce the social effects of this type of normative discourse (which may have repressive effects). And Pierre Legendre's discourse has had a definite influence on actors employed in various agencies for social intervention (from judges to social workers). Armed with these normative injunctions, they have no hesitations in pressurizing psychiatrists into 'resymbolizing their patients'. The unfortunate psychiatrists find themselves being put in the position of the guardians of the temple of the symbolic, and they obviously do not want to be in that position. They quite understandably fear that they might become a sort of new priesthood.

It has to be said, however, that Pierre Legendre is not responsible for the social effects of his discourse. He is simply saying what he has to say, and everyone is free to take from it what they like, depending upon what they are willing to hear and upon the period, situation and circumstances in which they live, and all these factors are eminently variable. Everyone knows that what allows us to castigate any given discourse at the moment can later be used to defend it. Let us be quite clear about this: we cannot explain a discourse merely by taking its social effects into consideration, unless we adopt a position as untenable as that of blaming Spinoza for anti-Semitism, or Nietzsche for Nazism. There is in fact only one serious philosophical option, and that is to look at the discourse in terms of its internal logic. I will therefore give Pierre Legendre's discourse the benefit of the doubt, assume that it does have something to say (whatever use is made of it) and discuss it purely in terms of its internal consistency.

What, then, is Pierre Legendre saying? To get away from Freud's scientific myth, Legendre looks to the law in an attempt to find a rational basis for the father in the West. He demonstrates that one of the things, now relatively forgotten, that helped to lay the foundations of Europe can be traced back to the canon law elaborated between the eleventh and thirteenth centuries. It founded Europe by reformulating Roman law in Christian terms, and this led to the emergence of a state and a law based upon genealogical principles. 'The construct of the Law allowed the Churches to so arrange things that sons – the sons of both the sexes – could succeed sons.' These constructs bring into play 'the logical principle that we in the West call the Father, and on to which we pin the civil law'.[10] In Roman law at least, there is no paternal function that is not bound up with power in the *polis*. As Legendre himself puts it (1988: 172), this is a 'vital consideration', as the symbolic function proves to be established at the juridico-political level. On this point, I refer the reader to the highly pertinent arguments that Legendre develops – at considerable length – to support his thesis. Legendre obviously reveals one of the major Western figures of the Subject in everything to do with the patriarchate or patriarchy [*le patriarcat*].

It must, however, be noted that there was a time when this canonization of the father caused Legendre a lot of problems, especially since, as Legendre himself explained in the mid-1970s (Legendre 1974), the subsequent secularization of the state adopted the terminology of *le patriarcat* and used it for its own purposes: 'By adopting the notions of sin so as to absolve human beings, the secular Law tries

[10] See Legendre (1996; 1985; 1988).

to replace the whole of religion and to fill in its gaps.' At this time, Legendre's verdict was quite clear. Modern secularization did nothing to change the old Inquisition: 'French law proves to be remarkably good at adapting its own traditions to social varieties of the industrial regime: as a result, the secular idea literally invaded various sites of power' (Legendre 1974). The capitalist industrial state, which is based upon a patriotic bureaucracy and promotes nationalism, must therefore be seen as a development of the patriarchate or patriarchy initiated by the canonization of the Father.

The very thing that caused Legendre so many problems in 1974 seems to have become the solution to them twenty years later. In 1974, Legendre was denouncing 'the omnipotence of an all-powerful father, the terrifying bearer of the supreme symbolic [. . .] the boss-father and the teacher-father [. . .] made in the image of the progenitor-father, who is in a symmetrical relationship with a sovereign State worshipped by French subjects'. In 1996, he could claim that what is meant by the 'humanization of man' is the 'scaffolding that constructs the image of the Father'. It is a well-known fact that one good oxymoron can always 'resolve' the problem of completely incompatible meanings. But if we wish to avoid purely rhetorical solutions, it has to be noted that there has been a complete change: the father who was the 'terrifying bearer' has become the most important factor in the 'humanization' of man . . .

Let me report here a minor but amusing misreading, a sort of aural slip of the tongue. I mention it because it seems to me to show how our author adopts contradictory positions. In his study of the origin of images, Legendre (1994: 226) reports that a theologian called Pierre Le Chantre (*circa* 1110–97) taught that 'whatever the Pope prescribes is fair and equitable'. The author (who ought to have found this amusing) makes no allusion to the obvious paronym that links his name to that of the theologian, but I suspect he is giving a very subtle hint as to the existence of a reduplication that affects him personally: wherever there is a Pierre Legendre [*gendre*: son in law] to denounce the Father, there is also a Pierre Le Chantre [*chantre*: bard, eulogist] to sing his praises . . .

Be that as it may, one suspects that Legendre is falling into the same trap as Heidegger, who denounced all the utilitarian 'enframing' [*Gestell*] of the world in his doctoral thesis of 1916 on Duns Scotus only to swear allegiance to the worst 'enframing' of all (Nazism). Legendre is obviously not singing the praises of something *Völkisch*, but he has completely changed his position on the patriarchate. In *L'Amour du censeur*, he criticises the medieval order of the canonists and actually describes it as an Inquisition, but in his later work he claims that, in the absence of a dogmatic order, there cannot be anything but unreason and barbarism.

The problem therefore begins when Legendre attempts to turn the genealogical principle of the patriarchate and patriarchy – and he is right to exhume it – into a Subject that is still fully valid today. This is supposedly the Subject that can prevent us from lapsing into the barbarism that always threatens the social bond and that does sometimes destroy it. Given that he makes great use of this concept, Legendre should know that historical constructs are always the products of local circumstances. The stage we build to exhibit the Subject is always contingent and constructed with what is available in our region or our tradition (in this case, Roman law reformulated as canon law). If we turn some Subject into an absolute, there is a great danger that we will become something resembling that subject's priest, spokesperson or prophet. If there is one pitfall we must avoid at all cost, it is falling into the symbolic form we are trying to explain. If we do that, we find ourselves in the process of becoming a subjected subject, in other words a proselyte subject, and will be unable to take the Subject as an object of study.

There is only one way to avoid the danger of essentializing a local figure: we must get back to the basic linguistic blueprint of the basic triangle of enunciation: I, you and he/she.[11] We have to go back to language simply because there can be no unconscious without language. If we are to consider the subject of the unconscious, we must look at the subject of language. We must therefore scrape away all the other strata – be they (pseudo-)anthropological (as is the case with Freud and his myth of the *Urhorde*) or juridical (Legendre) – until we reach the deepest level of symbolism: the semiosis which is consubstantial with our neotenic being, and which applies regardless of the specific juridical regime in which it is manifested. If we do not reach this semiotic level, there is a great danger that we will

---

[11] I have attempted elsewhere (Dufour 1990) to demonstrate that even the most uncontrolled use of language implies a trinitarian enunciation: no matter what he says, no speaking subject can speak without saying an 'I' to a 'you' and about a 'he'/ 'she'. Insofar as he is a speaking being, the subject inhabits from the outset a trinitarian enunciatory space, where the three main persons of speech are knotted together and where the basic symbolic relationships of space and time are inscribed. There can be no access to symbolization unless the subject passes through the basic structure of a trinitarian enunciation.

reduce the symbolic to one determinate juridico-political form. Ultimately, Legendre's theory of the construction of the subject relies solely upon the agency of the juridical: 'Instituting subjectivity means fabricating the juridical framework that can take care of the subject's desire' (Legendre 1994: 354). The symbolic is therefore reduced to 'normativity' or to various 'dogmatic constructs of the social'.[12] Legendre is certainly careful to point out (1985: 360) that 'the intervention of the law is incomprehensible unless we recognize that juridical science is closely bound up with the element that structures human life: speech'; but at no point does he undertake an analysis of that structural element, nor does he analyse the essential link between the living and the speaking. Legendre's entire argument is not based upon the two levels of the biological and the symbolic. He bases it on three levels, and I cite: 'The biological, the social and the unconscious'. To assume, however, that these three levels are the starting point of all thinking in this domain is, in my view, highly debatable:

- The first level – the biological – appears to be more or less acceptable and unproblematic, provided that, when we apply the term 'living' to human beings, we define it with reference to the specific feature of human neoteny (prematuration and organic incompleteness), as Lacan never fails to define it. Without this feature, we cannot understand that language is grafted (through a process of substitution) onto that lack of completion.
- The second level of the social raises serious problems of consistency, as the deepest roots of the social are in part biological: the gregariousness characteristic of human beings, which is also found in the hominoids, is typical of the species as such. In a word, it seems to me impossible to define the social without reference to gregariousness.
- As for the unconscious, how can we view it as an independent entity which can be apprehended in itself? It is in fact traversed by the social from the outset – as we can easily see from the fact that the notions of totem and of the Name of the Father refer to social forms of the unconscious. The 1960 Bonneval Colloquium made it even more difficult to regard the unconscious as something which exists independently, as it has to be seen as an effect of language. It

[12] Given that everything is no more than a dogmatic construct, there is little difference between a choreographed ballet and the goose step used in military parades (see Legendre 1978).

is well known that, after Bonneval,[13] Lacan put forward a formula that became famous during the heyday of structuralism: 'The unconscious is structured like a language.' It is therefore difficult, to say the least, for anyone claiming to be a Lacanian to divorce the unconscious and its effects from their site of production, namely language.

Ultimately, it seems to me that Legendre's three levels are consistent only insofar as they allow him to put the juridical in a position to tie everything together. That this has heuristic effects is undeniable, but it is also very dogmatic. Because it is neutralized, controlled and smothered by the juridical, the symbolic appears to be nothing more than a dead spot, or, at best, a locus for the father insofar as he is dead. Legendre refers to it as a 'Text without a subject'. When the symbolic is reduced to the juridical, it can no longer be the site where the permanent warfare that characterizes the fate of living human beings is continued by other means. What disappears in this dogmatic construct is a Heraclitean symbolic traversed by conflicting dogmas and legitimacies, a symbolic traversed by repeated attempts to escape the domination of Subjects. These struggles are of course recycled and incorporated into the struggles of newly emergent Subjects, but they constantly run across the symbolic and make it a site that swarms with a wealth of multiform and contradictory texts, images, sounds and representations.

The 'lesson' (this is the generic title Legendre gives his books) is, in my view, clear: if we are not to confine the symbolic within a juridical cage, we must get beyond juridical constructs and get down to semiosis. We must reach, thanks to an eidetic reduction, the semiotic blueprint, or in other words a level that is free of all ideological, historical and dogmatic implications and involves only relations between terms. This blueprint does nothing more than establish a system of logical relations which can be satisfied in many different ways and does not essentialize any term. This stance presupposes a real bracketing out (*epoche*) of the objective world, as defined both by the Sceptics and by Husserl's phenomenology. Husserl, for instance, recommends (1988: 20) 'an "inhibiting" or putting out of play of all

---

[13] The Bonneval Colloquium on the relationship between language and the unconscious was an exceptional encounter between psychoanalysts (Green, Lantéri-Laura, Laplanche, Leclaire, Perrier . . .) and philosophers (Lefebvre, Ricoeur, Hyppolite, Merleau-Ponty . . .). The proceedings were published in 1966 under the direction of Henri Ey.

positions taken towards the already-given Objective world and, in the first place, all existential positions (those concerning being, illusory, possible being, being likely, probable, etc.)'. Basically, we must not become fixated on one of the possible forms the Subject can take in the world, or, for that matter, any one of the three terms of the (semio-)logical triangle. The first term, or I, has been essentialized, as in the various *personalisms*, past and present. We also know that the second term ('you') can be essentialized; the philosophies of Martin Buber and Lévinas might supply the model. Legendre essentializes the third term, or party, of the 'he'/'she'. Whilst he does identify one major form of Subject in Western culture, he cannot see its other forms. He fails to see that, as I have tried to demonstrate, all the various figures of the Subject necessarily imply the genealogical principle. The father, that is, obviously lies at the origin of all Subjects because the *he* is a signifier which replaces an origin that can never be found. Every name given to this *he* is therefore designed to found that origin. Being a temporal marker, this father can take multiple forms: there is no more reason to base the father on the Totem rather than on the Subject of canon law, *physis*, the king, the fatherland, the republic or the little father of the peoples . . .

It transpires that Legendre's attempt to reduce the father in the Oedipus complex to a given juridical form is vain, if only because that form has played a decisive role in the history of the West. Behind the father and beneath the Oedipus complex, we find not a local form, but a basic semiotic blueprint relating to our status as speaking beings. That semiotic blueprint is also the only reasonable alternative to, and escape from, Freud's symptom and its Oedipal form.

One way to avoid this dogmatism of the father that we see developing is to go in the opposite direction, to attempt to reject the Oedipus complex outright and to ignore everything about it that we should be retaining. As I have already said, we cannot reject the figure of the father, which is central to Freudianism, without rejecting Freudianism in its entirety. Yet we often hear it said that the goal of analysis, or even 'the ethics of psychoanalysis', is to 'demote' the father. In one very specific sense, this is perfectly true, as the goal of the analysis does, as Serge Leclaire used to say, depend upon our ability to speak in the first person. *In the long run*, we therefore have to get rid of the third person who speaks within us, namely the father. But we can do so only *after* we have spoken in the third person. If we get rid of the father before we do that, we find ourselves in the position of the psychotic, as Lacan's remarks about the foreclosure of the Name of the Father indicate so clearly. Before we can escape the law, we must enter its domain. Without the law, there can be no possibility of transgression.[14] Psychoanalysts who are tempted by the radical postmodernist stance have therefore to take a decision: they can go on being Freudians and accept the role of the father, together with sexual and generational differences, or they can invent another theory of, for example, sexual non-difference. In which case they break their ties with Freud. There is no alternative.

Psychoanalysis and the old temptation of incest

It might be said that Lacanianism is the alternative to Freudianism. And at the moment there actually is a 'Foucauldo-Deleuzean-Lacanian' alliance, and its half-statements and disavowals suggest that it accepts that there is no distinction between the sexes. When I say 'Foucauldo-', I am referring to the rather discreet pro-gay stance taken by Foucault towards the end of his life. It has now come back to us from the United States in the exaggerated form of the so-called queer tendency (Halperin 1995). When I say 'Deleuzean-', I am referring to Deleuze's anti-Oedipal theses (Deleuze and Guattari 2004), and to his problematic of 'becoming' (man's 'becoming woman' and man and woman's 'becoming animal' (Deleuze and Guattari 1992).[15] And when I say 'Foucauldo-Deleuzo-Lacanian', I am referring to what we now find in certain Lacanian circles, even though is not always overt: a surrender to incestuous desire in an attempt to escape generational and sexual differences.

There ought to be something surprising about a situation in which those who are supposed to have understood something about incestuous desire and about the need to inscribe it in the symbolic are the first to succumb to it. But is it really so surprising? Is there any place where the notions of 'the incestuous society', 'proscription of incest' and 'social incestocracy' are more present than in psychoanalytic societies? The first to realize this was Serge Leclaire, who was one of the most eminent psychoanalysts of his generation. It is when

[14] On Lacan's 'transcendence' of the law/desire dichotomy, see 'Kant with Sade' (Lacan [1963a]). See also the discussion led by J. Rogozinski (1999).

[15] On 'becoming', see chapter 10 of A Thousand Plateaus (Deleuze and Guattari 1992). Deleuze specifically states (pp. 237, 238) that becoming escapes relations: 'A becoming is not a correspondence between relations . . . Becoming is not an evolution, or at least not an evolution by filiation. Becoming produces nothing by filiation.'

analysts work on the psychical implications of the generational sequence by looking at sexual difference that the danger of them being retroactively invaded by what they have discovered – incestuous Oedipal desire – is at its greatest. Serge Leclaire very quickly realized that we have never actually escaped incest. He meant that, although there is such a thing as a *law* based upon the prohibition of incest, we have never actually escaped a 'socio-incestocratic' order. 'It is thanks only to an inversion [. . .] that we have become accustomed to placing the prohibition of incest at the centre of our societies [. . .] it would be easy to denounce the social-incestocratic order that psychoanalysis reproduces in its history and practice because it has failed to analyse it' (Leclaire 1981: 235f). Psychoanalysis has created, he asserts, 'a micro-society whose order is transparently incestuous, and those who investigate the discontents of our civilization could learn a lot from it'. In this collection of articles, which Leclaire wanted to publish before Lacan died, he brings to 'the attention of exegetes' the two bolts in what he calls 'the psychoanalytic State'. There is an incestuous bolt and a narcissistic bolt. The 'incestuous bolt' is 'the effect of that part of Freud's heritage which has never been paid for', by which he means 'AnnaFreudianism' and the endogamous practices of the first psychoanalysts. The 'narcissistic bolt' is that which, in Lacanianism, eventually gave rise to an order based upon a system of relations between psychoanalysts who tried to overcome their anxiety by devoting themselves to what he called the unifying Idol, promoted to the rank of the Other. There was no threatening outside to this order, and difference was excluded. When Lacan died, it quickly became apparent that the 'narcissistic bolt' was nothing but the first stage in the forging of a new incestuous bolt. What we have here is another instance of the transmission of psychoanalysis via the daughter. Which gives us a familiar picture: being a son-in-law [*beau-fils*], the daughter's husband reproduces and resurrects the father as best he can, whilst the illegitimate sons aspire to being better looking [*plus beau*] than him . . .

Lacan's inheritance has rightly been described as an example of *epikleros* transmission.[16] According to Vernant (1965: 145f), the transmission by *epikleros* was practised in ancient Greece when a man did

---

[16] We owe the application of this term in psychoanalysis to Jean Allouch (1991: 196f). This might tend to indicate that the latter had perfectly well understood the incestuous affairs of psychoanalysis before giving in, in his turn, ten years later, to the social-incestocratic order by promoting sexual non-differentiation . . .

not have a son who could inherit the *kleros* or family estate. One of his daughters stayed in the paternal home to tend the family altar. She was described as an *epikleros* because she remained true to the paternal *kleros*. If she married, her husband had to abandon all ambition of establishing his own home so as to allow her to fulfil her duties in her father's home. 'In this way, the daughter could give birth to a child who resembled her true father.' This familial endogamy, which did not conform to the Greek ideal, was very present in family institutions because 'the *epikleros* combined both aspects of Hestia: the father's virgin daughter and the wife who embodied his lineage's reservoir of life' (1965: 147).[17] The *epikleros* fulfilled the 'dream of a purely paternal heredity that always haunted the Greek imagination' (1965: 133). Although the *epikleros* daughter obviously did not commit incest in the literal sense, the estate was passed on endogamously from father to daughter. Whilst the father–daughter relationship is analytic theory's poor relation, it nonetheless implacably dominates the psychoanalytic institution and definitely reveals the paternal function for what it is. It is very fragile and quite capable of being inverted: it can become *an imperative that prescribes incest*. When the woman, who is the mobile element in the social bond, becomes the stable element in the paternal home, the result is something resembling 'mausolization'. God knows the 'psychoanalytic State' now encounters a form that never ceases the haunt the state itself. When this form of intergenerational transmission is cathected, it obviously discourages all future discourse. Discourse becomes literally inaudible; it is silenced from the outset when it is reduplicated by the voice of a dead father, which wells up and is immortalized thanks to the ventriloquism of the priestess of the mausoleum. This is somewhat reminiscent of Edgar Allan Poe's *Tales (The Facts in the Case of M de Valdemar, The Mesmeric Revelation)*. Lacan loved those tales.

The least we can say is that there is a long-standing predisposition towards incest within psychoanalysis. It is a constituent element of the psychoanalytic institution, and it causes it to alternate between the (official) proscription of incest and its (repressed) prescription. It annuls sexual and generational differences by conflating all positions and dissolving the differences between the sexes and between generations. What we have to try to understand is how and why what was essentially an unconscious prescription is sometimes now

---

[17] Hestia was the Greek domestic goddess. The Roman equivalent was Vesta (hence the Vestal virgins).

recommended more and more literally. It is probable that post-modernity gives free expression to a perversion that both asserts and denies something by using the enunciatory form of disavowal. Octave Manonni formulates it in canonical form: 'I know, but . . .' (Manonni 1969). In any case, this is not a purely theoretical problem. It is a very practical, that is to say, clinical problem pertaining to the handling of what used to be called the 'standard treatment': either the analyst gives the subject to understand [*fait entendre*] that what she wants is impossible, or he tells the subject [*fait entendre*] what she wants to hear.

How to erase Lacan's formulae for sexuation

We can therefore say that the Foucauldo-Deleuzeans are making a takeover bid for psychoanalysis. One 'detail' has to be settled if the bid is to succeed: they have to circumvent Lacanianism by making Lacan say something he never said. Just as they had to remove the Oedipus complex from psychoanalysis, they now have to attempt to perform a very complicated surgical operation on Lacan. It involves doing away with the concept of the Name-of-the-Father or, at the very least, demonstrating that it has nothing to do with either the difference between the sexes or the difference between the generations – which is not easy. That is, however, what certain 'Lacanians' are trying to do, in roundabout ways and by re-examining one of Lacan's major con-tributions: the so-called formulae for sexuation.[18] In a word, they are attempting to turn the phallus into a function expressed not by two formulae, but by a continuous function. They can then move from one formula to the other without any hiatus. The Foucauldo-Deleuzean-Lacanian alliance is trying to make one of Lacan's key

[18] See section VII of the seminar of 1972–3 (Lacan 1998). These formulae employ a logical script in which the 'man' side refers to universal propositions, whilst the 'woman' side refers to singular propositions. In plain language, they mean that man's distinctive characteristic is his ability to establish *links* inside large organizations (churches, armies, parties . . .) even though *one*, the leader, is exempt (that is, escapes castration). The 'woman' side is not based upon any exception, and therefore cannot establish large organizations in which we can recognize ourselves. Women are there-fore not completely subordinated to the phallic function (Lacan says that they are 'not-whole' ['*pas-toutes*']) and experience two *jouissances*: a phallic *jouissance* and an Other *jouissance*). To be schematic and to simplify things still further, men – the men and the women who regard themselves as such – constantly propose laws and general-izations (which may prove to be pointless), whilst women insist and remain in an idiolect and the singular.

formulae – 'there is no such thing as a sexual relationship' – mean that there is no distinction between the sexes.[19]

This thesis is of great interest to certain gay and lesbian movements, which are demanding nothing less than the codification of a new basic right: the right to choose our sex. Being the hysterological subject of the postmodern condition, I will create the whole process and I will go so far as to 'manufacture' my gender all by myself. I might even take my case to court because, despite my inalienable freedom, there always has to be a judge to ratify my new condition. I will use my new 'human right' to declare the sex I have just chosen, quite independently of my biological sex . . .

Is this really Lacanian?

Are we all the same sex and are we therefore all homosexual, whether we like it or not?

All I can do is emphasize how far we have come – in the wrong direction – since the days when the man Elisabeth Roudinesco calls 'the first Lacanian' could explain: 'the most difficult thing we [psychoanalysts] still have to do is to complete the transition from a homosexual society to a heterosexual society' (Leclaire 1998). Leclaire was trying to say that, because men have always dominated social relations by coming to an arrangement amongst themselves, we still do not know what the other sex is or what the other sex can really do. At the very moment when Leclaire was noting with some alarm (this was in 1978, or just as he was working on the 'social incestocracy') that we had never really emerged from a homosexual society, other Lacanians were, in short, refusing to emerge from it and trying to make everyone part of that society.

How can we take a new approach to this question? One starting point is as good as another. For the purposes of the argument, let us say that my starting point is the real – something exists before I do. It is not in fact ridiculous to postulate that the real – which in this context means 'the living' – comes first and that speaking beings come later, or may come later. All too often, it is forgotten that Lacan does sometimes define the real in positive terms as, for example, 'that which returns to the same place'. In the seminar on anxiety (29 May 1963), he states that

---

[19] I am repeating some of the themes of the lecture I gave at the colloquium held to mark the centenary of Lacan's birth by the École Lacanienne de Psychanalyse (Cité des Sciences et de l'Industrie de Paris–La Villette, 6–7 May 2001). Several philosophers were invited to speak on the theme 'there is no such thing as a sexual relationship'. Parts of my lecture were published in no. 10 of the special issue of *Essaim* (Autumn 2002, Érès, Ramonville) devoted to *Des Sexes différents*.

the 'real' implies 'the union of two sexual cells' and implies that one is 'male' and that the other is 'female'.[20] Like the movement of the planets, this always has the same effect, namely generation. The only way for mortals to escape their mortal condition is to prolong the human farce for another generation. If we take the real as our starting point, there are therefore two sexes. There are two sexes because there are two texts, or two genetic scripts that we can now read with confidence: XY for men and XX for women. Humanity is subject to the law that presides over the evolved organization of living beings, namely the law of *sexion*. I use the term to indicate that humanity experiences a primal division between the sexes. From the point of view of the real, we are therefore either one sex or the other, and the reality of sex means precisely that: *sexion*. This is the real because it corresponds to the organic condition of living beings, or of those living beings that are usually indifferent to what is said about them – which might be a cause for celebration.

Such, then, is the reality of sex [le *réel du sexe*], as defined in positive terms. But it can also be defined in negative terms, as when Lacan defines it in terms of the impossible. We might put it this way: when we end up as one sex, it 'really' is impossible to go over to the other. That is the price that had to be paid for the division of *sexion*. Of course we can add whatever we like to our bodies, or remove whatever we like. We can modify our 'look' as much as we like by using products (such as hormones) and artifices, or even prosthetics or grafts. Because we are neotenic and have unfinished bodies, we love finishing off our bodies with prosthetic extensions. But we cannot change anything to do with our sex because we cannot change anything to do with our text. In that sense, the real is the impossibility of escaping our sex. This is the Aristotelian impossibility of the *tertium non datur* (the excluded third). If a proposition is true, its negation is false, and there is no third possibility. It is the same with sex: if we are one sex, we are not the other and there is no third possibility. There is therefore, I insist, no *real* third possibility of changing our sex, but there are, of course, *non-real* possibilities.

It is in fact quite obvious that the living beings I am talking about can, given that they can speak, come to terms with this real – or refuse

[20] Cf. the unpublished seminar on 'Anxiety' (29 May 1963): 'We are talking here about something real [un *réel*], or that something that preserves what Freud articulates about life's property at the level of his Nirvana principle; in order to reach death it must once more pass through forms that reproduce those that gave the individual the opportunity to appear thanks to the conjunction of two sexual cells.'

to do so. There is no legal reason to prevent someone of one sex, in other words, of one text, from saying that they are of the opposite sex, of both sexes at the same time, or of an infinity of sexes. Because a neotenin is a speaking being who constantly invents epirealities, there is the imaginary possibility of playing with [*jouer avec*], or outwitting [*déjouer*], the real inevitability of sexion. It is only from this point of view, or from the point of view of what passes for logic in these imaginary constructs, that the sexual can be said to be a continuum. At the imaginary level, everything is therefore possible in sexual terms. It is possible to say one thing and its opposite – and people have been happily doing so since time immemorial. And everyone knows that a neotenin's sex games are no fun unless there is at least an element of perversion, and that perversion usually begins with certain inversions.

When it comes to the symbolic field, there are two possible ways of positioning ourselves, the real inevitability of our sex notwithstanding. Lacan's sexuation formula defines two *genders*, or two symbolic ways, of playing the part of the man and of playing the part of the woman – and I mean 'playing' in the sense of 'make-believe'. Because they can speak, those who carry in their cells the text characteristic of, say, a male mammal can go in the direction of whatever semblance suits them: they can play at being either a man or a woman. And because they can speak, those who carry the female text can play at being either a woman or a man.

It is because of the existence of these two formulae and of what they refer to that there is no such thing as a sexual relationship. We have only to compare the two logical formulae to see that there is no such thing – one formula relates to the universal proposition of playing at being a man, and the other, to the singular proposition of playing at being a woman. There is only one way to understand 'there is no such thing as a sexual relationship': it means 'there is no logical relationship between the genders'. Obviously we cannot leap to the conclusion that individuals do not meet when they rub whichever mucous membrane they choose to rub up against another. Everyone knows that. Of course 'there is no logical rapport between the genders', but that is precisely why individuals meet. The fact that there is no logical relationship between the genders has never been an obstacle to physical encounters between individuals, whatever their sex and what results from it, namely a relationship involving their sexual organs. Basically and as Lacan himself said, commenting on his own formula, you can still have a good fuck even when, or especially when, there is no sexual relationship.

We can even understand that, in both genders if I may put it that way, the relationship which unites a man and a woman remains, for better or worse, dominant. This is probably because, even though we meet only as the result of a misunderstanding or accident, the most serious misunderstanding is that which occurs between the sexes. All it takes is a meeting between a man of the male gender and sex and a woman of the female gender and sex – and such meetings do still occur from time to time – for them to be able to make babies without any intervention on the part of either the Holy Spirit or the techno-logical spirit, which is now trying to replace spirituality by offering to make babies in test tubes. In a word, the reality of sex can still come to terms with the symbolic non-relationship between the genders: it is because of the irremediable misunderstanding between the genders that the sexes go on meeting and perpetuating the adventure.

I am saying that the encounter between the sexes is, at bottom, nothing more than one example of the non-relationship between the genders. We are therefore in a position to understand that, if two men or two women came together by rubbing the appropriate mucous membranes together, that would do the job just as well. What is worse, or perhaps better, is that it is a matter of choice: given that there is no logical relation between the genders, it is quite possible that, when I am fucking, I am basically fucking by myself. And perhaps that is the real question: am I not always alone when I am fucking? We may not be a single sex [un seul sexe] but we are alone when we have sex [seul dans le sexe]. And if that is the case, there is no reason why I should not have sex alone, or why there should not be two of us involved . . . or three, or four, or fifteen, or twenty . . . The fact that there is no sexual relationship opens up a whole range of coital possibilities.

We must conclude from all this that, whatever my real sex may be, I can speak and therefore I have the right to opt for either gender. I am talking here about one of the speaking subject's basic rights which, depending on the period, can be either totally or partly denied or accepted by 'history', and therefore totally or partly inscribed in that period's historical law [droit historique]. I am speaking here of a man's inalienable right to play the part of the man or the part of the woman, and of a woman's right to play the part of the woman or the part of the man, and I define 'play the part of' in the broadest possible sense. So we can play with sexual difference – Anne Garréta's admirable novel

Sphinx (1986) provides adequate proof of that.[21] But before we can play with it, it has to exist. That, however, is not a sufficient reason for me to be able to choose my sex. *Gender* is a construct (which can be singular, historical or grammatical) that can be deconstructed. I can, in other words, choose my gender.[22] This is a matter for what Kant calls the *problematic* modality of judgement, which pertains to what is possible; sex is a matter for the *assertoric* modality of judgement, which pertains to what is real. This is a fundamental difference, and we must not forget it, especially at a time when 'gender studies' tends to take up so much room (especially in American universities) and tries to conceal, or even challenge, the reality of sex.

Basically, whilst we all have a basic right to choose our gender, that right does not include the right to choose our sex because it is impossible to choose our text – quite simply because, as *sexion* is a given, my text has already been chosen when I am born, or when I come into being. The outcome is what I see as a proposition that cannot be ignored: the right to choose my sex as a referent for my text is not on the human rights agenda. The demand to be able to choose our sex cannot be inscribed within the human race's extraordinary capacity for escaping its natural determinations. No matter what is said today, there are no grounds for thinking that culture can set us free from all the states of nature. What a living culture can do, apart from providing the neotenin with a few prostheses that allow him to have a slightly better life in time and space, is to shake off the subjections that political theologies and onto-theologies have always tried to pass off as natural: subordination to gods, kings, masters, the mighty . . . Humanity's irresistible march towards democracy provides confirmation of what Tocqueville called the tendency towards 'equality of condition'. Of course equality of condition is still restricted to the symbolic and juridical domains. And of course our emancipation from all supposedly natural conditions is far from complete: social Darwinism and contemporary neoliberalism still see the social and economic domination of 'the fittest' as natural. But the fact remains that the tendency towards equality of condition has allowed us to do away with, or alleviate, many subjections that used to be considered

[21] The novel shows us how the game starts: with a language game, that is to say, a grammatical game. *Sphinx* was written under Oulipien constraints: all marks of gender have been removed from the descriptions of the two main characters in the novel.

[22] The choice is of course largely unconscious. I speak of a 'choice of gender' in the sense in which Freud speaks of a 'choice of neurosis' (*Neurosenwhal*).

natural. Some would have us believe that we can do the same with sex. Of course, men's supposedly natural dominance over women is eminently open to criticism, because it is in fact a social construct. But the relationship between the sexes cannot be reduced to a mere social relationship in which men dominate women. There is always something left over, and that something is anatomical. *Sexion* cannot be dissolved into the social. It has its own consistency and it has major implications for the constitution and differentiation of subjects. We cannot, in other words, ignore natural determination.[23] The fact that, like it or not, we find ourselves in the body of a girl or in the body of a boy even before culture comes into play is adequate proof of that. That is why, before we start blowing the trumpet of human liberation, we have to think about the natural determinations that no long march can transcend, unless we change the definition of humanity itself.

The right to choose our sex is therefore nothing to do with human rights. This proposition has an immediate corollary: if I made the right to choose our sex a human right, I would be in a highly absurd position of telling the subject to choose when the choice has already been made for her. Now, as Lacan reminded his young colleagues, housemen at Sainte-Anne, in 1967: 'It is the mad who are the totally free men' (Lacan 1967b). That is how it is: only the mad are truly free, and if I demanded and obtained the right to choose where there is no choice, I might be free but I would certainly be mad. The one who might possibly give me that right, or at least the one from whom I might ask for the possibility to choose, is the one known as the legislator. Perhaps we can understand why the legislator might be somewhat reluctant to put subjects – the subjects with rights who make up a social whole – in that position.

Choosing our sex in the market

Efforts are, however, being made to do just that. Indeed, a lot of effort is going into it. As I have already tried to demonstrate elsewhere

---

[23] This is, however, what Pierre Bourdieu does (2001). He attempts to demonstrate that the distinction between men and women is not so much a biological fact as a social construct. By reducing sexual relations to the social relations that allow men to dominate women, he paves the way for the postmodernist demand for the negation of all organic differences. This thesis is, of course, often evoked by 'sexual liberation' movements which think that the critique of social domination justifies the right to choose our sex. I will not dwell on this question: Thierry Vincent (2002) has already made a rigorous critique of Bourdieu's thesis.

(Dufour 1996a), we cannot rule out the possibility that, thanks to the progress of democracy and with a little hysterological encouragement, the legislator might be in a position put the subject in a situation of madness.

Something is insinuating itself into these debates about the right of gender, and we need to be very clear about what it is. This something is the demand for the right to choose our sex. It is not surprising, in my view, that it should be making itself heard now. Why? Because we are in a democracy, in other words in a situation where we are beginning to grant the subject the same self-referential definition we once granted the Subject.

Now this definitional transposition leads to, and provokes, certain pretensions. As I have already indicated, it has authorized the deployment of a total freedom (for commodities, amongst other things) and has allowed the unbridled development of neoliberalism. It allows more than that: we are now behaving as though self-foundation in the symbolic justified self-foundation in the real. Today's demand is for the right to choose our sex; tomorrow's demand will surely be for self-generation through cloning. The demands are consistent because there is a link between the right to choose our sex and the triumph of the market.

Those who clash swords over this issue are well aware that there is a correlation between the market and the demand for the right to choose our sex – whatever their opinion may be. I will take only two very different texts that appeared in the summer of 2000: Henry Frignet's book on transsexualism (Frignet 2000) and Michel Tort's essay on the symbolic (Tort 2000). Henry Frignet notes that the erasure of the reference to sex and the promotion of gender are 'concomitant with' the worldwide expansion of North America's economic model, but he does not expand upon this interesting comment. Michel Tort, who takes a very different view, notes that psychoanalysis is now being used to identify the forms of desymbolization that are supposedly at work. They include the demand for the erasure of the differences between the sexes, and Tort mentions the danger of both science *and* the market. Tort silences the critics of science, but his book has nothing to say about the market he has just evoked. It neither demonstrates nor refutes that the market has a role to play here, rather as if that was something too difficult or delicate to talk about. Yet this is precisely what we have to examine: the relationship between the demand for the erasure of sexual difference and the triumph of the market.

As we know, the market's goal is to transform every part of the world into a place which is devoted to the commodity. Ultimately, no domain must remain untouched by commodities: no region in the world, and no 'region' of international exchange, be it economic, social, cultural or artistic. The same now applies to the psychical regions, where identities are cobbled together. Given that it obeys the logic of continual expansion, we might say that the market is greatly interested in the existence of identities, including sexual identities, which are extremely flexible, variable and shifting. It is in the market's objective interest to make identities flexible and precarious. Because its logic forces it to expand the commodified zone to infinity, the market is now dreaming of being able to provide kits of all kinds, including identity kits: discourses, images, models, prosthetics, products . . . Ideally, the market must be something that can provide everyone – anywhere and at any time – with all the products that supposedly correspond to instantaneous desires that can be immediately satisfied.

Deleuze correctly identified this tendency when he demonstrated that schizophrenia, which is a form of radical deterritorialization, is bound up with the extension of capitalism (Deleuze and Guattari 2004). It should also be noted that Lacan's suggestion that it is the mad who are truly free is quite consistent with Deleuze's remarks about the schizo and successful deterritorialization. The great difference, which is worth noting, is that Deleuze turns the problem – the extension of schizophrenia – into the solution. He basically attempts to transform the subjective impasses which result from the absence of the Other into a solution (or 'positivities', to use his terminology). Why? Probably because Deleuze, who was fascinated by the incredible dynamism of capitalism, thought that the solution to the extension of capitalism was to go even faster than it does. The attempt to overtake capitalism in order to prevent it from reterritorializing the flows that had been set free was one aspect of Deleuze's vitalism. That is why the schizo, who is excluded from all possible territorialities, becomes *the* revolutionary. Turning the schizo into a revolutionary might, with hindsight, be understood as a post-'68 attempt to find – at any cost – a replacement for a proletariat that was already beginning to look very tired during the merry month of May. But it was also an attempt to give the schizo the status of a new Subject. The schizo as new Subject! Someone had to come up with the idea.

And this is precisely what is happening now, as sexuation is deterritorialized and cut loose from its biological moorings. The market is indeed very interested in the disappearance of the classic subject-form, which is both critical and neurotic, and in its 'paranoiac' terri-torialization, which once protected individuality, biological sex and the generational order. The schizoid revolution is basically taking place under the aegis of the market. The existence of transient individual-ities is perfectly consistent with the existence of a market that can supply and continually renew a stock of identity prosthetics. The market is an expert on surfing flows and plugging everything into everything else. For the market, hackers, rappers, computer nerds and anyone else who can produce strange objects, even if he is a schizoid Deleuzean, are all the more welcome in that their products and their various fads can easily be transformed into new commodities. A world of commodities that are constantly being replaced is the best of all pos-sible worlds for interacting fluid identities (which can be either schizo, divided, multiple – or mobile).

The market's only ambition is to annexe those domains that once escaped it, either because they were in the private domain or because they were a matter for state intervention. Education and health, for example, are seen less and less as problems pertaining to the public interest, and increasingly in market terms. The market now has its eyes on a different world. Its new target is a private real which has remained outside the system of political representation for almost three hundred years. Nothing has calibrated this 'other part' since the Enlightenment. This realm has to do with the 'self-belonging' which the psychoanalyst Guy Le Gaufey identifies so well in his 'anatomy of the third person' (1998). This 'part' or 'share' [*part*] – which we can describe as badly put [*mal dite*], not say 'accursed' [*maudite*], as Bataille puts it – has, since the eighteenth century, drifted through magnet-ism, Mesmerism, somnambulism, hypnosis and then transference.[24] The 'personation' [*personnation*][25] and sexuation, which were taken care of by psychoanalysis in the modern period, are what are at stake in this share. This is what the market has to recuperate and introduce into the realm of the commodifiable. We cannot rule out the possibil-ity that, as they see their patients scattering or becoming more volatile than they might otherwise be, some psychoanalysts will indeed

[24] On this point, see also Gauchet and Swain (1997).

[25] The concept of 'personation' relates to any person's ability to accede to the 'I' and the ways in which that person accedes to it. Cf. Le Gaufey (1998: 122), who refers to the concept of '*personnaison locutoire*' ('locutory personation') in Damourette and Pichon's dictionary (1911–50, vol. II: 153).

attempt to keep their market share and will come to terms with their dogma as best they can, in a bid to keep their flock and even win over new converts who might otherwise escape them. With this rebranded psychoanalysis on the one hand and the techniques of the identity market on the other, we may be witnessing one of the last struggles for control over the market in sexuation. That the market has a good head start is quite obvious from the growing number of television pro-grammes in which participants are invited to discuss their sexual prac-tices, their choices in matters sexual[26] and their life choices. There is obviously already a good market for personation and sexuation. We can safely predict that the market's ideal is the ability to produce sub-jects who can buy and consume as many identities as possible, and every imaginable personation and sexuation.

I do not suppose that Adam Smith actually foresaw this, but, to put it in the brightly ribald style of a Raymond Queneau, 'the invisible hand of the market' is probably now feeling its way into the pants of the postmodern zouave. Watch out for the market's wandering hands. As the field of the market expands, we may lose a lot of things. First, our perception of the distinction between the sexes. And then love. The market cannot embrace things as outdated as love – and love for the opposite sex still provides the model. If the market takes charge of sexuation, love will suffer at the expense of *jouissance*. Lacan was well aware of this: 'Any order and any discourse that has anything to do with capitalism leaves aside what I will simply call things to do with love' (Lacan 1972b).

A question about psychoanalysis in the postmodern period

If, as I do, we think about psychoanalysis 'within the limits of mere reason',[27] we have to note that it is concerned primarily with ontogene-sis and psychogenesis. And it therefore relates the subject's every ques-tion to his own desire. Doing so was eminently subversive in regimes in which the subject was symbolically subjected to the Other, but there is a danger that it will become politically correct in our market democ-racies, where everything is based, ultimately, upon the self-referred subject. The psychoanalytic gesture of referring the subject back to his desire now raises a serious political problem (I use 'political' in the

---

[26] According to *Le Monde* (23 February 2001), French television channels showed 551 programmes about sexual choices in 2000.

[27] I allude, of course, to Kant's *Religion within the Boundaries of Mere Reason* (1998).

Greek sense of pertaining to the life of the *polis*). If a subject who has been referred back to his desire *really* wants to have a child by artificial insemination, *really* wants to have a sex change, *really* wants to be cloned and *really* wants to modify our species' genetic characteristics, I do not think that he is raising a question that relates solely to his desire. He is also, and above all, raising a question that is bound up with the destiny of the *polis*, the *phylum*, in other words the human tribe. That is why referring the subject back to his desire is no longer enough, as we are no longer dealing with ontogenetic and psychogenetic questions, but with phylogenetic questions, in other words with problems relating to the species, its survival and its destiny. Why should we rely upon the free will of one out of many speaking subjects to settle issues of a phylogenetic order which concern the destiny and survival of the species, even if he has talked to his psychoanalyst?

Make no mistake about it: the denial of *sexion* poses a threat to the Freudian subject himself. Especially when it is denied by the psychoanalysts themselves – which only goes to prove that postmodern ideas have now penetrated the bastions of modernity. For the moment, their propagation has been restricted to one psychoanalytic society, but it will spread from there. The claim that we should stop transmitting what is wrongly seen as an old norm prevents us from seeing that something else is in fact being promoted and turned into a real norm: *unisex*. And it seems to me that the dogmatization and juridicalization of psychoanalysis is not an adequate response to this development. Both putting the symbolic father to death and defending the patriarchate seem to me to be inadequate responses to the challenges postmodernism poses in the psychical realm.

There appear to be two threats to psychoanalysis. They are at once very different and quite symmetrical: there is a possibility that psychoanalysis will degenerate into being one of the many forms of postmodern therapy, but there is also a possibility that it will be transformed into a dogma. It is possible to ward off both threats. It just takes a few psychoanalysts to stand up and, taking care to avoid both the Charybdis of denial and the Scylla of dogmatization, to begin to explore the new psychical economy of the postmodern period. And it does seem that some of them have started on this decisively critical work.

4 Neoliberalism as Desymbolization: A New Form of Domination

The postmodern desymbolization we are currently witnessing is often bitterly resented by many strata of society. It is no exaggeration to say that a feeling of deep crisis is affecting the soundest of minds. And yet we can observe a singular paradox: the more we suffer as a result of this desymbolization, the less we are convinced that it might not be a cause for celebration. We have a tendency to say that of course postmodernity and the 'fading' of the Subject are making it more difficult for us to be together and to be ourselves. But modernity, which was full of Subjects, was by no means exempt from serious disturbances. We have only to recall the terrible massacres that were carried out in the twentieth century in the name of the idols that were then at the height of their power: the nation-state, the republic, the proletariat or the race . . . In that sense, the final disappearance of the last great scarecrow and of its ultimate meaning should be a source of relief rather than anything else – even if it does result in new forms of psychic and civil disorders in our societies. Ultimately, the disappearance of the Other is nothing more than the predictable effect of a radical deterritorialization. It is probable that this fading away of the symbolic will have deleterious, disturbing and prejudicial effects, especially on the younger generations. But we wonder, however, if a brief symbolic breakdown that can be redeemed by cults or some exceptional exploit, soothed by a minor addiction to Prozac or some less legitimate product, and punctuated by a few bouts of maladjusted omnipotence and a few mistimed changes of sexual orientation will do any more damage than the combined effects of the cult of Mary,

This chapter was written in collaboration with Patrick Berthier. An earlier version appeared in *Le Débat* in January 2002.

civic instruction and the veneration of Marianne . . . We have, in short, a tendency to say to ourselves that the destruction of the symbolic humbug of old (religion, the patriarchy, the family, the nation . . .) may result in nothing more than a painful but salutary awakening for subjects as we make the sudden transition from modernity to postmodernity.

Basically, we should not confuse the end of transcendence with the end of the transcendental. We would lose nothing. It is of course true that we no longer have any external law to guide us (and subjugate us), but this might be our only opportunity to find our own internal laws. We have always known, or at least since Rousseau, that, as the word's etymology indicates, autonomy does not mean the end of the law; it means that we have to look for laws that we can prescribe for ourselves: 'Obedience to a law which we prescribe ourselves is liberty' (Rousseau 1973: 196). It might, then, be the case that we are being offered a historical chance: access to autonomy.

If that were true, we would still have to be able to (1) take that chance, and (2) know how to make use of it. There is, unfortunately, nothing to indicate that we are heading in that direction. The autonomy programme is a strictly philosophical requirement. It certainly does not mean letting individuals loose in culture with nothing and no one to guide them; on the contrary, it requires careful preparation and involves a great deal of what used to be called 'spiritual guidance' – one thinks of the efforts of the Cynics, Epicureans, Stoics and Sceptics. But the current trend is to believe that the collapse of idols leads automatically to freedom.

We have to decide: is this the hour that precedes Nietzsche's 'bright noon', or the hour of a philosophical nihilism that has finally arrived at some lucidity? Or is it the twilight hour of 'weary nihilism'? We are familiar with the irreconcilable difference between the two nihilisms. A lucid nihilism takes as its starting point the idea that the old metaphysical foundations of values were never anything more than fictions built over a void. It commits us to an extremely demanding and often salutary exercise: how can we begin to think again, now that we have no intellectual foundations? The other nihilism, or what Nietzsche himself terms 'weary nihilism' (1968: §23), refers to that uncertain moment when all values become grey. That moment now appears to be a social and a historical fact, as we can see from a phenomenon that has spread throughout our populations: the rejection of all hierarchies of values (both those pertaining to private interests and those that are based upon the *res publica*), or even the rejection of all values.[1] This is the 'weary', or even 'exhausted' nihilism that gives a central role to 'whatever refreshes, heals, calms, numbs [and] emerges into the foreground in various guises' (§23). That key position is currently occupied by the commodity. Apparently it can now bring forth a profusion of objects to fill the ontological void.

The two levels are, as we know, closely connected. Nietzsche himself held that if we did not turn the death of God into a great renunciation and a perpetual victory over ourselves, we would have to pay for our loss. Which nihilism are we dealing with? Are we dealing with a new liberation and do we have to take the advantage it offers (even if it is due to the deterritorialization brought about by the commodity), or are we entering into a new alienation? We cannot avoid the conclusion that we no longer know what to think. There is every indication that we have become trapped into an antinomy of reason.[2] There is only one way out of it: we have to wrestle with it in order to resolve it. I have been saying that we are being desymbolized, and I therefore owe it to myself to undertake a careful examination of the opposite thesis: what I see as desymbolization may be a manifestation of a new resistance to all forms of domination. We therefore have to make a new investigation into the notion of domination.

Domination

Writing in the 1960s, Bourdieu settled the question of domination in a way that is still widely accepted in sociology, and further afield in all the human and social sciences: any cultural act is an act whereby one class dominates another.[3] Bourdieu also laid down a subsidiary precondition for perfectly successful domination: the act of domination must be forgotten. The legitimacy of the dominant culture is asserted all the more easily when it succeeds in making us fail to recognize the arbitrariness it implies (Bourdieu and Passeron 1970: 38). As we know, this paradigmatic case against culture became very popular in the 1960s and replaced the previous paradigm, which derived from the Enlightenment. The earlier paradigm was based on the emancipation

---

[1] As François Meyronnis notes in his theoretical narrative (2003): 'nihilism is precisely the period when nihilism ceases to be an opinion . . . and becomes the world's dominant regime.'

[2] See Kant (1999), Book I, division 2, chapter 2, 'The antinomy of pure reason'.

[3] This is perfectly obvious in a proposition that at least has the virtue of clarity: 'All pedagogic action is, objectively, symbolic violence insofar as it is the imposition of a cultural arbitrary by an arbitrary power' (Bourdieu and Passeron 1970: 5).

that would result from universal access to knowledge and culture. That paradigm held good for two hundred years, from Kant to Condorcet to Henri Wallon.[4] With the rise of the new paradigm in the 1960s, the culture (science, literature, art . . .) which once guaranteed the salvation of all, and especially the oppressed, became nothing more than an instrument of power and alienation. Thanks to an astonishing inversion, the goal that everyone was supposedly pursuing became the one thing we had to distrust at all cost. The slogan 'knowledge equals power' was on everyone's lips at the time, and the work of Foucault (who was very sympathetic to the thesis but never actually adopted it) provided the historical and philosophical underpinnings for Bourdieu's sociological studies. One day, we will have to admit that this very reductionist thesis has had a profoundly devastating effect on culture in general. Our schools are now paying a heavy price for it.[5]

As desire is not a sociological issue, Bourdieu overlooks what I see as the essential question of why it is that human beings are always attracted to cultural acts that allow them to be so easily alienated. Why do they let themselves be dominated so easily? What do they think they will get out of it? How did it all begin? Bourdieu never has anything to say about these questions. For the second time in this book, I therefore find myself criticizing Bourdieu for attempting to explain the complexity of the world in purely sociological terms. What is worse, he tries to turn a reductionist sociology, in which everything is reduced to the ruled/ruler relationship, into a metascience. It is conceivable that he sheds light on an important element in culture (its social impact), but in doing so he overlooks the important point: what culture is in ontological terms (in relation to human nature) and what culture is in itself (its specific levels of scientific, semiotic or aesthetic consistency). Basically, we cannot consider the question of culture's symbolic effects without taking into account its constituent dimensions.

In order to do so, we can take as a starting point one basic fact. Kant put it very well: 'unlike the animals, man needs a reason of his own. Having no instinct, he has to work out a plan of conduct for himself'

[4]This paradigm can be summed up as 'we must defeat ignorance'. A useful account of its diffusion will be found in Duveau (1948).

[5]Which prompts Marie-Claude Blais to remark that 'so-called theories of reproduction helped to devalue school work in the 1970s and afterwards, particularly as a result of the influence of Pierre Bourdieu's theories' (Blais, Gauchet and Ottavi 2002: 169).

(2003: 2). In other words, the human being is what we would now call a neotenin, and his nature is incomplete. His nature does not allow him to perfect himself, and he must therefore abandon it in order to realize himself. To the extent that he is an unfinished being, he is dependent upon an other who can compensate for the human being's incompleteness. And, to the extent that he is forced to seek out that other being, *the first domination to which the human being succumbs is of an ontological nature.* We can put this in different terms: her nature is not enough to keep her alive, and she must at all cost encounter the whole of language and culture before she can be complete. Lacan, whose conception of the symbolic was very different from Bourdieu's, used to say (1956b: 392): 'Man is, prior to his birth and beyond his death, caught up in the symbolic chain.' And, to make it perfectly clear that the human being is therefore 'caught' in an essential domination and an inescapable dependency, he adds elsewhere (1956a: 414) 'the subject, while he may appear to be the slave of language, is still more the slave of a discourse.' Symbolic slavery: the expression is all the more striking in that the human being has no way of escaping her radical domination by language, unless she loses her humanity and plunges into barbarism.

It is only when this first (ontological) domination has been established that we can say that domination is, for human beings, a socio-political phenomenon. Marx allows us to understand the complexity and subtlety of this socio-political domination by showing that it is a reality that asserts itself by concealing itself. The expression 'socio-political domination' refers to all the means that certain groups of individuals use to dominate others in economic, political and/or cultural terms, and all the means that these dominant groups use to conceal their particular interests by passing them off as universal interests. The defining characteristic of this form of domination is its contingency: it works so long as the dominated can be fooled. When a human group stops being mystified by a concealed domination and suddenly realizes that, as in the story, the emperor is wearing no clothes, that group usually escapes its domination sooner or later, though it may of course immediately come under another.

Two dominations

There are therefore two very different kinds of domination. One is primal and we cannot escape it; we can, in certain circumstances, escape the other. The difficulty is that, in social practices, these very different kinds of domination are closely linked, which explains why we often confuse the two or so easily reduce one to the other. Either we emphasize the person's ontological dependency and play down her socio-political domination, or we indulge in great metaphysical flights of oratory about Being, which pay so little attention to socio-political domination that they can actually fail to notice the very worst forms of domination – one thinks of Heidegger's ontology, which quite happily accommodated itself to Nazism. Alternatively, we insist on concentrating solely upon socio-political dominations and fail to see, or even deny, the very specificity of culture.

Seeing the close connection between these two forms of domination presupposes, then, a delicate operation, which does not emphasize one at the expense of the other. My explanation is this: certain groups exploit the human being's ontological determination (which is necessary) in order to establish their socio-political domination (which is contingent). How? Quite simply by monitoring access to meaning as closely as possible and by blocking the roads of approach. That is why there are specific institutions corresponding to each form of socio-political domination. They are designed to keep a close watch on authorized meanings. The dominant groups find that they have a responsibility to guarantee that individuals have access to the symbolic function, not as a result of some philanthropic concern but because of their desire to control subjects. We might say that language and symbolic systems are unconditionally available to all speaking subjects, but only provided that they are subject to strict controls. In that sense, modernity's societies were disciplinary societies, as Foucault has demonstrated in his work of the 1960s (on asylums and prisons) and of the 1970s (on the biopower that emerges once life becomes the object of political decision-making).

The fact that power takes control of life does not, however, mean that the two forms of domination merge. And that is precisely the mistake that is made by those who see desymbolizing acts as ways of resisting socio-political domination. In reality, such acts merely undo the symbolic function. All that naked violence, for example, can do is to destroy the innermost sources of the person's humanity. To believe that attacking this primal core of humanity will rid us of socio-political domination is a tragic misunderstanding. No revolution is worth that – as was, alas, demonstrated by the madness of Pol Pot's attempt to eradicate the symbolic function in order to do away with all socio-political domination.

Neoliberalism and desymbolization

If we damage this core of humanity, there is in fact a danger that quite the opposite will happen. At the moment, the danger is that we might see the triumph of the most aggressive of all possible dominations: what is generally known as neoliberalism. The great novelty of neoliberalism, as compared with earlier systems of domination, is that the early systems worked through institutional controls, reinforcements and repression, whereas the new capitalism runs on deinstitutionalization.[6] Foucault probably did not see this coming. Being fully preoccupied with studying the ways in which power takes control of life (health care, education, forms of punishment . . .), he failed to see that a very novel domination had been gradually established from the end of the Second World War onwards. Foucault's exemplary studies of disciplinary societies in fact appeared at the moment when those societies were lapsing into decadence. They applied to an object that had already become very fragile even as he was studying it.[7] That is why Foucault's studies of disciplinary societies led to a huge misunderstanding, even though they are well founded. The highly committed militant actions of the day did not take it into account that the institutions they were targeting were the very apparatuses that the most aggressive fraction of capitalism wished to destroy. It no longer wanted to assert itself by placing disciplinary controls on life; it wanted a completely new form of domination, and the events of the 1960s (in California, Italy, and England; and in France during May '68) hastened its introduction. The new capitalism was in the process of discovering and implementing much less coercive and less costly ways of guaranteeing its own success: it is no longer reinforcing the secondary domination which has produced submissive subjects. It is destroying institutions and putting an end to primal domination in such a way as to produce individuals who are supple, insecure, mobile and open to all the market's modes and variations.

[6] As Robert Castel well realized (see especially Castel, Castel and Lovell 1979), the remarkable thing is that this deinstitutionalization began in asylum-like institutions with very high levels of surveillance.

[7] The same misunderstanding occurred with Goffman in the United States, where *Asylums* was seen as a study in liberation, whereas it was in fact a project for deinstitutionalization (Goffman 1961; the French translation was published in 1968). The project was put into practice in California from 1966 onwards, after a certain Ronald Reagan was elected Governor . . .

The only 'acceptable constraints' are now those of 'commodity exchanges' (Taguieff 2001: 14). The only acceptable imperative is the imperative stating that commodities must circulate. Any institution whose cultural and moral references can come between individuals and commodities is now unwelcome. The new capitalism was very quick to see how it could exploit protests. And so, neoliberalism is now promoting 'an imperative to transgress prohibitions' that gives its discourse an 'aura of libertarianism' based upon the proclamation of the autonomy of all and 'the indefinite extension of tolerance in every domain' (Taguieff 2001: 15). That is why it brings deinstutionalization in its wake: we need not only 'less State', but less of anything that might block the circulation of commodities.

The immediate result of this deinstitutionalization is, of course, a desymbolization of individuals. We reach the absolute limit of desymbolization when there is no longer anything to secure and guarantee that the subjects are on the road to the symbolic function that governs the relationship of meaning and the search for meaning. That limit is never actually reached, but when the relationship of meaning breaks down, it always does so at the expense of humanity and discursivity and to the advantage of relations of force. The new capitalism's new target is the primal core of humanity, or the person's symbolic dependency. It is therefore not surprising that our social space should increasingly be invaded by ordinary violence punctuated by momentary crises marked by hyper-violence and catastrophic accidents, which are now an ever-present possibility thanks to environmental conditions. The circle is complete: neoliberal logic produces subjects who, because they obey the law of 'might is right', reinforce that logic.

It is perfectly obvious that these precarious new subjects are also victims. That is precisely what the vibrionic advocates of 'zero tolerance' want us to forget; they are perfectly happy to tolerate massive corruption in business and politics, and their main concern is to protect the nice parts of town. On the other hand, we must not forget that these victims also victimize others. Playing 'greater tolerance' off against 'zero tolerance' is therefore a very bad solution, which can only make the situation worse and not better. The refusal to see what is at stake in the newly precarious subjective condition of the neoliberal era, or, worse still, the insistence that these desymbolized individuals represent a new form of resistance, is an indication that we have gone blind and really have lost our way. The phenomenon appears to me to stem from a compassion which is miserabilist in ethical terms but fashionably 'politically correct' in neoliberal social democracies, and from a cheap literary fascination with the limit-acts, which are often so popular with the children of the bourgeoisie as they rebel against their own milieu. Nothing can come of these revolts. And we do not have to look very far to see that, if there is one social reality that the new capitalism accepts without a blink, although it is destroying so many others, it is the existence of all kinds of mafias which shamelessly use the most ruthless methods. Capitalism has always been able to get along with what Marx called the lumpenproletariat (Marx and Engels 1973). Marx had no illusions about it: it was incapable of conducting an organized political struggle, being made up of 'decayed roués of doubtful origin and uncertain means of subsistence . . . ruined and adventurous scions of the bourgeoisie . . . discharged criminals, escaped galley slaves, swindlers, confidence tricksters, *lazzaroni*, pickpockets, sleight-of-hand experts, gamblers, *maquereaux*, brothel keepers . . .' (Marx 1973: 197). The lumpenproletariat has now lost its status as a local historical curiosity on the margins of capitalism.[8] Its characteristics are more widespread and have come to categorize certain social forms. A more tangible continuity is in the course of being established between the little gangs which operate in cities by sucking the blood of the poorest populations and by preventing the subsisting republican institutions (schools and public transport, for example) from functioning normally; the small, medium-sized and big mafias which make 'dirty' money (out of drugs, prostitution, the arms trade, political corruption . . .); the financial networks which have no qualms about recycling the money through tax havens; and certain political networks where business mixes with the mafia, sometimes openly (even in Europe itself; one thinks of Berlusconi's Italy).

Neither zero tolerance nor greater tolerance will work. The only solution is a new symbolization that will allow the precarious new subjects to recover their human dignity. We therefore have to launch the struggle against desymbolization, which presupposes that we can identify its contemporary forms with some precision.

---

[8] This non-class did have its hour of glory. In *The Eighteenth Brumaire of Louis Bonaparte*, Marx analyses Bonaparte's seizure of power as a *coup d'état* carried out with the help of 'the Society of 10 December organised into secret sections . . . the whole indeterminate fragmented mass, tossed backwards and forwards' (1973: 198).

What is desymbolization?

The word refers, first and foremost, to one of the effects of the contemporary pragmatism, utilitarianism and 'realism' which want to
'slim down' symbolic exchanges by stripping away the symbolic
burden that weighs them down. Desymbolization refers to a process
designed to rid symbolic exchanges of that which is in excess of them
and which at the same time institutes them: their foundations.
Human exchanges are in fact framed by a body of rules whose principle is not 'real'; it refers to 'values' which are postulated. Those values
derive from a culture (a repository of moral principles, aesthetic
canons, models of truth, and so on) and, as such, can differ from, or
even come into conflict with, other values. Now the 'new spirit of capitalism' is pursuing an ideal of fluidity, transparency, circulation and
renewal which cannot be reconciled with the historical weight of these
cultural values. In that sense, the adjective 'liberal' describes the condition of a man who has been 'liberated' from all ties with values.
Anything relating to the transcendent sphere of principles and ideals
has been discredited because it cannot be converted into commodities
or services. (Moral) values have no (market) value. As they are worthless, there is no justification for their continued survival in a world
that has been completely commodified. What is more, they still
provide a basis for possible resistance to the advertising propaganda
that demands minds that must be 'free' of all cultural residues if they
are to be fully efficient.[9] Desymbolization has a purpose: it wants to
eradicate the cultural component in exchanges, because that is always
specific. The desymbolization we are now experiencing takes three
forms: venal, generational and nihilistic.

Venal desymbolization

The term *numismatic* – pertaining to coins – comes from the Greek
nomos, which means 'law'. Money originally had, therefore, something to do with the law. It follows that, if we devalue money, we
devalue the law. A single example is enough to demonstrate the pertinence of this precept: the abandoning of the gold standard, which
guaranteed the value of European currencies in the inter-war period,

[9] The 2002 dispute between the Vivendi group and French film-makers was a typical
example. Vivendi's goal is to make all 'cultural exceptions' impossible . . . in the name
of pluralism and equality.

has been shown to be one of the factors that triggered totalitarianism (Goux 2000: 245). Or, in 2002, Europeans lived through an almost allegorical moment of desymbolization without striking a blow. They adopted the euro. A currency is in fact a 'fiduciary' sign; it is, that is, based on the credit we place in it. The trusting belief that a scrap of paper with pictures on it can represent a value was based on two things: the gold standard, the ultimate and primary reference (a psychoanalyst would call it 'anal') enshrined in a precious metal which was sanctified and totemized; and the spiritual reference, the symbolic imprint of the effigies and devices which guarantee the unity of the community, or even preserve its soul. These two origins – the founding matrix and the foundation myth – have been greatly weakened. One was weakened in 1972, when the dollar ceased to be convertible into gold because the US Federal Reserves were melting away, thanks mainly to the war in Vietnam; the second was weakened on 1 January 2002, thanks to the appearance of a currency with no motto, no portrait of a 'great man', and no stated cultural value. There are still faces on the coins, but the higher value notes, which are promissory notes pledged against values and property, depict nothing but doors, windows and bridges . . .

Now, money is not just money. The French language makes a distinction between *argent* [money] and *monnaie* [currency, coin]. A *monnaie* is not just a sign of *argent*: it also symbolizes a whole set of patrimonial values that are transmitted from seller to buyer. Over the years, the franc distributed a gallery of little pictures which, from Pasteur to Pascal and from Descartes to Delacroix, placed all transactions under the aegis of the 'French genius', which was indissociable from the 'franc'. American currency has similar characteristics. They are now largely forgotten but they are still part of its history. Dollar bills carry an explicit reminder of the debt ('This note is legal tender for all debts') that the payment has just cleared. As the anthropologist Marcel Mauss taught us long ago, debt lies at the origin of all symbolic meaning. The dollar also depicts the origins of the nation (portraits of the founding fathers) and makes a statement of belief (*In God We Trust*). Given the current state of affairs, the euro claims to have been set free from all these eminently symbolic characteristics. We sometimes hear it said that Europe needed a strong symbol and that the euro gave it one. But how can anyone fail to see that, in order to do so, it first had to strip itself of all explicitly cultural references. If the euro is going to symbolize Europe from now on, it will do so in purely practical banking terms that are quite devoid of emblematic references.

The euro is a universal equivalent which is not based on anything, a pure countermark which has no origins and is used for purely functional exchanges. It is, if we can put it that way, the very symbol of desymbolization: all values have been reduced to monetary values. With the coming of the euro, money [*argent*] becomes the only value. The one thing that still bore the seal of the symbolic has disappeared from our transactions. The euro thus represents a sort of intermediary stage between the old fiduciary monetary system and the electronics of credit cards. When digital money leads to the complete disappearance of all symbolization, money will be reduced to mere figures. At the very moment when Europeans were happily getting ready to adopt the euro, their thinkers gathered at UNESCO to describe the inexorable 'twilight of values'.[10]

Once *argent* is no longer symbolized by *monnaie*, there is nothing social about it and it becomes just a neutral heap of coins representing both the beginning and the end of all social relations. The desymbolization we are experiencing is putting all social subjects in a potential position of grabbing as much 'liquid' currency as possible. The expression 'liquid' is telling. When we have a pure circulation of neutral values, there is no longer any such thing as 'dirty money', even if we do sometimes speak of money laundering. All there is is money. You either have it, or you don't.

In that respect, we are now seeing the emergence of a youthful realism that sheds a crude light on what society really has taught our young people: that the only power that exists is the power of money. Thanks to a 'semiotic reversal' (Goux 2000: 244), the sign becomes the thing itself, in the absence of what it once referred to and which gave it its value. This *monnaie* becomes both immaterial (no gold) and an orphan (no mother, no Marianne to symbolize the republic). It is therefore not surprising that more and more adolescents are stealing and indulging in risky operations with breathtaking ease. To take only one tragic example. On 26 December 2001, a young man was shot dead by the police during a bank hold-up in Vitry-sur-Seine. The youths of the estate where he lived took to the streets and put the neighbourhood to fire and sword for a whole week, claiming that their pal had not done anything wrong. As one of them explained, all he had done was to 'go and get some money'.[11] After all, what could be more

---

[10] See the contributions of Gianni Vattimo, Jean Baudrillard, Peter Sloterdijk and Michel Maffesoli to UNESCO's Dialogues du XXᵉ Siècle (8 December 2001).

[11] See *Le Monde*, 4 January 2002.

natural than going to a bank to 'get some money'? The expression reveals a whole climate. Money is no longer something you earn [*gagner*], unless you win it [*gagner*] in a game of chance. You go and get it in the same way you go and get the groceries. This logic is not *sui generis*. It is not something dreamed up by the bad lads from the *banlieues*. It is the direct result of the neoliberal anthropology, which is reducing humanity to a collection of calculating individuals motivated only by their rational self-interest and in unbridled competition with one another. That which has no foundations can have no claim to legitimacy, and it has been demonstrated that money [*argent*] no longer has any foundations; it has literally represented nothing ever since the speculative economy, which allows money to 'reproduce', as Marx puts it, became brutally divorced from the 'real economy'.

There is a direct link between this violence and our monetary deficiency and, whilst the euro is obviously not to blame for this, it is the most obvious index of the link's existence. The paradox is that an anomic currency [*monnaie*], which is pledged against nothing and symbolizes nothing, will, it is claimed, provide access to 'this powerful convoy of commodities to which our civilization has been reduced' (Fukuyama 2001). It also promotes the 'risk society' proclaimed by neoliberal thinkers.[12] In a climate worthy of the old westerns, in which money was nothing more than cash lying around and social agents were bank-robbers who had to get their hands on it, hold-ups and armed robberies are no more than risks like any other risks, and they are taken by those who take neoliberalism literally.

Generational desymbolization

Just as labour no longer defines economic value according to the new theories of finance, it no longer defines any social position within the production of wealth. There is certainly no shortage of consumer goods, but jobs are becoming scarce and insecure, and many of them are being deskilled. This is the way it is. A whole generation is trapped in a sort of airlock between school and work. Its needs are growing but it has no resources of its own. It no longer constitutes just an age cohort that can be identified with adolescence; it forms a new kind of social category. It is new because it is quite impossible to see it as part

[12] On MEDEF's new enthusiasm for 'libertarian' philosophers and economists, see *Le Monde*, 16 January 2002. [The Mouvement des Entreprises de France is the most important employers' association in France.]

of the working class, even though many of these young people are from a working-class background. Many of them are the children of workers, but they themselves are not workers. A whole age cohort has been reduced to idleness. It is a sort of inactive third estate, and our schools are charged with looking after these young people for as long as possible. Thanks to a paradoxical inversion, leisure and exemption from labour, which were once the supreme privileges of the ruling classes, have been degraded and transfigured: they are now the fate of young people who have been abandoned by the wayside. Pierrot le Fou's famous line – *Qu'est-ce que j'peux faire? J'sais pas quoi faire.* ['What can I do? Dunno what to do'] – has become the silent refrain of a population of non-productive consumers.

'Young people' – it is a vague and elastic category – find themselves isolated in two ways. They are isolated in chronological terms because it is impossible for them either to project themselves into the future or to refer to a past: the answer to the punks' '*no future*' is a tacit and more subdued '*no past*'. They are cut off in the present because it is impossible for them to see their elders as anything other than equals. The old vertical relationship between the generations has become a horizontal relationship between contemporaries. Symbolic difference has been declared redundant.

Families are no longer agents of socialization and therefore tend simply to supply whatever the media and advertising prescribe. The generational difference between parents and children, and between teachers and pupils, is beginning to disappear, both within the family – which is an affective and financial entity – and in schools. Everyone is now on equal terms. According to Hannah Arendt, who made this the central thesis of her political anthropology, the fact of being born as newcomers in an old world placed the elders, as we have seen, under an obligation to *institute* the young. The American 'modernization', whose proliferation she predicted, consists essentially in short-circuiting all transmission. The traditional role of parents was to show their children a world which, in many cases, we join only because we have to. In the unprecedented situation in which they now find themselves trapped, what is basically the austere and thankless task of bequeathing a cultural heritage they do not really possess becomes almost impossible. Parents are still the old world's old people, and that is a necessary precondition for their transcendence if young people are to rejuvenate what they have inherited of their own accord and responsibility.

With the old the young should find out who they are talking to, in the twin senses of 'talking to each other' and of being 'curbed', or even 'snubbed'. Parents are the people who say 'no', who initiate and permit a certain 'work of negativity' which frustrates the youthful craving for omnipotence. Their role has become difficult, not only because it is very unattractive at a time when everyone, and especially the elders, are faced with a categorical imperative to 'be young', but also because the ability to say 'no' that they incarnate can no longer be exercised in the name of the principles on which the world is supposedly based. They therefore have to accept the criticisms and rebellions born of the frustrations that their 'no' inevitably provokes. This symbolic precedence, which stems from the fact that authority is made incarnate for someone, is now, and probably for the first time, being denied. The result is the sabotaging of what I have termed the 'symbolic serfdom' of man, and it paves the way for a certain contemporary nihilism.

Nihilistic desymbolization

Because they find it so difficult to enter a world of work which is becoming more and more hypothetical and enigmatic, and because their historical and generational signposts are so confused, young people are being grouped into serial aggregates that simply do not supply them with the structure and foundations of a social class. We are dealing with something resembling a non-class, which is defined in negative terms by what it is not. The term 'exclusion' captures it rather well: some young people actually are excluded from social activity. This is why it seems inadequate to analyse juvenile violence in terms of the class struggle. This violence is not a revolt against exploitation (when there are no jobs, there is no surplus-value) and its goal is not emancipation (there is no ideology of salvation at work here). These young people are unreservedly in favour of consumerism and consumerist values and they are not denouncing some alienation (left to themselves, they tend rather to fall back upon a gregarious identity politics – the phenomenon of rival 'gangs' is an excellent example). Their exactions are, in political terms, meaningless. *Avoir la haine* ['having hate'] is an expression of a mood that is as imperious as it is ill-defined, and not a social demand. The only thing that could possibly recuperate this violence is a hypocritical populism which is openly reactionary when it denounces young people for being a 'dangerous class', and supposedly progressive when it turns them into a redemptive young guard made up of 'exterminating angels'.

Nothing can transform revulsion into revolt because the strength of neocapitalism lies, paradoxically, in the weakness of its governments.

Neoliberal governance is a will to non-government,[13] and is quite in keeping with the idea that less political government means greater economic productivity. The deliberate and technical weakening of power has a perverse effect that did not escape the sagacious Arendt (1972: 184): 'Every decrease in power is an open invitation to violence.' In this context, 'power' is the expression of a 'will'. Now contemporary power 'wills' nothing more than to adapt as best it can to an economic situation and an evolution that transcend it. 'Modernization' (of firms, schools, institutions . . .) looks like a gigantic tropism on a planetary scale, like a sort of natural law or a blind and irresistible thrust on the part of evolution. It is now force of circumstance that demands the submission and adaptation of the living, rather than the holders of a power which has become soft and floppy, secondary and managerial. The absence of any real government, in other words of an institution whose legitimacy is of necessity unrelated to economic interests, abolishes authority and at the same time makes power invisible. The weakening of the state does not presage the withering away of socio-political domination, far from it; it presages the transition to a new form of sly and deceitful domination, which makes actual power something that has no name and no shape and cannot be localized: 'we have a tyranny without a tyrant' (Arendt 1972: 178). The weakening of the state leads to the open promotion of anomie, and the removal of all taboos and of anything else that might check the pure impetuosity of our appetites. When citizenship is restricted to civil society,[14] which is no more than the sum total of conflicting individual interests, the essential dialectic between the social body and its representation becomes impossible. Neoliberal anthropology's famous slogan of laisser-faire was already an admission, and its ultimate success would be the opening up of a new and completely empty societal space in which value – we now have to speak of it in the singular – is passed from hand to hand, without further ado and with no concerns as to the modality of its transmission: the 'fittest' can quite legitimately take advantage of all situations, whilst the 'least fit' are simply abandoned, or even left for dead. This represents a powerful challenge to civilization, because it implies a dereliction of the traditional biopolitical duty that requires all states to protect their populations.

[13] Cf. Michel Foucault's 1979 lectures at the Collège de France on the 'birth of biopolitics' (Foucault 2004). Some were broadcast on France-Culture in the week of 14–18 January 2002.

[14] Bernard Cassen so defines civil society, quoting Hegel, in Le Monde Diplomatique, no. 576, June 2001, p. 28.

Some refuse to enter this hyper-realist space in which naked values are exchanged directly. Then they go down the road dictated by the dereliction of duty, which leads to 'gratuitous' or purely reactive violence.[15] When the locus of power and its representatives are invisible, we have to fall back on some scapegoat. Xerxes had the sea whipped to punish it for being stormy. Our young delinquents burn, loot and assault people with the same impotent rage because they cannot get at those who are responsible for their banishment.

We are faced with a vicious circle of nihilism: when anomie is neo-capitalism's condition of possibility, it becomes *nihilism* for both those who profit from it and those who suffer because of it.

Postmodernism does not just mean the collapse of our ego-ideals, nor is it a mass rising against idols. Those who believe that we live in a period of a painful but salutary awakening are easily satisfied. We are actually living in an era which is producing a 'new man' or an acritical and near-psychotic subject thanks to an ideology that is just as aggressive as, but probably more effective than, the great ideologies of the last century (communism and Nazism). What neoliberalism wants is a desymbolized subject who is neither subject to guilt nor able to rely upon a critical free will. It wants a free-floating subject who is not weighed down by any symbolic ties; it is trying to establish a unisex and non-gendered subject who has been cut loose from 'his' moorings in the only world that is real: the world of sexual difference and generational difference. When all the symbolic references that can validate human exchanges are challenged, the only things that remain are commodities exchanged against a backdrop of generalized venality and nihilism. This is where we are being invited to take our place. Neoliberalism is making capitalism's old dream come true. Not only has it extended the territory of the commodity to the four corners of a globe (this goes by the name of globalization), where everything (water, the human genome, the air, living species, health, organs, national museums, children . . .) can be bought and sold. It is also in the process of recuperating what used to be private affairs and a matter for individual discretion (subjectivation, personation, sexuation . . .) and bringing them into the commodity's orbit.

---

[15] Like the four boys, aged between thirteen and twenty-seven, who injured nine people by causing an explosion in a village hall. Their explanation was that they 'wanted to piss people off'. See *Le Monde*, 4 January 2002.

In that respect, we have reached a crucial turning point because, when the subject-form which was constructed in the course of great historical struggles comes under attack, it is not just the institutions we share that are in danger: it is also, and above all, *what we are*. It is not only our cultural heritage that is in danger; it is our very *being*. This is obviously much more serious: we can always make up for the loss of the goods we shared by producing new goods, but there is no cure for the loss of our very being. This is probably what the possibility of the absolute triumph of neoliberalism and the great battles to come will centre on: if the subject-form is destroyed, there will be nothing to hold back the limitless development of the political form of the final stage of capitalism: a total capitalism in which everything, including our very being, will be dragged into the orbit of the commodity.

What else is there to be said? Perhaps the most important thing of all. It can be summed up in two suggestions, and they happen to be contradictory. Invoking one last Kantian antinomy is my way of paying tribute to reason. And I have to admit that I cannot resolve it.

On the one hand, I have to admit that the extension of postmodernity means that there is less and less room for the critical subject and his old neuroses. How, then, are we to react to the programmed death of the modern subject? I feel that our sole option is to try to protect it like an endangered species, in the hope that better days will come, even if it means making it go underground to rediscover the stimulating practices of resistance networks.

As for the postmodernism's innumerable invitations, *I would prefer not to* . . . (Melville 1987).

I cite the polite formula with which Melville's Bartleby invariably greets all requests. It is solemn and laconic, but it is also final and quite devastating. ' "I would prefer not to" ', writes Blanchot (1975), 'belongs to the infinite patience where the destroyed come and go.'

On the other hand, I have to admit that the tragic destruction of that man provides us with an unexpected opportunity. We in fact find ourselves in an exceptional intellectual situation. Everything is topsy-turvy. We have to rebuild everything, starting with a new critical intelligence and a new understanding of the unconscious. We are in much the same position Descartes found himself in in Amsterdam in 1631, a few years before he wrote *Le Discours de la méthode*: 'In this great city where I am living, with no man apart from myself not being involved in trade, everyone is so intent on his profits that I could spend my whole life without being seen by anyone' (Descartes 1953: 941). Descartes, being a man who could remain calm in the most desperate situations, is the theoretical character we need here; when everyone else feels obliged to be involved in trade, he enjoys 'complete freedom'. It is when his doubts are greatest that he rediscovers, thanks to those very doubts, the harshest of philosophical exercises; but it was to found a new certainty.

Descartes's capitalist Amsterdam has now conquered the world. It is not just that everyone in this planetary city is now involved in trade; trade is now involved in everyone in the sense that it shapes us all. A few communicating philosophers are called upon to make reports from time to time. But, basically, no one is interested in that endangered species. It's not surprising: we are worthless.

Let us take advantage of this fact.

As we make our forced retreat, we – the destroyed – enjoy an absolute freedom.

For my own part, I am by no means resolved to use this leisure to practise one of the many arts of dereliction; I will use it to try to understand the ins and outs of the new ideology that is emerging. It is already apparent that, despite its pleasingly democratic appearance, it is probably as virulent as the terrible ideologies that were unleashed in the West during the twentieth century. It is not in fact impossible that, after the hell of Nazism and the terror of communism, a new historical catastrophe is in the offing. We may have leaped out of the frying pan and into the fire. For neoliberalism seeks to create a new man, just as the above-mentioned ideologies wanted to create a new man. Changes in the great fields of human activity – the market economy, the political economy, the symbolic economy and the psychical economy – are now so convergent as to indicate that a new man is beginning to emerge. He has lost his faculty of judgement and is encouraged to enjoy without desire.

This is not, in my view, a time for the foolish optimism of the impatient, who are too quick to rejoice at the deterritorialization brought about by the commodity and by the collapse of the idols. Nor is this a time for a pessimism nostalgic for times which have gone for ever. If there is such a thing as a modern categorical imperative, it is this: we must resist the consolidation of total capitalism.

Bibliography

Dates in square brackets refer to the original date of publication; in these cases, page numbers, when given, belong to the later published collection.

Agamben, Giorgio (1998) *Homo Sacer: Sovereign Power and Bare Life*, tr. Daniel Heller-Roazen, Stanford, CA: University of Stanford Press (original publication 1995).

Allouch, Jean (1991) *Le Transfert dans tous ses errata*, Paris: EPEL.

Althusser, Louis (1993) *The Future Lasts a Long Time*, tr. Richard Veasey, London: Chatto & Windus (original publication 1992).

Amorim, M. (1996) *Dialogisme et altérité dans les sciences humaines*, Paris: L'Harmattan.

Amorim, M. (2000) 'O branco da violência', *Carta Capital* (São Paulo), 2 August.

Arendt, Hannah (1961) *Between Past and Future: Six Exercises in Political Thought*, London: Faber.

Arendt, Hannah (1972) *Crises of the Republic*, New York: Harcourt Brace Jovanovich.

Assoun, Paul-Laurent (1995) *Freud, la philosophie et les philosophes*, Paris: PUF.

Bachelard, Gaston (1943) *L'Air et les songes*, Paris: Corti.

Badiou, Alain (1999) *Deleuze: The Clamor of Being*, tr. Louise Burchill, Minneapolis: University of Minnesota Press (original publication 1997).

Baltier, E. and Rochex, J.-Y. (1988) *L'Expérience scolaire des nouveaux lycéens*, Paris: Armand Colin.

Barrot, Adrien (2000) *L'Enseignement mis à mort*, Paris: Librio.

Barthes, Roland (1982) *Camera Lucida: Reflections on Photography*, tr. Richard Howard, London: Cape (original publication 1980).

Baudelaire, Charles (1972) 'The painter of modern life', in *Selected Writings on Art and Artists*, tr. P. E. Charvet, Harmondsworth: Penguin, pp. 390–436 (original publication 1863).

Bautier, E. and Rochex, J.-Y. (1988) *L'Expérience scolaire des nouveaux lycéens*, Paris: Armand Colin.

Beckett, Samuel (2003) *The Unnamable*, in *Trilogy*, London: Calder (original publication of Beckett's own English translation 1959).

Beckouche, Pierre (2001) *Le Royaume des frères. Aux sources de l'État-nation*, Paris: Grasset.

Benjamin, Walter (2002) 'The work of art in the age of its technological reproductibility', in *Selected Writings, Vol. 3: 1935–1938*, eds. Howard Eiland and Michael W. Jennings, Cambridge, MA and London: Belknap Press of Harvard University Press, pp. 101–33 (original publication 1936).

Benveniste, Émile (1971) *Problems in General Linguistics*, tr. Mary Elizabeth Mach, Coral Gables: University of Miami Press (original publication 1966).

Berthier, P. and Dufour, D.-R. (1996) 'Tractatus pédagogico-philosophique', in *Philosophie du langage, esthétique et éducation*, Paris: L'Harmattan.

Bident, Christophe (1998) *Maurice Blanchot. Partenaire invisible*, Seyssel: Champ Vallon.

Blais, M.-C., Gauchet, M. and Ottavi, D. (2002) *Pour une philosopie politique de l'éducation. Six questions d'aujourd'hui*, Paris: Bayard.

Blanchot, Maurice (1959) *Le Livre à venir*, Paris: Gallimard.

Blanchot, Maurice (1973) *Le Pas au-delà*, Paris: Gallimard.

Blanchot, Maurice (1975) 'Discours sur la patience', *Le Nouveau Commerce*, 30–1, pp. 19–44.

Boltanski, Luc and Chiapello, Éve (1999) *Le Nouvel Esprit du capitalisme*, Paris: Gallimard.

Boudinet, Gilles (2001) *Pratiques tag*, Paris: L'Harmattan.

Bourdieu, Pierre (1998) 'L'Essence du néolibéralisme', *Le Monde Diplomatique*, March.

Bourdieu, Pierre (2001) *Masculine Domination*, tr. Richard Nice, Cambridge: Polity (original publication 1998).

Bourdieu, Pierre and Passeron, J.-C. (1970) *Reproduction in Education, Society and Culture*, tr. Richard Nice, London and Beverly Hills: Sage.

Bové, José (2001) 'Les Mensonges de Mike Moore', *Le Monde*, 12 June.

Brohm, Jean-Marie and Perelman, Marc (2002) 'Football: de l'extase au cauchemar', *Le Monde*, 17 June.

Cassin, Barbara (1995) *L'Effet sophistique*, Paris: Gallimard.

Castel, F., Castel, R. and Lovell, A. (1979) *La Société psychiatrique avancée. Le modèle américain*, Paris: Grasset.

Charles, Gilbert (2000) 'Le Procès de la Ritaline', *L'Express*, 26 October.

Charlot, B., Bautier, E. and Rochex, J. Y. (1992) *École et savoir dans les banlieues et ailleurs*, Paris: Armand Colin.

Chassaing, Jean-Louis (1999) 'Élodie au corps peint', *Le Discours Psychanalytique*, 22 October.

Chassaing, Jean-Louis (2000) 'Faire son trou: se re-marquer', *Cahiers de l'Association Internationale*, May.

Comte, Auguste (1966) *Catéchisme positiviste*, Paris: Garnier-Flammarion (original publication 1852).

Damourette, E. and Pichon, E. (1911–50) *Des Mots à la pensée. Essai de grammaire de la langue française*, Paris: Éditions d'Artrey.

Delannoi, G. and Taguieff, P. A., eds (1991) *Théories du nationalisme. Nation, nationalité, ethnicité*, Paris: Kime.

Delcourt, Marie (1981) *Oedipe ou la légende du conquérant*, Paris: Les Belles Lettres (original publication 1944).

Deleule, D. and Guery, F. (1972) *Le Corps productif*, Paris: Mame/Repères.

Deleuze, Gilles (1998) *Essays Critical and Clinical*, tr. David W. Smith and Michael A. Greco, London: Verso (original publication 1993).

Deleuze, Gilles and Guattari, Félix (1992) *A Thousand Plateaus: Capitalism and Schizophrenia*, tr. Brian Massumi, London: Continuum (original publication 1980).

Deleuze, Gilles and Guattari, Félix (2004) *Anti-Oedipus*, tr. Robert Hurley, Mark Seem and Helen R. Lane, London: Continuum (original publication 1972).

Demorgon, Jacques (1996) *Complexité des cultures et de l'interculturel*, Paris: Anthropos.

Descartes, René (1953) *Oeuvres et lettres*, Paris: Gallimard, Bibliothèque de la Pléiade.

Destutt de Tracy, Antoine Louis Claude (1970) *Éléments d'idéologies*, Paris: Vrin (original publication 1801–5).

Duby, Georges (1985) *Le Dimanche de Bouvines*, Paris: Gallimard.

Duclos, Denis (1996) *Nature et démocratie des passions*, Paris: PUF.

Dufour, Dany-Robert (1988) *Le Bégaiement des maîtres*, Strasbourg: Arcanes.

Dufour, Dany-Robert (1990) *Les Mystères de la trinité*, Paris: Gallimard.

Dufour, Dany-Robert (1996a) *Folie et démocratie*, Paris: Gallimard.

Dufour, Dany-Robert (1996b) 'Sur le devenir fou des démocraties', *Le Débat*, March–April.

Dufour, Dany-Robert (1998) *Lacan et le miroir sophianique de Jacob Boehme*, Paris: EPEL.

Dufour, Dany-Robert (1999) *Lettres sur la nature humaine*, Paris: Calmann-Lévy.

Dufour, Dany-Robert (2000) 'Modernity, postmodernity and adolescence', *Journal for the Psychoanalysis of Culture and Society*, Autumn.

Dumont, Louis (1991) *Homo aequalis II: L'Idéologie allemande. France–Allemagne et retour*, Paris: Gallimard.

Dupuy, Jean-Pierre (2002) *Pour un catastrophisme éclairé*, Paris: Seuil.

Duveau, G. (1948) *La Pensée ouvrière sur l'éducation pendant la Seconde République et le Second Empire*, Paris: Dunat-Montchrétien.

Eco, Umberto (1979) *The Role of the Reader: Explorations in the Semiotics of Texts*, Bloomington: Indiana University Press.

Ehrenberg, Alain (1998) *La Fatigue d'être soi*, Paris: Odile Jacob.

Ey, Henri (1966) *L'Inconscient. VIe Colloque de Bonneval*, Paris: Desclée de Brouwer.

Ferry, Luc (2003) *Lettre à tous ceux qui aiment l'école*, Paris: Odile Jacob/ Sceren-CNDP.

Finkielkraut, Alain (2000) 'La Révolution culturelle à l'école', *Le Monde*, 19 May.

Flahault, François (2003) *Pourquoi limiter l'expansion du capitalisme*, Paris: Descartes.

Foucault, Michel (2003) *'Society Must be Defended'. Lectures at the Collège de France 1975–76*, tr. David Macey, London: Allen Lane (original publication 1997).

Foucault, Michel (2004) *Naissance de la biopolitique. Cours au Collège de France*, Paris: Gallimard/Seuil.

Frau-Meigs, Divina and Jehel, Sophie (1997) *Les Écrans de la violence*, Paris: Economica.

Freud, Sigmund [1905] 'Three essays on the theory of sexuality', in Freud (1953–73), vol. VII, pp. 123–246.

Freud, Sigmund [1908a] 'On the sexual theories of children', in Freud (1953–73), vol. IX, pp. 205–26.

Freud, Sigmund [1908b] 'Hysterical phantasies and their relation to bisexuality', in Freud (1953–73), vol. IX, pp. 155–66.

Freud, Sigmund [1909] 'Five lectures on psychoanalysis', in Freud (1953–73), vol. XI, pp. 1–55.

Freud, Sigmund [1910] 'A special type of choice of object made by men', in Freud (1953–73), vol. XI, pp. 163–76.

Freud, Sigmund [1912] *Totem and Taboo*, in Freud (1953–73), vol. XII, pp. 1–162.

Freud, Sigmund [1913] 'The claims of psychoanalysis to scientific interest', in Freud (1953–73), vol. XIII, pp. 163–90.

Freud, Sigmund [1914] 'On narcissism: an introduction', in Freud (1953–73), vol. XIV, pp. 68–104.

Freud, Sigmund [1915] 'The unconscious', in Freud (1953–73), vol. XIV, pp. 159–204.

Freud, Sigmund [1916–17] *Introductory Lectures on Psychoanalysis*, pt 3, in Freud (1953–73), vol. XVI.

Freud, Sigmund [1921] 'Group psychology and the analysis of the ego', in Freud (1953–73), vol. XVIII, pp. 65–144.

Freud, Sigmund [1923] 'The ego and the id', in Freud (1953–73), vol. XIX, pp. 1–62.

Freud, Sigmund [1924] 'The economic problem of masochism', in Freud (1953–73), vol. XIX, pp. 155–72.

Freud, Sigmund [1925] 'Some psychical consequences of the anatomical distinction between the sexes', in Freud (1953–73), vol. XIX, pp. 241–60.

Freud, Sigmund [1933] *New Introductory Lectures on Psychoanalysis*, in Freud (1953–73), vol. XXII.

Freud, Sigmund [1939] *Moses and Monotheism*, in Freud (1953–73), vol. XXIII.

Freud, Sigmund [1940] *An Outline of Psychoanalysis*, in Freud (1953–73), vol. XXII, pp. 139–208.

Freud, Sigmund (1953–73) *The Standard Edition of the Complete Psychological Works of Sigmund Freud*, translated under the general editorship of James Strachey, 24 vols, London: Hogarth Press and the Institute of Psychoanalysis.

Freud, Sigmund (1985) *The Complete Letters of Sigmund Freud to Wilhelm Fliess, 1887–1904*, ed. and tr. Jeffrey Moussaieff Masson, Cambridge, MA: Belknap Press of Harvard University Press.

Freud, Sigmund (1993) *The Correspondence of Sigmund Freud and Sandór Ferenczi, vol I, 1905–1914*, ed. Eva Brabant, Ernst Falzeder and Patrizia Giamperi-Deutsch, tr. Peter T. Hoffer, Cambridge, MA: Harvard University Press.

Frignet, Henry (2000) *Le Transsexualisme*, Ramonville: Érès.

Fukuyama, Francis (2001) 'Nous sommes toujours à la fin de l'histoire', *Le Monde*, 16 January.

Garréta, Anne (1986) *Sphinx*, Paris: Grasset.

Gauchet, Marcel (1985) *Le Désenchantement du monde*, Paris: Gallimard.

Gauchet, Marcel (2002) *La Démocratie contre elle-même*, Paris: Gallimard.

Gauchet, Marcel and Swain, Gladys (1997) *Le Vrai Charcot*, Paris: Calmann-Lévy.

Gauchet, Marcel, Ottavi, D. and Blais, M.-C. (2002) *Pour une politique de l'éducation*, Paris: Bayard.

Gavarini, Laurence (2001) *La Passion de l'enfant*, Paris: Denoël.

Gay, José María Perez (1991) *El Imperio perdido*, Mexico: Oceana.

Geuens, Geoffrey (2003) *Tous pouvoirs confondus. Capital, État et medias à l'heure de la mondialisation*, Paris: EPO.

Goffman, Erving (1961) *Asylums: Essays on the Social Situation of Mental Patients and Other Inmates*, New York: Doubleday.

Goux, J.-J. (2000) *Frivolité de la valeur. Essai sur l'imaginaire du capitalisme*, Paris: Buisson.

Groebel, Jo (1998) 'The UNESCO global report on media violence', in *Children and Media Violence*, Stockholm: UNESCO.

Grossman, E. (2002) 'Peindre l'évanouissement de la forme', *Europe*, February.

Halperin, David M. (1995) *Saint Foucault: Towards a Gay Hagiography*, New York and Oxford: Oxford University Press.

Hegel, G. W. F. (1975) *Hegel's Aesthetics: Lectures on Fine Art*, 2 vols, tr. T. M. Knox, Oxford: Clarendon Press (original publication 1835).

Heidegger, Martin (1975) 'Aletheia', in Heidegger, *Early Greek Thinking*, tr. David Farrell Krell and Frank A. Capuzzi, San Francisco: Harper & Row (original publication 1946).

Horkheimer, Max and Adorno, Theodor W. (1973) *Dialectic of Enlightenment*, tr. J. Cumming, London: Allen Lane (original publication 1944).

Husserl, Edmund (1988) *Cartesian Mediations*, tr. Dorion Cairns, Dordrecht: Kluwer Academic (original publication 1930).

Jonas, Hans (1984) *The Precautionary Principle: In Search of an Ethics for the Technical Age*, Chicago: University of Chicago Press.

Josephson, Wendy (1995) *Television Violence: A Review of the Effects on Children of Different Ages*, Ottawa: Patrimoine Canadien.

Kafka, Franz [1916] 'Before the law', tr. Willa and Edwin Muir, in Kafka (2005), pp. 3–5.

Kafka, Franz (2005) *The Complete Short Stories*, ed. Nahum N. Glatzer, London: Vintage.

Kant, Immanuel [1784a] 'An answer to the question "What is Enlightenment?" ', tr. H. B. Nisbet, in Kant (1991b), pp. 54–60.

Kant, Immanuel [1784b] 'Idea for a universal history with a cosmopolitan purpose', in Kant (1991b), pp. 41–53.

Kant, Immanuel (1964) *Philosophie de l'historie*, tr. Stéphanie Piombetta, Geneva and Paris: Gonthier (original publication 1780).

Kant, Immanuel (1967) *Philosophical Correspondence 1759–99*, Chicago: University of Chicago Press.

Kant, Immanuel (1991a) *Critique of Judgement*, tr. James Cree Meredith, Oxford: Oxford University Press (original publication 1790).

Kant, Immanuel (1991b) *Kant: Political Writings*, ed. Hans Heiss, Cambridge: Cambridge University Press.

Kant, Immanuel (1993) *Critique of Practical Reason*, tr. Lewis White Beck, intr. Robert Merrihew Adams, Upper Saddle River, NJ: Prentice-Hall (original publication 1788).

Kant, Immanuel (1998) *Religion within the Boundaries of Mere Reason*, tr. Allen Wood and George de Giovanni, Cambridge: Cambridge University Press (original publication 1792).

Kant, Immanuel (1999) *Critique of Pure Reason*, tr. and ed. Paul Guyer and Allen W. Wood, Cambridge: Cambridge University Press (original publication 1781/1787).

Kant, Immanuel (2002) *Groundwork for the Metaphysics of Morals*, tr. and ed. Thomas E. Hill Jr and Arnulf Zweig, Oxford: Oxford University Press (original publication 1785).

Kant, Immanuel (2003) *On Education*, tr. Annette Churton, Mineola, NY: Dover (original publication 1803).

Kant, Immanuel (2004) *Prolegomena to Any Future Metaphysics*, ed. and tr. Gary Hatfield, Cambridge: Cambridge University Press (original publication 1783).

Kant, Immanuel (2006) 'On a recently prominent tone of superiority in philosophy', tr. Peter Heath, in *Theoretical Philosophy after 1781*, ed. Henry

Allison and Peter Heath, Cambridge: Cambridge University Press (original publication 1796), pp. 425–46.

Kojève, Alexandre (1981) *Esquisse d'une philosophie du droit*, Paris: Gallimard.

Koyré, Alexandre (1957) *From the Closed World to the Infinite Universe*, Baltimore: Johns Hopkins University Press.

Lacan, Jacques (1938) 'Les Complexes familiaux', in *Encyclopédie française*, vol. 8 on 'La Vie mentale'.

Lacan, Jacques [1949] 'The mirror stage as formative of the I function as revealed in psychoanalytic experience', in Lacan (2006), pp. 75–81.

Lacan, Jacques [1956a] 'The instance of the letter, or reason since Freud', in Lacan (2006), pp. 412–44.

Lacan, Jacques [1956b] 'The situation of psychoanalysis and the training of psychoanalysts in 1956', in Lacan (2006), pp. 384–411.

Lacan, Jacques [1958a] 'The direction of the cure and the principles of its power', in Lacan (2006), pp. 489–542.

Lacan, Jacques [1958b] 'On a question preliminary to any possible treatment of psychosis', in Lacan (2006), pp. 445–88.

Lacan, Jacques [1963a] 'Kant with Sade', in Lacan (2006), pp. 645–70.

Lacan, Jacques (1963b) *L'Angoisse* (unpublished).

Lacan, Jacques (1967a) *La Logique du fantasme* (unpublished).

Lacan, Jacques (1967b) 'Petit Discours aux psychiatres de Sainte-Anne' (unpublished).

Lacan, Jacques (1968) 'A qui s'adresse *Scilicet*', *Scilicet* 1, pp. 3–13.

Lacan, Jacques (1970a) 'Allocution prononcée pour la clôture du congres de l'École Freudiennes de Paris, le 19 mai 1970, par son directeur', *Scilicet* 2–3, pp. 391–9.

Lacan, Jacques (1970b) 'Radiophonie', *Scilicet* 2–3, pp. 55–102.

Lacan, Jacques (1972a) 'Conference lecture at the University of Milan, 12 May' (unpublished).

Lacan, Jacques (1972b) 'Ou pire . . .', seminar 3 Feb. (unpublished).

Lacan, Jacques (1973a) 'Les Non-dupes errent' (unpublished).

Lacan, Jacques (1979) 'The neurotic's individual myth', tr. Martha Noel Evans, *Psychoanalysis Quarterly* 48 (original publication 1953), pp. 405–25.

Lacan, Jacques (1991) *L'Envers de la psychanalyse*, Paris: Seuil.

Lacan, Jacques (1992) *The Ethics of Psychoanalysis, 1959–1960. The Seminar of Jacques Lacan*, Book VII, ed. Jacques-Alain Miller, tr. Dennis Porter, London: Routledge (original publication 1986).

Lacan, Jacques (1994) *The Four Fundamental Concepts of Psychoanalysis*, tr. Alan Sheridan, Harmondsworth: Penguin (original publication 1964).

Lacan, Jacques (1998) *On Feminine Sexuality, the Limits of Love and Knowledge, 1972–1973. (Encore). The Seminar of Jacques Lacan*, Book XX, ed. Jacques-Alain Miller, tr. Bruce Fink, New York and London: Norton (original publication 1975).

Lacan, Jacques (2006) *Écrits*, tr. Bruce Fink, New York and London: Norton (original publication 1966).

Lebrun, Jean-Pierre (1997) *Un Monde sans limite*, Ramonville: Érès.

Lebrun, Jean-Pierre (2001) *Les Désarrois nouveaux du sujet*, Ramonville: Érès.

Leclaire, Serge (1981) *Rompre les charmes*, Paris: InterEditions.

Leclaire, Serge (1998) *Écrits pour la psychanalyse II*, Paris: Seuil/Arcanes.

Le Clezio, J. M. G. (1988) *Le Rêve mexicain ou la pensée interrompue*, Paris: Gallimard.

Lefort, Claude (1978) *Les Formes de l'histoire. Essai d'anthropologie politique*, Paris: Gallimard.

Le Gaufey, Guy (1998) *Anatomie de la troisième personne*, Paris: EPEL.

Legendre, Pierre (1974) *L'Amour du censeur*, Paris: Seuil.

Legendre, Pierre (1978) *La Passion d'être un autre. Études pour la danse*, Paris: Seuil.

Legendre, Pierre (1985) *Leçons IV. L'Inestimable objet de la transmission. Étude sur le principe généalogique en Occident*, Paris: Fayard.

Legendre, Pierre (1988) *Leçons IV, suite. Le Dossier occidental de la parenté. Textes juridiques indésirables sur la généalogie* (collaboration with Anton Schutz, Marc Smith and Yan Thomas), Paris: Fayard.

Legendre, Pierre (1994) *Dieu au miroir. Étude sur l'institution des images*, Paris: Fayard.

Legendre, Pierre (1996) *La Fabrique de l'homme occidental*, Paris: Mille et Une Nuits.

Le Goff, Jean-Pierre (1999) *La Barbarie douce: la modernisation aveugle des enterprises et de l'Etat*, Paris: La Découverte.

Le Goff, Jean-Pierre (2002) *La Démocratie post-totalitaire*, Paris: La Découverte.

Levy, Pierre (1990) *La Technologie de l'intelligence*, Paris: La Découverte.

Lipovetsky, G. (1983) *L'Ère du vide*, Paris: Gallimard.

Loraux, N. (1997) *La Cité divisée*, Paris: Payot.

Luca, G. (2001) *Héros-limite*, Paris: Gallimard.

Lurçat, Liliane (1998) *La Destruction de l'enseignement élémentaire et ses penseurs*, Paris: Éditions François-Xavier de Guibert.

Lyotard, Jean-François (1983) *The Differend: Phrases in Dispute*, tr. G. van der Abbeele, Minneapolis: University of Minnesota Press (original publication 1983).

Lyotard, Jean-François (1986) *The Postmodern Condition: A Report on Knowledge*, tr. Geoffrey Bennington and Brian Massumi, Manchester: Manchester University Press (original publication 1979).

Mahelli-Rechtman, Vannina (2002) *Le Statut de l'interprétation freudienne et sa critique dans l'épistémologie freudienne*, Paris: Université de Paris VIII.

Maffesoli, Michel (1996) *The Time of the Tribes*, tr. Don Smith, London: Sage (original publication 1988).

Mairet, G. (1997) *Le Principe de souveraineté*, Paris: Gallimard.

Manonni, Octave (1969) *Clefs pour l'imaginaire ou l'autre scène*, Paris: Seuil.

Marx, Karl (1973) *The Eighteenth Brumaire of Louis Bonaparte*, tr. Ben Fowkes, in *Surveys from Exile*, ed. D. Fernbach, Harmondsworth: Penguin (original publication 1869).

Marx, Karl (1976) *Capital*, vol. 1, Harmondsworth: Penguin (original publication 1867).

Marx, Karl and Engels, Frederick (1973) *Manifesto of the Communist Party*, tr. Samuel Moore in *The Revolutions of 1848*, ed. D. Fernbach, Harmondsworth: Penguin (original publication 1848).

Melman, Charles and Lebrun, Jean-Pierre (2002) *L'Homme sans gravité. Jouir à tout prix*, Paris: Denoël.

Melville, Herman (1987) *Bartleby, The Scrivener*, in *The Piazza Tales and Other Prose Pieces*, vol. 9 of *The Writings of Herman Melville*, ed. Harrison Ford, Evanston and Chicago: Northwestern University Press and University of Chicago Press (original publication 1853).

Meyronnis, François (2003) *L'Axe du néant*, Paris: Gallimard.

Michéa, Jean-Claude (1999) *L'Enseignement de l'ignorance*, Castelnau: Climats.

Michéa, Jean-Claude (2002) *Impasse Adam Smith*, Castelnau: Climats.

Micheli-Rechtman, V. (2002) 'Le Statut de l'interpretation freudienne et sa critique dans l'épistemologie freudienne', doctoral thesis, Université de Paris-VIII, Saint-Denis.

Michon, Pierre (2002) *Corps du roi*, Paris: Verdier.

Millot, P. (2003) 'La Reconfiguration des universitiés selon l'OCDE', *Actes de la Recherche en Sciences Sociales* 148, June.

Milner, Jean-Claude (1984) *De l'école*, Paris: Seuil.

Ministère de l'Éducation Nationale (1998) *Quels savoirs enseigner dans les lycées?* Paris: Ministère de l'Éducation Nationale.

Moreira, Paul (1995) 'Les Enfants malades de la publicité', *Le Monde Diplomatique*, September.

Muray, Philippe (2000) 'Sortie de la liberté', *Critique*, July–August.

Neill, Alexander Sutherland (1960) *Summerhill: A Radical Approach to Child Rearing*, New York: Hart.

Nietzsche, Friedrich (1968) *The Will to Power*, tr. Walter Kaufmann and R. J. Hollingdale, ed. Walter Kaufmann, New York: Vintage (original publication 1906).

Nietzsche, Friedrich (1971) *The Gay Science*, tr. and commentary Walter Kaufmann, New York: Vintage (original publication 1887).

Nietzsche, Friedrich (1982) *Daybreak: Thoughts on the Prejudices of Morality*, tr. R. J. Hollingdale, Cambridge: Cambridge University Press (original publication 1881).

Nietzsche, Friedrich (1990) *Beyond Good and Evil*, tr. R. J. Hollingdale, intr. Michael Tanner, Harmondsworth: Penguin (original publication 1886).

OMS (2001) *La Santé mentale Nouvelles conceptions, nouveaux espoirs.* Geneva: L'Organisation Mondiale de la Santé.

Ottavi, Dominique (2001) *De Darwin à Piaget. Pour une histoire de la psychologie de l'enfant,* Paris: CNRS.

Otto, W. F. (1954) *The Homeric Gods: The Spiritual Significance of Greek Religion,* tr. Moses Hadas, London: Thames & Hudson (original publication 1934).

Padovani, Marcelle (2001) 'Quand l'Italie privatise ses musées', *Le Nouvel Observateur,* 6 December.

Pascal, Blaise (1966) *Pensées,* tr. A. J. Krailsheimer, Harmondsworth: Penguin (original publication 1661).

Pierre, José, ed. (1980) *Tracts surréalistes et déclarations collectives, tome I: 1922–1939,* Paris: Le Terrain Vague.

Plon, M. (2001) 'L'In-conscient et la politique', in P.-L. Assoun and M. Zafiropoulos, eds, *Les Solutions sociales de l'inconscient,* Paris: Anthropos.

Pommier, Gérard (2000) *Les Corps angéliques de la postmodernité,* Paris: Calmann-Levy.

Popper, Karl (1996) *The Lessons of this Century. With Two Talks on Freedom and the Democratic State,* London: Routledge.

Porge, Érik (1994) *Vol d'idées? Wilhelm Fliess, son plagiat et Freud,* Paris: Denoël.

Porge, Érik (1996) *Freud–Fliess,* Paris: Anthropos.

Porge, Érik (1997) *Les Noms du père chez Jacques Lacan,* Ramonville: Érès.

Rancière, Jacques (1995) *La Mésentente,* Paris: Galilée.

Rank, Otto (2004) *The Myth of the Birth of the Hero: A Psychological Exploration of Myth,* tr. Gregory C. Richter and E. James Lieberman, Baltimore: Johns Hopkins University Press (original publication 1909).

Renaut, Alin (2001) *Kant aujourd'hui,* Paris: Champs-Flammarion.

Renaut, Alin (2002) *La Libération des enfants. Contribution philosophique à une histoire de l'enfance,* Paris: Calmann-Levy.

Rogozinski, Jacob (1999) *Le Don de la loi. Kant et l'énigme de l'éthique,* Paris: PUF.

Rohatyn, Felix G. (2003) 'Le Capitalisme saisi par la cupidité', *Le Débat* 123, January.

Roudinesco, Elisabeth (1990) *Jacques Lacan & Co.: A History of Psychoanalysis in France 1925–1985,* tr. Jeffrey Mehlmann, London: Free Association Books (original publication 1986).

Roudinesco, Elisabeth (1997) *Jacques Lacan,* tr. Barbara Bray, Cambridge: Polity (original publication 1993).

Rousseau, Jean-Jacques (1973) *The Social Contract,* in *The Social Contract and Discourses,* tr. G. D. H. Cole, London: Everyman (original publication 1762).

Roussel, L. (1992) *La Famille incertaine,* Paris: Odile Jacob.

Sauvagnat, F., ed. (2001) *Divisions subjectives et personnalités multiples,* Rennes: Presses Universitaires de Rennes.

Schnapper, Dominique, ed. (1992) *L'Europe des immigrés. Essais sur les politiques d'immigration*, Paris: François Boarin.

Smaïl, Paul (2001) *Ali le magnifique*, Paris: Denoël.

Smith, Adam (1996) *The Wealth of Nations*, 2 vols, Chicago: University of Chicago Press (original publication 1776).

Soros, George (1998) *The Crisis of Global Capitalism: Open Society Endangered*, New York: Public Affairs.

Taguieff, P.-A. (2001) *Résister au bougisme*, Paris: Mille et Une Nuits.

Théry, I. (1998) *Couple, filiation et parenté aujourd'hui. Le Droit face aux mutations de la vie privée*, Odile Jacob/La Documentation Française.

Tort, Michel (2000) 'Quelques conséquences de la différence "psychanalytique" des sexes', *Les Temps Modernes*, June–July–August, pp. 176–215.

Vasari, Giorgio (1998) *Lives of the Painters*, tr. and intr. George Bull, Harmondsworth: Penguin (original publication 1550).

Vattimo, Gianni (1988) *The End of Modernity: Nihilism and Hermeneutics in Postmodern Culture*, tr. Jon R. Snyder, Baltimore: Johns Hopkins University Press (original publication 1985).

Vernant, Jean-Pierre (1965), *Mythe et pensée chez les Grecs*, vol. 1, Paris: Maspéro.

Vernant, Jean-Pierre (1972) 'Oedipe sans complexe', in Jean-Pierre Vernant and Pierre Vidal-Naquet, *Mythe et tragédie en Grèce ancienne*, 2 vols, Paris: Seuil (original publication 1967).

Vernant, Jean-Pierre (1974) *Mythe et société en Grèce ancienne*, Paris: Maspero.

Vernant, Jean-Pierre (1979) *Religions, histoires, raisons*, Paris: Maspero.

Vincent, Thierry (2002) *L'Indifférence des sexes*, Ramonville: Érès.

Weil, Patrick (2002) *Qu'est-ce qu'un Français? Histoire de la nationalité française depuis la Révolution*, Paris: Grasset.

Yourcenar, Marguerite (1951) *Mémoires d'Hadrien*, Paris: Plon.

Index